OXFORD WORLD'S CLASSICS

══

EDMUND GOSSE

Father and Son

══

Edited with an Introduction and Notes by
MICHAEL NEWTON

OXFORD
UNIVERSITY PRESS

OXFORD
UNIVERSITY PRESS

Great Clarendon Street, Oxford OX2 6DP

Oxford University Press is a department of the University of Oxford.
It furthers the University's objective of excellence in research, scholarship,
and education by publishing worldwide in

Oxford New York

Auckland Bangkok Buenos Aires Cape Town Chennai
Dar es Salaam Delhi Hong Kong Istanbul Karachi Kolkata
Kuala Lumpur Madrid Melbourne Mexico City Mumbai Nairobi
São Paulo Shanghai Taipei Tokyo Toronto

Oxford is a registered trade mark of Oxford University Press
in the UK and in certain other countries

Published in the United States
by Oxford University Press Inc., New York

British Library Cataloguing in Publication Data

Data available

Library of Congress Cataloging in Publication Data

Gosse, Edmund, 1849–1928.
Father and son/Edmund Gosse; edited with an introduction and notes by Michael Newton.
p. cm.—(Oxford world's classics)
Includes bibliographical references.
1. Gosse, Edmund, 1849–1928—Childhood and youth. 2. Authors, English—19th
century—Family relationships. 3. England—Social life and customs—19th century.
4. Authors. English—19th century—Biography. 5. Plymouth Brethren—England—Biography.
6. Zoologists—Great Britain—Biography. 7. Gosse, Philip Henry, 1810–1888. 8. Fathers
and sons—England. 9. Apostasy. I. Newton, Michael, 1965– . II. Title. III. Oxford world's
classics (Oxford University Press)
PR4725.G7Z5 2004 820'.809—dc22 [B] 2004049285

ISBN 0–19–284066–5

1

Typeset in Ehrhardt
by RefineCatch Limited, Bungay, Suffolk
Printed in Great Britain by
Clays Ltd, St Ives plc

OXFORD WORLD'S CLASSICS

FATHER AND SON

EDMUND WILLIAM GOSSE was born in 1849, the only child of
Emily Gosse (née Bowes) (1806–57), a writer of Christian tracts,
and Philip Henry Gosse (1810–88), an eminent naturalist and
author. Both Edmund's parents were ardent members of the
Christian sect, the Plymouth Brethren. In 1857, following his
mother's death, Gosse went to live with his father in St Marychurch
in Devon. Gosse came up to London in 1867, where he began work
as a cataloguer at the British Museum. It was at this time that Gosse
rejected his father's Christianity. Gosse pursued a very successful
career as a 'man of letters', writing numerous literary critical studies, biographies, and books of essays. He was instrumental in intro-
ducing Ibsen and Gide into English culture; championed the work
of Swinburne (and wrote a bowdlerized biography of the poet);
and was prominent in the re-evaluation of John Donne. However,
accusations of carelessness marred his reputation as a serious
scholar. Gosse married Ellen Epps in 1875; together they had two
daughters and one son. He worked as a translator at the Board of
Trade (1874), a lecturer in English literature at Trinity College,
Cambridge (1884–9), and as librarian at the House of Lords
(1904–14). He received many honours and was knighted in 1925. He
numbered Robert Louis Stevenson, Thomas Hardy, and Henry
James among his friends. His literary masterpiece is *Father and
Son* (1907), an impassioned and witty analysis of his childhood
and adolescence, and of his relationship with his scientific and
evangelical father. He died in 1928.

MICHAEL NEWTON is the author of *Savage Girls and Wild Boys: A
History of Feral Children* (Faber, 2002) and of a book on *Kind Hearts
and Coronets* (BFI, 2003). He has taught for Princeton University,
Central Saint Martins College, and University College London.

OXFORD WORLD'S CLASSICS

*For over 100 years Oxford World's Classics have brought
readers closer to the world's great literature. Now with over 700
titles—from the 4,000-year-old myths of Mesopotamia to the
twentieth century's greatest novels—the series makes available
lesser-known as well as celebrated writing.*

*The pocket-sized hardbacks of the early years contained
introductions by Virginia Woolf, T. S. Eliot, Graham Greene,
and other literary figures which enriched the experience of reading.
Today the series is recognized for its fine scholarship and
reliability in texts that span world literature, drama and poetry,
religion, philosophy and politics. Each edition includes perceptive
commentary and essential background information to meet the
changing needs of readers.*

CONTENTS

Acknowledgements   vii

Introduction   ix

Note on the Text   xxix

Select Bibliography   xxxvi

A Chronology of Edmund Gosse   xxxix

FATHER AND SON   1

Appendix 1. From *A Memorial of the Last Day on Earth of Emily Gosse* by P. H. Gosse   187

Appendix 2. From *Omphalos* by P. H. Gosse   196

Appendix 3. From *The Life of Philip Henry Gosse FRS* by Edmund Gosse   202

Appendix 4. Two letters from Sir James Frazer to Edmund Gosse   205

Explanatory Notes   207

ACKNOWLEDGEMENTS

I would like to thank Judith Luna and the editing team at Oxford University Press for their incredible patience. Thanks to Philip Horne for all his excellent and scholarly advice, and thanks to David Grugeon for the *Signals*. I am also grateful to the staff at: the Special Collection section of the Brotherton Library at the University of Leeds; the London Library; and the British Library; and to Professor John Sutherland for suggesting that I might ask to edit *Father and Son*. I would like also to thank Lily Kim for reminding me of what I ought to know: that is, the themes of this book are still living ones. Thanks to Richard Hamblyn who gave me a line, and with whom I shared by telephone the daily sufferings of an editor, to Lee Sands, who gave me another good line, and to Greg Dart for his fulminations against the puritans. Especial thanks to Liz Newton, my mother, for her biblical advice; and thanks to my father for other advice and support.

I dedicate this edition to Christopher Hamilton, someone who happily combines only the very best features of both father and son.

INTRODUCTION

I

Edmund Gosse knew everyone; no one really knew Gosse. He dined with André Gide; corresponded with Henrik Ibsen; gossiped with Henry James; joked with Robert Louis Stevenson; and had tea with Thomas Hardy. When, in a quest for an academic position, he applied to Trinity College, Cambridge, for a lectureship, Tennyson, Browning, and Matthew Arnold wrote his letters of reference.

Old age covered Gosse with honours, transforming him into that pitiful thing, the unsmiling, public man. He was the official representative of letters; a tame author. His friend, A. C. Benson, sighed over Gosse's bloodless biography of Algernon Charles Swinburne: 'It is the life of a fearless and ebullient little man, written by a man in an armchair who is afraid of everyone and everything—the shadow of fear lies over the whole book—fear of critics, fear of relations, fear of readers, fear of press-cuttings.'[1] In the 1910s and 1920s, to young writers he was a memento mori for the imaginative soul: might theirs wither like Gosse's? There he emphatically was: a dismaying embodiment of the old guard. He had crucified poetry on the cross of respectability. No one believes a laureate will write a good poem, and Gosse was the laureate of *belles lettres*.

Yet the good companion, the public figure, none of that conveys the inner stresses that turned Gosse's life into the affair of depth and shadow it truly was. Melancholy softened his outline, and made of his self-importance something ineffably depressing. That sadness came from a conflict that makes Gosse's story one of the most significant of the nineteenth century. And not just of the nineteenth century: Gosse's struggle resonates in our culture too, in ways that may yet surprise us.

In one of Max Beerbohm's wickedly accurate caricatures, we find the perfect image of Gosse's doubleness. It is called 'The Old and the Young Self'. The child Gosse, a small, yearning figure dressed like a Tolstoyan peasant, with a wild gesture cries out the words 'Are you saved?' to the aged Gosse, one stiff, bespectacled figure in

[1] Quoted in Ann Thwaite, *Edmund Gosse* (London: Secker & Warburg, 1984), 479.

evening dress among many. Old Gosse looks past the embarrassing disturbance. The child pleads; the man turns a stony face to him. Above all, that question—'Are you saved?'—disturbs the public function: this is not bonhomie, or literary gossip, or urbane dinner-party chat. It is an appeal to the soul, and the soul should never appear in polite company.

Beerbohm's image shows two Gosses: one is old, tight, enclosed; the other is a child, energetic, ardent with a terrible knowledge. And yet it is old Gosse that wrote this book about the other. Somehow he had kept that child still alive in him. It was the part of him that no one knew. The old man looks a terribly unpromising author, hardly someone for the young to love, or the rebel to cherish. None the less _Father and Son_ (1907) stands as one of the great paeans to youth, one of the twentieth century's indispensable acts of rebellion.

There are other reasons why we should still read _Father and Son_. It is brilliantly written, and full of gentle wit. It is an unmatched social document, preserving for us whole the experience of child-hood in a Protestant sect in the high Victorian period. It is a vital record of the impact of evolutionary theories on the religious mind. Above all, it is one of our best accounts of adolescence, particularly for those who endured and found themselves within, or despite, a religious upbringing. In a secular country, in the early twenty-first century, such a theme may seem a dead dilemma. Of course, the truth is that in our age of fundamentalisms—Christian and Muslim—Gosse's book is more relevant than ever.

Perhaps the chief barrier to enjoyment of _Father and Son_ is the personality of the son himself. Young Gosse's ghastly priggishness complicates our reaction to his story. He can be, as he himself admits, a precocious and irritating little boy. He is the kind of child who points out to a visiting carpenter the smartness of his family's wallpaper (p. 106), or who can wag a finger at his father with outraged piety, ' "Papa," I said, "don't tell me that she's a pedobaptist?" ' (p. 126).

This priggishness derives from his melancholy solitude. He is a boy who might be left by his father like 'the domestic cat, in an empty house for the neighbours to feed at intervals' (p. 46). He begins as a child simply lonely, and goes on to become lost, with his father, in a loneliness _à deux_. Gosse the father's habit of isolation made young Edmund lonely too, and probably lies behind that suave sociability that defined Edmund's adult life. Interestingly, Edmund Gosse finds a source of pain in his later need for people—that 'magnetism of humanity which has been the agony of mature years' (p. 156).

So young Gosse has the only child's precocity, his loneliness too, and above all that pressured sense of self held tensely within the loving aspirations of his parents. The paradox of the only child is that his parents' attention both privileges and destroys him. A sense of specialness oppresses the young Gosse, and his loneliness can be such that it can seem that he stands outside of childhood, removed from it by a heavy gauze of parental love: 'It was not in harshness or ill-nature that he worried me so much; on the contrary, it was all part of his too-anxious love' (p. 115).

Melancholy and repressed anger inform this book. Young Gosse is both prig and rebel. And Gosse the writer knows this: he looks back on his childhood with the 'tender contempt' that Dennis Potter, another childhood memorialist and a dramatizer of *Father and Son*, recommended for such glances.

II

The story of *Father and Son* is soon told. The book describes the early life of Edmund Gosse in a Plymouth Brethren home. His mother, who dies early, is an evangelist and writer of Christian tracts. His father, who takes him to live in Devon, is a zoologist and a student of marine life. The book reveals the father's response to the new evolutionary theories, and shows the son's gradual break with his father and with the Christian faith. It is a brilliant, and often comic, record of the small diplomacies of home: those indirections, omissions, insincerities, and secrecies that underlie family relationships. It is also a painful record of apostasy. In a secular age, it might be difficult to imagine just how bewildering that loss of faith could be, how it seemed to set the soul adrift in a hostile and directionless world.

Yet *Father and Son* is not a conventional autobiography. As the book's subtitle points out, it is rather 'a study of two temperaments'. Perhaps, in describing the book as a 'study', with all the coolness that implies, Edmund Gosse attempts to distance himself from too radical a critique of his father. The word 'temperament' appears twice in the opening pages of the book, to reappear intriguingly at its end.

However, at times Gosse will pause and remind us that this is not 'another memoir of public individuals' and that he is not going to rewrite his parents' biographies. Late in the book, he resists the impulse to describe his school days in more detail, since 'this is not an autobiography' (p. 157). Gosse is subtly directing us as to how we ought to read his book. He tells us that this story (despite its fantastic moments) is no fiction; that 'chronicle or fiction' has never provided figures like those encountered in his childhood (p. 73).

While the infant Gosse's first and second words were 'Papa' and 'Mamma', his third word was 'book'. So it is that, fittingly, *Father and Son* is a work of literary responses, in which, finally, the Bible itself is taken as just another text. Gosse's book exists through a constant relationship to other books, that break in through allusion, quotation, or analogy. Gosse was a natural critic. Literature, that began as an escape, became an official and inescapable function. To understand his experience, he makes for the library.

Yet in the process of literary allusion, Gosse can reveal tensions hidden within his text. Consider the moment in which Gosse compares Miss Marks to the Dickens characters, Mrs Pipchin and Miss Sally Brass (p. 57). This is to cast himself as Paul Dombey, the doomed child-hero of *Dombey and Son* (1846–8) and indeed the similarities are striking, since both are sensitive 'old-fashioned' children with dead mothers and stern fathers. Or what is one to make of those several feminizing and vaguely sexualized moments in which Edmund describes himself as a princess locked in a tower (p. 22), or Bluebeard's wife (p. 119), or St Teresa (p. 115), or an Andromeda chained to the rocks (p. 82)? Not all Gosse's allusions are as packed with complexity as these, but the alert reader would be wise to look out for additional meanings whenever the author invokes another book.

As well as being a real, or at least a remembered experience, the miserable childhood and the adolescent loss of faith were literary tropes of the period, appearing in the autobiographies and autobiographical fictions of many Victorian and Edwardian writers. The most famous such books were: John Stuart Mill, *Autobiography* (1873); William Hale White, *The Autobiography of Mark Rutherford, Dissenting Minister* (1881); and Samuel Butler, *The Way of All Flesh* (1903). Gosse's book can be seen as written self-consciously within this very loose genre. However, Gosse did not need to turn to Samuel Butler to pick up the sarcasm that best and most subtly expressed his rage. For Gosse, anger could be transformed into a kind of elegance; the humour in his book mingles sympathy with the sneer of contempt.

Gosse's literary antecedents offer him other models. His auto-biography belongs to one stream of turn-of-the-century writing that presents identity as emerging from an assertion of autonomy. In *The English Novel in History, 1895–1920*, David Trotter describes a modern self that claims itself through a break with its class, familial, marital, or religious allegiances.[2] What is common to *Father and Son* and those other major religious autobiographies is the sense that identity, that once existed within the needs, beliefs, and speech of the group, becomes something asserted by a lonely and individual self in its own rhetoric and its own choices. For in *Father and Son*, religion is a language, a way of taking the world within a mix of 'Biblical and colloquial phrases' (p. 79). It is a language that permits such flour-ishes as ' "Oh! blessed Child, you're wonderin' to zee old Pewings here again, but He have rolled away my mountain!" ' (p. 113). But for young Edmund religious discourse is a 'mechanical address' that reveals 'the emptiness of my language' (p. 129). The son's spirit does not go with his father's words. Gosse murmurs, 'And yet—I doubt' (p. 131); the cadence of that sentence unveils the heart of his book.

Of course, what Edmund Gosse actually does is to choose a counter-rhetoric. As he does so, he loads the last chapters of the book with biblical allusion and metaphor, his language still super-saturated with the words of the religion he professes to reject. Yet to use the Bible so is to display a mastery that amounts to a rejection; see, it says, I truly know this no longer needed thing. So Edmund Gosse spurns (without losing hold of) the language of the Bible and the Brethren in order to adopt the language of the poet, the pagan, the rational scientist.

By 1907, Edmund Gosse was already offering the public an historical text, almost an anthropological account of recent religious history. So distant did the lives of the mid-Victorians already feel. Quite often, he pauses to remind us of the historical and cultural distance between the reader and the world he presents to us, so mid-Victorian, almost so seventeenth century.

Writing of the Plymouth Brethren, Gosse was also presenting a

[2] See David Trotter, *The English Novel in History, 1895–1920* (London and New York: Routledge, 1993), 27–48.

religious sect whose cultural life was defined by exclusivity and secrecy. This desire to shun the world meant good literary copy. In writing *Father and Son*, Gosse would be providing an insight into a world that he knew would have been hidden from most of his readers, even those who were members of less rigorous Protestant sects.

The 'Brethren' began in the winter of 1827–8 with a break by four Dublin Protestants from all existing established and dissenting churches. The movement spread as one of the men, John Nelson Darby, travelled in 1831 via Oxford to Plymouth, where a similar minded group had founded the 'Providence Chapel'; from here the Brethren spread across the country, becoming particularly strong in the west country: an Assembly Room was founded in Torquay in 1834, and around 1850 the St Marychurch Assembly, where the Gosses worshipped, started up. At Plymouth, the Brethren began to demonstrate their separateness from the world, first of all in sacrificing gifts of jewellery, and increasingly, following a split in the little church between 'Exclusive' and 'Open' Brethren, in a sense that they should seclude themselves, keeping meetings closed and private. In *The Life of Philip Henry Gosse*, Edmund Gosse describes the beliefs of the Brethren:

The tenets of this body are perhaps well known. They may be best described by a series of negations. The Brethren have no ritual, no appointed minister, no government, no hierarchy of any kind; they eschew all that is systematic or vertebrate; their manner of worship is the most socialistic hitherto invented. Their positive tenets are an implicit following of the text of Holy Scripture, the enforcement of adult baptism, subsequent upon conversion and preliminary to the partaking of the Lord's Supper in both kinds, the loaf of bread and the cup of wine being passed from hand to hand in silence, every Sunday morning.[3]

Much Victorian religious experience involved a constant debate between faith and doubt. The Brethren could never allow this uneasy and productive dialogue. Instead they valued fixity and the unchangingness of true faith. It is from the conflict between fixity and change that the force of Gosse's book emerges.

[3] Edmund Gosse, *The Life of Philip Henry Gosse, F.R.S.* (London: Kegan Paul, Trench, Trübner, 1890), 213.

III

The book is called *Father and Son*, and indeed motherlessness is central to it. The mother is the absent one, and her absence informs young Edmund's story.

Emily Bowes, Edmund's mother, was of American descent, born in England; she seems, before her marriage, to have been a strong young woman, effectively being the person who kept her family going. There are moving accounts of Emily Gosse in her husband's memorial of her last illness (see Appendix 1), and in Anna Shipton's hugely popular memoir, *Tell Jesus* (1863). Anna Shipton, who suitably enough was brought to God by the study of rock pools, seems to have been a little enamoured of Emily. She describes her as young-looking, delicate featured, with a childlike smile. We see her watching over her young son: 'Many a lesson might nurses and governesses have learned from her.'[4]

Later in her book Anna dreams of Emily in 'a panorama of glorious significance'.[5] Angels give Emily a heavy purple robe that achingly bears her emaciated body down; the robe slowly vanishes, and she is given another shining robe. She then allows herself to be dressed like a happy child; her face loses all trace of pain. And then young Edmund appears in the dream: 'The sight of her child appeared to arrest the happy pilgrim. She paused. Immediately the angelic hands were withdrawn . . . A basket of fruit was near her. She seemed to search amongst it for the ripest, and chose . . . a pomegranate. When the child had received the fruit she appeared satisfied; and her angel attendants resumed their office of leading her onwards.'[6] The world of the Brethren was one of such significances, divine patterns, and intentions. Edmund Gosse left unrecorded what he made of this dream in which he figures.

To understand Emily Gosse properly, we must place her in the context of Victorian female piety. For some women religion offered the rare possibility of a public career, while to others it offered fulfilment through passivity and contemplation. Emily Gosse chose the path of activity, securing for herself a place in the social realm. Women like Emily Gosse, despite her son's insistence on her

---

[4] Anna Shipton, *Tell Jesus* (London: Morgan and Chase, 1863), 8.
[5] Ibid. 18.   [6] Ibid. 19–20.

isolation, were not lonely eccentrics but members of a community composed both of women and of men. Her pamphlets seek access to a religious or, indeed, 'unsaved' audience far beyond that of just the Plymouth Brethren themselves (as her sales ran into the hundreds of thousands).

Her chief task in *Father and Son* is to die. Philip Henry Gosse's dispassionately passionate account of his wife's death in the *Memorial* he wrote of her is incredibly painful to read. This is how a Christian woman died in the middle years of the nineteenth century. In his father's book, young Edmund's presence is shadowy, though at times we are reminded that the little boy is there watching his mother's death.

Edmund figures his later rejection of Christianity as a rejection of his father. But, of course, it also entails the guilt of denying his dead mother and refusing her dying wishes. Her loss is a burden that seals his fate, turning him for ever into the dedicated child of the Lord, and the boy whose mother has died. Her death translates into a sense of his own mortality. Edmund seems to be a frail child: his stepmother's relations remark that ' "the first thing you will have to do will be to bury that poor child" ' (p. 128). He appears to be dead when born (p. 8); later, death threatens him again (p. 33). And yet Edmund lives, and it is his mother who dies; his life inevitably requiring her further death as a figure of restricting love.

IV

Over and above the mother's absence is the father's oppressive and wonderful presence. Since the book's first publication, it has been a common reaction for readers to prefer the father to the son. In his biography of Gosse, Evan Charteris notes this fact, and declares it to have been one of Gosse's intended aims. He quotes a letter, written in 1924, in which Gosse asserts that 'the book is a monument to the memory of my father, an extraordinary man'.[7]

The father was pale-skinned, burly, 'heavy-limbed', though under average height; with a large face and full brown eyes. His lips were characteristically tightly closed. Despite his enthusiastic personality, he could be bashful and irritably anti-social. At times he was

---

[7] Evan Charteris, *The Life and Letters of Sir Edmund Gosse* (London: William Heinemann, 1931), 307.

formidable, grim, and scarily severe. 'The air of severity was increased by the habit of brushing his straight black hair tightly away from the forehead; it was occasionally removed by a cloud of immeasurable tenderness passing across the great brown lustrous orbs of his eyes. His smile was rare, but when it came it was exquisite.'[8] He had been an adventurer, who, aged only 17, had sailed for Newfoundland; a Canadian explorer; a traveller to Alabama and Jamaica; a Dorset prophet; a lover of sea-creatures; a prodigious author; a dweller by the ocean. Moreover, he had genuinely struggled with life: been destitute and reduced to living on his wits, stubbornly refusing what aid there was. His son's path through life seems, in comparison, easy, regular, and strewn with eager helpers.

The image of Gosse the father as an unloving and unlovely Victorian patriarch will just not do. His writings reveal a genuinely sweet character. Nor does he always seem at war with childhood. The father had been slow to grow up, a man who, according to his son, remained a child for a long time: 'I cannot exactly describe what it was that made this powerfully built and admirably equipped man sometimes strike one as having the immatureness and touching incompleteness of the nature of a child.'[9] Philip Henry Gosse's love of nature began in childhood, and he sustained this childhood interest throughout his life. In *Sea-Side Pleasures* (1853), both Emily and Philip Gosse write that: 'The rounded pebbles at your feet, washed so clean and looking so brightly polished by the action of the waves, tempt you to become a child again.'[10] The tone of that book is one of people who can feel pleasure, who can play (if a little earnestly), and who are not afraid of looking ridiculous. It is a book that contrives to make you see the world with an '*open eye*'.[11]

His *A Naturalist's Rambles on the Devonshire Coast* (1853) is wondering, curious, delightedly animated. Gosse senior was no dry stick; he writes with the subtlest and best of motives: that is, he seeks to transmit a pleasure. If that implies vague uplift and an earnest, bracing approach, then we should bear in mind also the father's commitment to 'precision' uncoloured by some pseudo-poetic tinge of jollity. Gosse is a scientist, first and last; a Christian, first and last;

---

[8] Gosse, *The Life of Philip Henry Gosse*, 207.
[9] Ibid. 335.
[10] Philip Henry Gosse and Emily Gosse, *Sea-Side Pleasures* (London: SPCK, 1853), 1.
[11] Ibid. 8.

if both of those things suggest aridity to us, then we must recognize that could be our blindness. Gosse senior was an enthusiast for science and for salvation, and we should hear the echo of those enthusiasms behind his son's words if we are to view their tragedy correctly.

Most interestingly, father and son are more alike than might be thought. So it is that Edmund can remark on how his father once watched the way in which his son walked to school 'by dancing along the curbstone sideways, my face turned inwards and my arms beating against my legs, conversing loudly all the time. This was a case of pure heredity, for so he used to go to his school, forty years before, along the streets of Poole' (p. 122).

Moreover, both father and son were 'bookish' children. The father youthfully tries to write verse, but 'His genius was not for poetry'.[12] The son's genius was not for poetry either, though he took longer to realize it. Like Edmund, Philip Henry Gosse developed an adolescent passion for literature. The father was introduced to Scott's *Lady of the Lake* and Byron in childhood; as a teenager, he became unbearably excited by Byron's *Lara*.

But in spite of, or perhaps because of, these similarities, we find, of course, that the book is most interested in the conflict between father and son. This conflict can be best traced by considering the two men's attitude to evolutionary theories.

It would be easy and misguided to imagine a simple state of war between the evangelicals and science. There is the example of Michael Faraday, the great scientist and committed Christian. Moreover, many evangelicals were interested in science and were often amateurs of botany, geology, zoology, or chemistry (the eighteenth-century tradition shows a strong connection between religious dissent and natural philosophy), although most were unresponsive to evolutionary theory. Yet the last book Philip Henry Gosse ever read was a biography of Darwin.

Despite the fact that the picture is more complex than might at first be thought, it remains the case that Gosse the father rejected the concept of evolution, while the son appears to have embraced it. In this divide, they reveal themselves. To understand what the division means, we should turn to the father's book attacking evolutionary theory, *Omphalos* (1857), and to the son's correspondence with Sir

---

[12] Gosse, *The Life of Philip Henry Gosse*, 69.

James Frazer, the famous anthropologist and author of *The Golden Bough*.

The writing of *Omphalos* in the immediate aftermath of his wife's death and the hostile public reception it received on publication stands as one of the most striking moments in *Father and Son*. P. H. Gosse really does seem to have believed that he had come up with an argument that refuted evolutionary theory and preserved for science the literal truth of Scripture. In its account of the many metamorphoses that animals and plants live through, his book does celebrate development and process. Yet it also clearly denies the idea that forms are unstable and mutable. In *Omphalos*, Gosse the father imagines God creating animals, and human beings, already in a state of full maturity.[13] He writes: 'In the preceding examples I have assumed that every organic entity was created in that stage of its being which constitutes the acme of its peculiar development; when all its faculties are in their highest perfection, and when it is best fitted to reproduce its own image.'[14] From this point onwards development is circular; in motion, but always fundamentally static.

This idea of a development already fully attained at its beginning reproduces in the biological sphere what Edmund Gosse feels was done to him as a child, both in the sense that his parents refuse to treat him as though he indeed were a child, and also in so far as they deny that he can choose for himself the kind of adult he wishes to be. Young Gosse fights for the right to change his mind, to step outside the circle of development and head off in a new direction of his own. But the father stunts young Gosse's development; the son is 'like a plant on which a pot has been placed' (p. 151). The father both denies his son's individuality in one way (it belongs within the circle of family life) and also denies his right to develop, almost the fact of development itself. Edmund is both denied as himself (he is the 'bud of his parents') and also denied as a child, an immature being who shall grow into something else.

This refusal to accept the fact of development also appears in P. H. Gosse's lingering within a religious belief that is out of time. It is as though he himself were caught in a rock pool left by the withdrawing tide of faith. In a secular and liberal age, he lives anachronistically as a Puritan figure from the seventeenth century:

[13] Philip Henry Gosse, *Omphalos* (London: Van Voorst, 1857), 294.
[14] Ibid. 292.

But it was mainly that he had nothing in common with his age. He was a
Covenanter come into the world a couple of centuries after his time, to
find society grown too soft for his scruples and too ingenious for his severe
simplicity. He could never learn to speak the ethical language of the nineteenth century; he was seventeenth century in spirit and manner to the
last.[15]

For Edmund Gosse, faith changes, like everything else; a belief can
become outmoded and fall away from the popular mind. For Philip
Henry Gosse, belief was unchangeable.

Against this view, Edmund Gosse embraces in *Father and Son* an
image of evolution and change. He reveals one way he may seek to
do this in a letter about that book to his friend, Sir James Frazer
(Frazer's replies to Gosse are included in Appendix 4):

If you come across an anonymous book called *Father and Son*, which is
just published by Heinemann, let me tell you that it is I who have written
it and that it contains some observations about the growth of moral (or
savage) ideas in children such as I should not dare to lay before you, but
such as I should be pleased if you thought of value. And with this squint-
ing and trepidatious hint, I leave you to more important studies.[16]

The letter to Frazer may reveal a great deal of what Gosse was
hoping to set out in his book. As the preface to *Father and Son*
declares, he has two aims: to diagnose a dying Puritanism; but also to
trace the process of development in an ordinary child. It is highly
likely that Gosse understood that development in terms informed
by an evolutionary psychology, one that relied on the theory of
'recapitulation'. This means that 'ontogeny' repeats (or recapitu-
lates) 'phylogeny', or, in simpler words, that the development of the
individual repeats the development of the human race. Recapitulation derived from embryology, which then believed that the human
foetus passes in the womb through the evolutionary stages of life on
earth. Then, by analogy, and not just by analogy, it was felt that the
growing child passed through physical and psychological stages of
savagery and barbarism on the way to a fully civilized adult maturity.
This sense of an atavistic return in childhood to primitive and original human experience informed the psychology of the day. And the

[15] Gosse, *The Life of Philip Henry Gosse*, 335; the entire original passage is quoted in
App. 3.
[16] Quoted without source in Thwaite, *Edmund Gosse*, 438.

anthropology too: it was not just the puritan Gosse senior who would have seen in Christmas celebrations the modern survival of 'horrible heathen rites' (p. 69).

So it is that young Gosse practises a form of natural magic that approaches 'the ideas of savages at a very early stage of development' (p. 26). And so it is that he believes that he will be able to walk on the sea, if he drinks of it, 'a perfectly irrational movement of mind, like those of savages' (p. 60). Such moments are not just curiosities designed to impress his famous anthropologist friend. They expose a fundamental difference from his father in their concepts of childhood. For all the religious training that young Gosse undergoes, recapitulation means that he remains intrinsically savage, pagan, and resistant. Moreover, he lives within a process of dark, inner evolutionary change over which his parents have no control.

The book declares itself to be a study of two temperaments. The word 'temperament' is a curious one. It suggests an innate and unchangeable set of predispositions. But where do these predispositions come from? What is their source? One obvious answer is that they derive from our parents. Indeed this sense that our temperament is something derived from our family inheritance is one strong if contradictory theme in Edmund Gosse's study.

Yet temperament may come from elsewhere, an unexpected and unaccountable gift, not formed by 'suggestion or training' (p. 22). To Gosse, the 'consciousness of self' (p. 22) charges the very existence of such instinctual promptings. The self finds its ultimate origin in the common experience of humanity, the savagery from which every individual child returns. The young child taps at strange moments into the universal consciousness of the human race as it has developed from its primitive origins to its sophisticated present form.

Yet the paganism that the young Gosse embodies as a child, later becomes something chosen, the ultimate rebellion against Christianity. Gosse's adolescent paganism fits with an over-valuation of art, which, from Matthew Arnold onwards, was seen by some optimistic souls as providing a beautiful and profound alternative to religion. Gosse shares something of that attitude, and really does pitch imaginative literature against Christianity. The 'pagan' spirit he finds in Michael Scott's novel, *Tom Cringle's Log*, is a sense of life, energy, and the free reign of the instincts. Against it, Christianity appears as dullness, restriction, and repression. The puritan censors fiction—although this may not be unique to evangelical families, as Kathleen Tillotson describes a general antipathy to the novel in mid-Victorian homes.[17] None the less, the parents suspect art, and it is art that sets young Gosse free.

This becomes clearest late in the book, where, in a series of vignettes, young Gosse must choose between his love of art and his father's religion. In each case, the struggle is brief: he desires the Greek gods, the plays of Shakespeare. 'The dangerous and pagan notion that beauty palliates evil budded in my mind, without any external suggestion, and by this reflection alone I was still further sundered from the faith in which I had been trained' (p. 146). Once again, young Gosse's unbidden instinct undermines the careful process of nurture. He may be a puritan by upbringing, but he is a pagan by nature.

Above all, Gosse is a pagan in so far as he is a reader. Despite the wide range of Christian material they read, the Brethren are ultimately readers of one book—the Bible; Edmund is the reader of many. Yet paganism, or, at least, anti-puritanism is as much a matter of how one reads a book as it is of what books one reads.

Recently critics have spoken interestingly of how Christian theology in the nineteenth century took on the language of evolutionary theory to explore how the meaning of Scripture might change over time. Such an idea would have been anathema to P. H. Gosse, for whom the unchanging nature of God and therefore of his Word were central to his faith. You might argue over the interpretation of Scripture, but this was not to imagine that interpretations might change with the times, but rather to show that human understanding might be weak in relation to Divine mystery. Only those already filled with the spirit of God could truly read and understand his Word. Professor Suzy Anger suggests that literary criticism was to follow the shift in theology. By the end of the century, an early Victorian sense of literary texts as possessing fixed meaning vanishes from the criticism of Pater and Wilde (both undoubtedly influential on Edmund Gosse). They do away with authorial intention, and focus on how meaning constantly shifts and alters. Did Gosse inherit this new approach to the literary text, one which furthermore favoured development and instability over fixity in religion, science, and the human

[17] See Kathleen Tillotson, *Novels of the Eighteen-Forties* (1954; Oxford: Oxford University Press, 1961), 18.

personality itself? Certainly Edmund Gosse knows the 'peculiar agony in the paradox that truth has two forms, each of them indisputable, yet each antagonistic to the other' (p. 61).

To read a book in a sense of its instability is to read imaginatively. Gosse accuses his parents of a lack of 'sympathetic imagination' (p. 41), the one positive value that literature may give us, and a root into the moral life. Gosse the son snidely notes of his father that as 'a collector of facts and marshaller of observations, he had not a rival in that age; his very absence of imagination aided him in this work' (p. 71). However, both men possessed the taste for the minute, the hidden, the unobtrusive. In *Father and Son*, this shows in the precision of description, pinning a person down in the memory. The belief is that the life of a thing emerges from attention to the detail. This is both P. H. Gosse's aesthetic credo and his son's.

In *Father and Son*, Edmund Gosse himself is a prodigious collector of facts, but, and this is not just filial self-satisfaction, he brings to those facts an imaginative sympathy that divides and vivifies his book. It is not just 'the troublesome pettiness of detail' (p. 80) that he wants, but the philosophic shape that comprehends those details. That philosophic shape entails a sense of the multiplicity of meanings in a book and in life.

Edmund Gosse attacks his father for his dogmatism, and it is facile and ultimately unrevealing to point out that the son's liberalism could run the risk of being as dogmatic in its refusal of dogma. In fact, there is a genuine difference here between father and son, between the puritan and the pagan. One wishes for the closed and certain thing; the other lives within indeterminacy.

V

The tacit subject of *Father and Son* is vocation. Gosse's parents choose a path in life for him, while every instinct he has, every facet of the 'temperament' alluded to in the book's subtitle, point him towards his vocation as a writer. He must break one 'vocation' imposed from without, and follow another of his own choosing.

Young Gosse's story is that of a person striving to live according to his temperament, and to follow the literary vocation that he most desires. When he discovers his aptitude for verse, he awakens his 'prosodical instinct' (p. 96), bringing to consciousness something already natural and dormant in him. On the other hand, he can never become an artist, because his drawings show 'no native skill' (p. 99). As Miss Marks asserts, ' "Even the Lord can't make a silk purse out of a sow's ear" ' (p. 121).

For this reason, it is painful and intriguing that Emily Gosse should appear as one who mortifies her instinct, as a natural novelist who on principle would not write a novel, and who also conquers her natural timidity in order to be a better evangelist for the Lord (p. 34). The father is much better suited than the son by temperament to the exigencies of his religion. But that is young Edmund's point. What is good for the father is not good for him. And even the father must do violence to his instincts in order to remain a good Christian. His 'every instinct' (p. 62) turns him in the direction of the new evolutionary theory. But then his absolute faith in Scripture constricts that move of his inner being. He searches his soul for 'the least unbending to human instinct', magnifying every trifling pleasure 'into a huge offence' (p. 66). In the end, 'he contrived to stifle with a deplorable success alike the function of the imagination, the sense of moral justice, and his own deep and instinctive tenderness of heart' (p. 169). Here instinct carries a moral depth, an inner goodness that religion perverts. Yet 'instinct' is also a key word in *Father and Son*, in so far as it gives the book an aptly scientific turn. Edmund Gosse's attack on Christianity is Darwinian, and, inadvertently perhaps, Nietzschean. For Gosse, Christianity perverts natural instinct, making a person turn against themselves in pursuit of an illusory ideal.

The book turns on two contradictions of instinct. First there is the cognitive dissonance produced in Gosse the father, by the collision of two contradictory modes of thinking and being, as his religion and his science break apart. The result is 'a dislocation of his intellectual system' (p. 70). Given this fracture in his world, Gosse senior fails to do what his son will later do, and rebel against the religion that upholds him. He lacks, what Edmund Gosse considers, 'the resolution of the larger nature' (p. 71) that enables one to trash one's deepest faith. And what of the 'large natured' Gosse the son? For him, the second contradiction in the book is his love and his hate for his father (and behind him, his mother), his desire to be loyal, and his need to be free. The book you are holding is the record of his attempt to forge together that split in his feelings.

The crime that Gosse's parents commit, if it is a crime, is to forget that their son is a child. It is as though particularly Gosse, the father, imagines his son's childhood as an impaired and imperfect state, a necessary if lamentable preparation for real adult life. The deathbed sealing of Edmund's dedication to the Lord is a terrible moment, as the young Gosse sinks under the burden, not only of his mother's death, but of his parents' expectations. Philip Henry Gosse may know that young Edmund is 'not what is styled adult' (p. 104), but still he believes him to be 'adult in a knowledge of the Lord' (p. 104).

In the brief period when young Edmund escapes his father's influence by being lodged with his cousins in Clifton, he 'lived the life of an ordinary little boy, relapsing, to a degree which would have filled my Father with despair, into childish thoughts and childish language' (p. 47). Gosse describes this brief happy state as having 'no history' (p. 47). What does he mean by this? Is it that for a while Edmund can escape the burden of being who he is, a young orphan? Or is it that falling back into this ordinary childhood, Gosse suddenly and delightedly no longer becomes a subject of aesthetic interest; that he is no longer the kind of boy who requires the explanation provided by a book?

Yet perhaps the Gosses' crime against their son is an extreme form of one that any adult may commit. For one purpose of *Father and Son* is to remind the reader of those fugitive, forgotten, and only half-understood experiences of child life. The child is alien to the adult, both then, and now, even in the act of literary remembrance that evokes again a child that both still exists in the writing adult and is simultaneously lost for ever. Adults approach children in a spirit of misapprehension: 'As a child develops, those who regard it with tenderness or impatience are seldom even approximately correct in their analysis of its intellectual movements, largely because, if there is anything to record, it defies adult definition' (p. 139).

In his consideration of vocation, the question Gosse poses for himself and us is whether identity derives from our parents, our past, or is it made by the individual in refutation of that past. Gosse claims the latter, while the autobiographical mode in which he writes, with its commitment to memory and to the very idea of 'formative experiences' and parental influences, argues for the other. This is a self-divided book. It chooses freedom while placing the origins of the self within the circumscription that the self rejects. The very title of the book shows that the self is always a self in so far as it is in relatedness, as one of a pair, father and son (the mother from whom one truly buds being lost from the picture). Young Edmund exists within this contradiction. To declare independence is an act of rejection that still yearns towards that which one claims independence from.

Near the beginning of the book, Gosse is his parents' creature, a child 'without individual existence' (p. 19). By the end of the book, he stands alone as an autonomous person. Father and son battle together, in a clash of two ways of imagining and living in the world. For the son, there is the sense of history and its contingencies; changefulness; and the relative nature of truth. For the father, there is the sense that truth is single, final, and irrefutable; that all readings should be literal.

Yet it is wise to recognize the deep force of the father's commit-ment. He stands in this book as a titanic competitor, a rival that young Gosse seeks vainly to outstrip. He moves us like a fact of nature. There he is; we cannot change him; he will not change. And beside his brooding stability, Gosse the son, with his liberalism, and his poetry, and his chosen multiplicity, feels to us insubstantial, vague, and shifting. Gosse the father is a single, simple thing; the son is everything and nothing, someone caught between cultures. So it is that at the end of the book, young Gosse becomes doubly double: both child and adult; both Christian and pagan. His adolescent soul is 'shadowy', 'undulating and so shapeless' (p. 173).

In *Father and Son*, Gosse includes an interesting passage on 'ori-ginality' and imitation (pp. 97–8). He asserts that the true path to creativity is through imitation, 'to imitate closely and carefully what is being said and done in the vicinity' (p. 98). In terms of the book as a whole it is an intriguing moment, for here Gosse reveals the primary tension in his account, which hestitates on the question of what identity is, and whence it derives. This is why the descrip-tion of infantile plagiarism (p. 99) and the anxiety of copying the father in mannerism and inclination are so central to the book. For later in the book, when Gosse describes his 'passion for imitation' (p. 116), where does that passion come from? He repeats the prayers and means them sincerely, and yet is equally sure that 'there never was a moment in which my heart truly responded' (p. 116). Here, and elsewhere, what is the authentic self of autobiography and of living? Where should we find it?

For Gosse, we find it in the Fall. *Father and Son* re-enacts that central Christian drama. It psychologizes Satan's sin of pride (the 'non serviam' of the creature who refuses to acknowledge the superiority of his creator) and refigures it as adolescent rebellion. Gosse peppers his book with petty revolts, from the 'passive resistance' of the early chapters (p. 101) to the final break with the father. Even in his acquiescence to his father's religion, there remains untouched by the experience, his 'innate and persistent self' (p. 116). Eventually 'there gushed through my veins like a wine the determination to rebel' (p. 142), and at school he becomes 'the liberator, the tyrannicide' (pp. 157–8).

As Satan rebels against God, so must Edmund against his father. Both claim an identity against the desires and wishes of that from which identity, and existence itself, derives. He ends the book too not just as the Satanic rebel, but as the Son in relation to the Father, a parody of sacrificed Jesus in relation to the parental God. Yet the very title of Gosse's book, and the whole premiss of the work itself, affirms that such gestures of defiance can only ever be broken and partial. We are our selves, but no one (only Jesus perhaps, in the mysterious light of the doctrine of the Trinity) is his own father; no one is 'the mother of themselves'.

Philip Henry Gosse fathered Edmund Gosse; but, in one sense, Edmund does father his own father. In taking the real man of history and experience and turning him into a character in a book, a figure in a literary fable of faith and doubt, Gosse writes his dad back into existence again, and, in an act of filial cruelty and love, re-evokes the lost father in the living tension of words. The book, he insists, derives its value from the light it may throw upon the 'unique and noble figure of the father' (p. 173). So it is that *Father and Son* is a loving attack, one that seeks to reconstitute and revivify the father that it deposes, as well as the lost child that he once oppressed with care. There they both are, linked for ever in the body of the book. Hate, like love, survives in remembrance.

Young Gosse chooses to reject his father and his childhood faith. He desires instead the world of his vocation; he becomes a writer. It is in one way a choosing of loneliness, as he cuts himself off from the oppressive protection of home. More lonely still is the sense that his identity from now on must be self-creating. In fact, as we have seen, he falls instead into the pre-emptory need for others, that 'magnetism of humanity which has been the agony of mature years' (p. 156). If we want to know the consequence of Gosse's break for autonomy, we must turn again to the figure described at the beginning of this introduction, to the man who wrote this book. There he remains, witty and well connected. A writer of one book of genius, but frightened; always social and always somehow sad. His young self beckons to him with the intractable question, 'Are you saved?', and the old self looks past him, embarrassed for a reply.

NOTE ON THE TEXT

The text of this edition is based on the first impression of the first edition of *Father and Son*, published anonymously on 25 October 1907 by William Heinemann. Opposite the title-page of this first impression is a photograph of Philip Henry Gosse, holding an open book, with Edmund on his knee; the image is entitled '*1857*'. Anonymous publication perhaps indicates some hesitation about owning up to the book, though in fact its authorship was something of an open secret in literary circles, and there are indications that from the first Heinemann wanted the facts of Gosse's authorship to leak out. (See Douglas Wertheimer, 'Gosse's Corrections to *Father and Son*, 1907–1928', *Notes and Queries*, 25: 4 (Aug. 1978), 327–32. This textual essay is heavily indebted to Wertheimer's excellent article.)

Gosse first had the idea for *Father and Son* following conversations with the writer George Moore, who glimpsed in *The Life of Philip Henry Gosse* (1890) the germ of a great book. Gosse began writing the book in October 1905, while staying in Florence; by February 1907 it appeared to be finished, though Gosse hung back from publication. He passed the manuscript to William Heinemann, his friend, as well as his publisher, in May 1907. This version of the book ended with Chapter 12. The twelve chapter structure is interesting, and may have been meant to evoke comparisons with epic, especially *Paradise Lost*. However, Heinemann felt that the book was unfinished. Gosse, at his request, wrote the epilogue, sending the completed book to Heinemann on 10 August 1907.

The book sold very well, and there were a further fourteen printings published in Gosse's lifetime. There were two further impressions in December 1907 and a fourth in March 1908. Gosse's name first appears on the title-page in the book's fourth impression. This impression carries a second short preface:

It is indicated to me that the slight veil of anonymity which I originally drew over this narrative was long ago torn to tatters, and that to pretend to preserve it would now be affectation.

Gosse's own copy of the book contains an autograph second paragraph to this preface. This reads:

On the title-page of this fourth impression of 'Father and Son', therefore the name of the author is set forth. At the same time, I take the opportunity to make a few slight corrections of matter of fact. I am thankful to say that, among the multitude of letters which I have received on the subject of this book, there has been none which have challenged the general accuracy of the record, and many which, to a striking degree, have confirmed the exactitude of my memory. The corrections, therefore, which I have made are trifling and do not interfere at all with the substantial character of the narrative.

                                                                    E.G.

March 1908.

(From this impression onwards, most versions of *Father and Son* published in Gosse's lifetime lose the fourth paragraph in the original preface with its allusion to Gosse's transparent anonymity.) As the autograph paragraph above suggests, the fourth impression also contains a number of corrections to the text of the first edition.

A popular edition of the book was published by Heinemann in October 1909, followed by the Booklover's edition published by Heinemann in November 1912 which reintroduces the missing fourth paragraph from the original preface. Most subsequent editions of the book, with the exception of a second, reset Booklover's edition published by Heinemann in October 1913, omit this paragraph. Both Booklover's editions add seven further illustrations to '*1857*' and the following 'Preface to the Booklover's Edition':

Many kind readers of previous impressions of this book have expressed a curiosity to know what some of the places and persons mentioned in it looked like more than half a century ago. Accordingly, I have searched in bureaux and albums for material with which to indulge a fancy which is flattering to me, and may even be helpful to the comprehension of my text. I can assure those who examine these illustrations that they are as scrupulously genuine as the narrative itself.

                                                                    E.G.

November 1912.

The indication that Gosse aims at a 'photographic realism' is a critically intriguing one.

The second reset Booklover's edition of October 1913 also shows some signs of Gosse's intervention, as it includes some further corrections to the text.

There were further printings of the popular edition in March 1916, September 1922, January 1925, and a Windmill Library edition in October 1928. These were all the editions to be printed in Gosse's lifetime.

Since Gosse's death, there have been many subsequent editions of *Father and Son*, and the work has been translated into many languages (the first French edition, translated by Auguste Monod, appeared in 1912). The first American edition was published by Charles Scribner's Sons in October 1907. There is a hilarious edition published as 'A Four Square Book' by Landsborough Publications in 1959, with a cover which contrives to make Gosse's work look very lurid indeed.

The first edition that forms the copy-text of the present edition of *Father and Son* was certainly seen through the press by Gosse, who took a strong interest in the fate of this book. There are none the less some errors that appear in the text: these have been noted below, and, where the error is one clearly produced by carelessness, corrected. In addition, certain typographic conventions have been regularized to conform to modern practice: the substitution of single quotation marks for double ones, and placing punctuation outside rather than inside closing quotation marks with single words and short phrases. This would ideally be all that is required of an editor. However, the situation is slightly more complex than this.

For Gosse himself noted corrections to the text in his own copy of the book. There are some fifty autograph corrections. It would be a valid editorial option to include all of Gosse's second thoughts, and create a text as close as possible to Gosse's final intentions. I have decided not to follow this course. There are several reasons for this. Firstly, Gosse, while noting these corrections, never systematically set out to incorporate them all into one later edition of the text, and, in one case, his correction has never been properly included in any subsequent text. This is despite the fact that he certainly intervened in the printing of later versions, adding prefaces, removing material from the first preface, making corrections. Gosse must have made at least some of the corrections prior to December 1908, as some of them are incorporated into the second and third impressions of the first edition published in that month. These corrections are those which are most likely to be of spelling mistakes or typing errors, though some errors like the misspelling of 'particulaly' were not changed until the popular edition of October 1909. This one piece of evidence would suggest that Gosse did reread the first impression and make corrections more than once, since having spotted this typographical error, it would be odd not to have included it in the changes made in the second, third, or fourth impressions. It is therefore possible that Gosse returned to the first edition and made other later sets of corrections, which were then mostly incorporated into the fourth impression of March 1908, the popular edition of December 1909, or the second Booklover's edition of October 1913. If Gosse reread the first impression as often as he instituted corrections, then this would entail perhaps as many as six rereadings of the text in the pursuit of further corrections. In other words, it is more likely that Gosse made most of the corrections during one reading prior to December 1908, and then added more at some point between then and October 1909, and perhaps October 1913. Gosse's sporadic and desultory approach to correcting the text means that it was not until the second Booklover's edition printed in 1913 that the majority of the textual changes indicated as desirable in his annotated copy of the book were incorporated into the text.

It would be a legitimate choice therefore to use this Booklover's edition as the basis for the copy-text for this edition. I have decided instead to stick to the first impression and to limit myself to correcting only the most obvious mistakes in that text. The corrections made by Gosse are undoubtedly productive of meaning, and are certainly interesting, and so, for the benefit of students, they are printed below. Although Gosse's list of changes are sometimes a matter of clearing up inaccuracies, often they place a different nuance in the prose. Their collective effect is to render the book less cautious. However, Gosse's initial hesitancy seems to me to be in itself an expressive feature of the text, and so the corrections to the prose have been left unamended. The intention is to produce a reading experience as close as possible to that of the book's very first readers. Peculiar features of the text of this edition (and there are very few) are noted in the Explanatory Notes at the end of this book. In addition to the errors listed below, many of Gosse's quotations are inaccurate, which would suggest that they are quoted from memory.

The following textual notes are mostly drawn from the Douglas

Wertheimer essay mentioned above. One error was corrected in the second impression, published in December 1907; some errors were corrected in the third impression of the book, published in December 1907; some in the fourth impression, published in March 1908; some in the first popular edition published in October 1909; some more in the December printing of the popular edition published in December 1910; and the last changes were made in the second Booklover's edition, published in October 1913. When a correction has been noted by Gosse it can be taken that, following its first appearance in the printed text, it was incorporated into later printings, unless otherwise stated. In most cases, I have decided not to list in which impression or edition Gosse's correction was first incorporated. Interested readers should refer to Wertheimer's article. In the following list, organized by page and line number, the first column indicates the reading in the first impression of the first edition, and the 'correction' follows in the second column.

5.4	being carried forward,	*in the first edition, the full stop is wrongly replaced by a comma. This may suggest carelessness on the part of the compositor, or a confusion carried into the text by a deleted phrase in the manuscript. Gosse did not correct this in his manuscript copy, but the error is corrected by the publication of the fourth impression in Mar. 1908.*
8.16	Mr. Balfour, an aged minister	Mr. Balfour, a valued minister
21.35	orgygia antiqua	*changed to* Orgygia antiqua *(2nd impression)*; orgyia antiqua *(4th impression)*; Orgyia antiqua *(in Popular edition, Oct .1909, and in Booklover's edition, Oct. 1913).*
35.17	just at a moment	just at the moment
41.29	Both of my parents	Both my parents

42.11	Jukeses and the Newtons	Habershons and the Newtons *(reading in the first impression in the library of the University of British Columbia, not in the BL and London Library edition used as copytext)*
42.26	Newton and Jukes	Newton and Habershon *(popular edition, Oct. 1909)*; Habershon and Jukes *(UBC first impression, fourth impression, and Booklover's edition, Oct. 1913)*
49.29	I was not allowed to	I was not permitted
52.32	I acquiesced, but	I acquiesced, although
55.25	Lord Beaconsfield's	Lord Chesterfield's *(corrected in later editions)*
56.14	Jukes or Newton	Habershon or Newton
62.22	of me, that	of men, that,
91.17–18	His surname I have forgotten	his surname was Jeffries
104.13	illusive way	allusive way
106.6	dismal depression	violent depression
107.17	sigh of decrepitude	sign of decrepitude
119.8	or endeavour	nor endeavour
121.22	Mary Brooks	Ann Brooks
124.5–6	I used to join	I was glad to join
134.2	with too full—a perception	with a too full—perception
135.11	fits of laughter	fits of hilarity
136.1–2	Cotman himself had touched	Cotman himself had painted
137.6	at the meeting	at the chapel
140.20	'On the Apocalypse'	'On the Pentateuch'
141.22–3	local vehicle 'the midge'	local vehicle, 'the midge'
141.28	horsechair cover	horsehair cover
148.7	had been made	had been hollowed out
148.21	and read a great block	and I read a great block
149.12	fond of talking	fond of talking,
150.14	she become	she became
151.37	It was my mother	It was my step-mother
159.11–12	in a way remarkable	in any way remarkable
165.26	reaching at last	reaching at length

166.7	Ben Jonson I could make nothing of	Of Ben Jonson I could make nothing
171.23	odes that were imitations	odes that were parodies
172.2	around me,	around me;
172.6	faintly-coloured sky	tender, coloured sky *(a correction that was never printed). Though the fourth impression of Mar. 1908 and the second Booklover's edition of Oct. 1913 both have 'tenderly-coloured sky', while the popular edition of Oct. 1909 has 'tender-coloured sky'.*
172.15–16	I had a little shame	I felt a little shame
173.1 and 6	son	Son *(both uses of the word on this page are corrected)*
173.4 and 8	father	Father *(both uses of the word on this page are corrected)*
173.13	father's	Father's
176.11–12	worth holding	worth proclaiming
176.17	great divines	great preachers
176.29	tempting errors	seductive errors
180.1	well aimed blows	well-aimed blows

SELECT BIBLIOGRAPHY

In *Father and Son*, Edmund Gosse refers to a large number of other texts, from the Bible through nineteenth-century poets such as Wordsworth, Coleridge, and Shelley, the Latin works of Virgil, the poetry of Christopher Marlowe, to the plays of Shakespeare, among many others. There are also generic and thematic similarities to John Stuart Mill's *Autobiography* (1873) and Samuel Butler, *The Way of All Flesh* (1903). An interested reader would discover a lot by reading *Father and Son* in the light of these inter-textual relationships.

Books on Emily Gosse

Gosse, Philip Henry, *A Memorial of the Last Days on Earth of Emily Gosse* (London: James Nisbet & Co., 1857).
—— and Gosse, Emily, *Sea-Side Pleasures* (London: Society for Promoting Christian Knowledge, 1853).
Shipton, Anna, *Tell Jesus: Recollections of Emily Gosse* (London: Morgan and Chase, 1863).

Select Works by Philip Henry Gosse

A Naturalist's Rambles on the Devonshire Coast (London: John Van Voorst, 1853).
The Aquarium: an Unveiling of the Wonders of the Deep Sea (London: John Van Voorst, 1854).
Omphalos: An Attempt to Untie the Geological Knot (London: John Van Voorst, 1857).
The Romance of Natural History (London: James Nisbet and Co., 1860).

Books and Essays on Philip Henry Gosse

Gosse, Edmund, *The Life of Philip Henry Gosse F.R.S.* (London: Kegan Paul, Trench, Trübner & Co., 1890).
Merrill, Lynn L., 'Philip Henry Gosse: "Feasting of the Eager Eyes"', in *The Romance of Victorian Natural History* (Oxford: Oxford University Press, 1989), 190–214.
Thwaite, Ann, *Glimpses of the Wonderful: The Life of Philip Henry Gosse* (London: Faber and Faber, 2002).

Biographies of Edmund Gosse

Charteris, Evan, *The Life and Letters of Sir Edmund Gosse* (London: William Heinemann, 1931).
Thwaite, Ann, *Edmund Gosse: A Literary Landscape* (London: Secker & Warburg, 1984).

Letters of Edmund Gosse

Bredsdorff, Elias (ed.), *Sir Edmund Gosse's Correspondence with Scandinavian Writers* (London: William Heinemann, 1960).

Brugmans, Linette F. (ed.), *The Correspondence of André Gide and Edmund Gosse, 1904–1928* (London: Peter Owen, 1960).

Mattheisen, Paul F., and Millgate, Michael (eds.), *Transatlantic Dialogue: Selected American Correspondence of Edmund Gosse* (Austin, Tex., and London: University of Texas Press, 1965).

Moor, Rayburn S. (ed.), *Selected Letters of Henry James to Edmund Gosse, 1882–1915* (Baton Rouge, La., and London: Louisiana State University Press, 1988).

The Victorians

Anger, Suzy (ed.), *Knowing the Past: Victorian Literature and Culture* (Ithaca, NY, and London: Cornell University Press, 2001).

Desmond, Adrian, *Archetypes and Ancestors: Palaeontology in Victorian London, 1850–1875* (London: Blond and Briggs, 1982).

Houghton, Walter, *The Victorian Frame of Mind* (New Haven: Yale University Press, 1957).

Sweet, Matthew, *Inventing the Victorians* (London: Faber, 2001).

Turner, Frank M., *Contesting Cultural Authority: Essays in Victorian Intellectual Life* (Cambridge: Cambridge University Press, 1993).

Wilson, A. N., *God's Funeral* (London: John Murray, 1999).

Victorian and Edwardian Religion

Bebbington, David, *Evangelicalism in Modern Britain: A History from the 1730s to the 1980s* (London: Unwin Hyman, 1989).

Bowler, Peter, *Reconciling Science and Religion: The Debate in Early Twentieth-Century Britain* (Chicago: University of Chicago Press, 2002).

Cutt, Margaret Nancy, *Ministering Angels: A Study of Nineteenth-Century Evangelical Writing* (Wormley, Herts: Five Owls Press, 1979).

De Laura, David J., *Hebrew and Hellene in Victorian England: Newman, Arnold and Pater* (Austin, Tex., and London: University of Texas Press, 1969).

Hogan, Anne, and Bradstock, Andrew (eds.), *Women of Faith in Victorian Culture: Reassessing the Angel in the House* (London: Macmillan, 1998).

Hutton, Ronald, *The Triumph of the Moon* (Oxford: Oxford University Press, 2000).

Jay, Elizabeth, *The Religion of the Heart: Anglican Evangelicalism and the Nineteenth-Century Novel* (Oxford: Clarendon Press, 1979).

O'Day, Rosemary, 'Women in Victorian Religion', in David Englander and Rosemary O'Day (eds.), *Retrieved Riches: Social Investigations in Britain, 1840–1914* (Aldershot: Scolar Press, 1995), 339–63.

Select Gosse Criticism to 1975

Braybrooke, Patrick, *Considerations on Edmund Gosse* (London: Drane's, 1925).

Gross, John, *The Rise and Fall of the Man of Letters* (London: Weidenfeld and Nicholson, 1969).

Nicholson, Harold, *The Development of English Biography* (London: Hogarth Press, 1927).

Pritchett, V. S., *The Living Novel* (London: Chatto and Windus, 1946).

Woolf, James D., *Sir Edmund Gosse* (New York: Twayne Publishers, 1972).

Woolf, Virginia, 'Edmund Gosse', in *Collected Essays*, iv (London: Hogarth Press, 1967).

Select Gosse Criticism since 1975

Brook-Davis, Douglas, *Fielding, Dickens, Gosse, Iris Murdoch and Oedipal Hamlet* (London: Macmillan, 1989).

Buckley, Jerome, 'Toward Early-Modern Autobiography: The Roles of Oscar Wilde, George Moore, Edmund Gosse, and Henry James', in Robert Kiely and John Hildebidle (eds.), *Modernism Reconsidered* (Cambridge, Mass.: Harvard University Press, 1983).

Henderson, Heather, *The Victorian Self: Autobiography and Biblical Narrative* (Ithaca, NY, and London: Cornell University Press, 1989).

Grylls, David, *Guardians and Angels* (London: Faber and Faber, 1978).

Malone, Cynthia Northcutt, 'The Struggle of *Father and Son*: Edmund Gosse's Polemical Autobiography', *Auto-Biography Studies*, 8:1 (Chapel Hill, NC, Spring 1993), 16–32.

Orel, Harold, *Victorian Literary Critics* (New York: St Martin's, 1984).

Pearlman, E., 'Father and Mother in *Father and Son*', *Victorian Newsletter*, 55 (Flushing, NY, 1979), 19–23.

Wertheimer, Douglas, 'The Identification of Some Characters and Incidents in Gosse's *Father and Son*', *Notes and Queries*, 23 (Oxford, 1976), 4–11.

Wertheimer, Douglas, 'Gosse's Corrections to *Father and Son*, 1907–1928', *Notes and Queries*, 25:4 (Aug. 1978), 327–32.

Woolf, James D., 'The Benevolent Christ in Gosse's *Father and Son*', *Prose Studies*, 3:2 (Sept. 1980), 165–75.

Further Reading in Oxford World's Classics

Darwin, Charles, *The Origin of Species*, ed. Gillian Beer.

Frazer, Sir J. G., *The Golden Bough*, ed. Robert Fraser.

Literature and Sciences in the Nineteenth Century, ed. Laura Otis.

A CHRONOLOGY OF EDMUND GOSSE

	Life	*Cultural and Historical Background*
1806	Emily Bowes born.	
1810	Philip Henry Gosse born.	
1815		Battle of Waterloo.
1819		Peterloo Massacre; birth of Victoria.
1829		Catholic Emancipation.
1830		Sir Charles Lyell begins publication of *The Principles of Creation* The first major railway opened, between Liverpool and Manchester.
1832		Great Reform Bill.
1833		Slavery abolished in British Empire; beginning of the Tractarian (the Oxford) Movement, as John Henry Newman launches *Tracts for the Times*.
1837		Queen Victoria crowned monarch.
1839		Charles Darwin, *Journal of Researches into the Geology and Natural History of the Various Countries Visited by HMS Beagle*
1840	Philip Henry Gosse, *The Canadian Naturalist*.	Newman's *Tract XC*
1841		Hugh Miller, *The Old Red Sandstone*
1844		Robert Chambers, *Vestiges of the Natural History of Creation* (published anonymously) Thomas Rust Cyprian, *The 'Brethren'*
1845		Famine widespread in Ireland until 1850.
1847	Philip Henry Gosse, *The Birds of Jamaica*.	Andrew John Jukes, *The Law of the Offerings in Leviticus I–VII*
1848	Philip Henry Gosse and Emily Bowes marry. They move to 13 Trafalgar Terrace, De Beauvoir Square in London.	Revolutions in Europe; Pre-Raphaelite Brotherhood founded.
1849	Birth of Edmund Gosse on 21 Sept.	Hugh Miller, *The Footprints of the Creator*
1851		Great Exhibition.
1852	The Gosse family visit Devon.	Matthew Arnold, *Empedocles on Etna, and other Poems*

1853 The Gosse family visit Weymouth in Dorset from Apr. to Dec. Philip Henry and Emily Gosse, *Sea-Side Pleasures*. Philip Henry Gosse, *A Naturalist's Rambles on the Devonshire Coast*. The family living in Huntingdon Street in Islington.

Andrew John Jukes, *The Characteristic Differences of the Four Gospels* Matthew Arnold, 'The Scholar Gypsy'

1854 The Gosse family spend two months in Tenby in Wales. Philip Henry Gosse, *The Aquarium: an Unveiling of the Wonders of the Deep Sea*.

Crimean War begins.

1855 Mar. to Sept., the Gosse family reside in Dorset and Devon. Emily Gosse, *The Young Guardsmen of the Alma; Abraham and his Children: or Parental Duties Illustrated by Scriptural Examples*.

Dissenters allowed to matriculate at Oxford. Charles Kingsley, *Glaucus: or the Wonders of the Shore* Andrew John Jukes, *The Two Ways*

1856 In Apr., Emily discovers that she has breast cancer.

End of Crimean War; birth of Freud.

1857 Death of Emily Gosse on 8 Feb.; Edmund spends just less than four weeks with his cousins in Clifton, before returning to Islington; in Sept., father and son move to St Marychurch, near Torquay in Devon. Philip Henry Gosse, *Life in its Lower, Intermediate, and Higher Forms: or, Manifestations of the Divine Wisdom in the Natural History of Animals; A Memorial of the Last Day on Earth of Emily Gosse; Omphalos*.

Indian Mutiny. 'M.C.H.' (C. H. Mackintosh), *Notes on the Book of Genesis*

1858

Jews admitted to Parliament. George MacDonald, *Phantastes*

1859 Philip Henry Gosse, *Evenings at the Microscope*.

Charles Darwin, *The Origin of Species*

1860 Philip Henry Gosse, *The Romance of Natural History*. Death of Edmund's paternal grandmother, Hannah Gosse; father and son meet Eliza Brightwen; Edmund starts school in St Marychurch; on 18 Dec. Philip Henry Gosse and Eliza Brightwen marry.

1863	Edmund goes to boarding school at Thorn Park in Teignmouth.	Anna Shipton, *Tell Jesus* Thomas Henry Huxley, *Evidence as to Man's Place in Nature* Charles Kingsley, *The Water Babies*
1864	Father and son attend an evangelical conference at the Freemason's Hall in London.	John Henry Newman, *Apologia Pro Vita Sua*
1865	In Nov., father and son visit Charles Kingsley in London; Edmund is taken to meet Sir Anthony Panizzi, Chief Librarian at the British Museum, regarding a job.	Lewis Carroll (Charles Dodgson), *Alice's Adventures in Wonderland*
1866	Philip Henry Gosse, *The Revelation: How Is It To Be Interpreted?* Edmund starts work as a librarian at the British Museum, lodging with family friends in Tottenham.	Algernon Charles Swinburne, *Poems and Ballads*
1867		Second Reform Bill. George MacDonald, *Dealings With The Fairies* Edward Crowley, *The Plymouth Brethren—So Called* Matthew Arnold, *New Poems*
1869		Matthew Arnold, *Culture and Anarchy*
1870	Edmund Gosse, *Madrigals, Songs and Sonnets*. On 21 Jan., Edmund writes the long letter to his father quoted at the end of *Father and Son*; he is moving among literary and artistic circles.	Civil Service in Britain thrown open to competitive examination; first Barnardo Home. John Lubbock, *The Origin of Civilization and the Primitive History of Man* Edward Dennett, *The Plymouth Brethren: their rise, divisions, practice, and doctrines*
1871	Philip Henry Gosse, *The Prophetic Times*. Edmund visits Norway.	Charles Darwin, *The Descent of Man in Relation to Sex* Sir Edward Burnett Tylor, *Primitive Culture*
1872	Edmund writes his first essays on Ibsen.	Charles Darwin, *The Expression of the Emotions in Man and Animals* Lewis Carroll (Charles Dodgson), *Through the Looking Glass*
1873	Edmund translates Ibsen's play, *Love's Comedy*, and also begins a correspondence with him. Edmund Gosse, *On Viol and Flute*.	John Stuart Mill, *Autobiography* Walter Pater, *Studies in the History of the Renaissance* Matthew Arnold, *Literature and Dogma*

1874	Begins a friendship with Robert Louis Stevenson.	
1875	Edmund marries Ellen Epps (Nellie Gosse) in Marylebone on 13 Aug.; begins work as a translator at the Board of Trade.	
1876	Nellie Gosse gives birth to a stillborn child. Edmund Gosse, *King Erik*.	Queen Victoria assumes title of Empress of India; Wagner's operas performed at the opening of the Bayreuth Theatre.
1877	Nellie Gosse gives birth to Emily Teresa Gosse.	Edison patents the phonograph.
1878		Algernon Charles Swinburne, *Poems and Ballads: Second Series*
1879	The Gosses have a son, Philip Gosse; Edmund begins a passionate friendship with Hamo Thornycroft, the sculptor. Edmund Gosse, *Studies in the Literature of Northern Europe*.	Henrik Ibsen, *The Doll's House* Thomas Hughes, *The Manliness of Christ*
1880		First women students at Oxford University; Papal bull, *Aeterni Patris*, encyclical declaration of Thomism as the official Catholic philosophy.
1881	The Gosses' last child, Teresa Gosse, born.	Thomas Carlyle, *Reminiscences* Henrik Ibsen, *Ghosts* 'Mark Rutherford', *Autobiography*
1882	Edmund Gosse, *Gray*.	Death of Charles Darwin.
1883	Edmund Gosse, *Seventeenth Century Studies*.	Fabian Society founded. John Addington Symonds, *A Problem in Greek Ethics*
1884	Edmund Gosse begins work as Clark Lecturer at Trinity College, Cambridge.	John Ruskin, 'The Storm Cloud of the Nineteenth Century' Henrik Ibsen, *The Wild Duck*
1885	Edmund Gosse, *From Shakespeare to Pope*.	Walter Pater, *Marius the Epicurean* John Ruskin begins *Praeterita*
1886	Churton Collins attacks Gosse in the *Quarterly Review* for careless inaccuracies in his book on English Literature, *From Shakespeare to Pope*. Philip Henry Gosse, *The Humanity of the Son of God*.	Daimler invents internal combustion engine using gasoline.
1887		Edison patents the Kinetoscope.
1888	Philip Henry Gosse dies. Edmund Gosse, *Life of William Congreve*.	Oscar Wilde, *The Happy Prince and Other Tales*

1889	Edmund finishes his position as Clark Lecturer.	First English performance of *The Doll's House*
1890	Edmund Gosse, *The Life of Philip Henry Gosse FRS; Northern Studies.*	Oscar Wilde, *The Picture of Dorian Gray* Sir James George Frazer, *The Golden Bough* (in two volumes)
1891	Edmund Gosse, *Gossip in a Library.*	First English performances of *Ghosts* and *Hedda Gabler* George Bernard Shaw, *The Quintessence of Ibsenism* Thomas Hardy, *Tess of the D'Urbervilles* Oscar Wilde, 'The Soul of Man Under Socialism' John Addington Symonds, *A Problem In Modern Ethics*
1892	Edmund Gosse, *The Secret of Narcisse.*	George and Weedon Grossmith, *The Diary of a Nobody*
1893	Edmund Gosse, *Questions at Issue.*	Thomas Henry Huxley, *Evolution and Ethics*
1895	Edmund Gosse, *In Russet and Silver.*	Max Nordau, *Degeneration*
1896	Edmund Gosse, *Critical Kit-Kats.*	Robert Louis Stevenson, *The Weir of Hermiston* Thomas Hardy, *Jude the Obscure*
1897		Queen Victoria's Diamond Jubilee. Havelock Ellis, *Sexual Inversion*
1899	Edmund's stepmother, Eliza Gosse, dies. Edmund Gosse, *The Life and Letters of John Donne.*	Start of Boer War. Arthur Symons, *The Symbolist Movement in Literature*
1900		Death of Oscar Wilde.
1901	Edmund Gosse, *Hypolympia.*	Thomas Hardy, *Poems of the Past and Present* William Blair Neatby, *A History of the Plymouth Brethren* T. Common (compiler), *Nietzsche as Critic, Philosopher, Poet and Prophet*
1902		End of Boer War. William James, *Varieties of Religious Experience* André Gide, *L'Immoraliste* Rudyard Kipling, *Just So Stories* Friedrich Engels, *The Origin of the Family* (trans. Ernest Untermann)
1903	Edmund Gosse, *The Challenge of the Brontës; English Literature: An Illustrated Record* (with Richard Garnett).	Ford Motor Company founded; Wright brothers' first successful powered flight. Samuel Butler, *The Way of All Flesh* G. E. Moore, *Principia Ethica* G. B. Shaw, *Man and Superman* André Gide, *Prétexts*

1903		W. B. Yeats, *Ideas of Good and Evil* Jane Ellen Harrison, *Prolegomena to the Study of Greek Religion*
1904	Edmund offered the job of Librarian at the House of Lords. Edmund Gosse, *Jeremy Taylor*.	G. Stanley Hall, *Adolescence*
1905	Edmund Gosse, *Coventry Patmore; Sir Thomas Browne; French Profiles*.	Einstein describes Theory of Relativity; Russian revolution. Oscar Wilde, *De Profundis* G. K. Chesterton, *Heretics*
1906	Edmund begins a one-year stint editing a literary supplement for the *Daily Mail*.	Rudyard Kipling, *Puck of Pook's Hill* Sir James George Frazer, *Adonis, Attis, Osiris* A. R. Orage, *Friedrich Nietzsche, the Dionysian Spirit of the Age*
1907	Edmund Gosse, *Father and Son*; *Henrik Ibsen*.	E. M. Forster, *The Longest Journey* J. M. Synge, *The Playboy of the Western World* André Gide, *Le Retour de l'enfant prodigue* Friedrich Nietzsche, *Beyond Good and Evil* A. R. Orage, *Nietzsche in Outline and Aphorism* Henry Adams, *The Education of Henry Adams* Bergson, *L'Evolution créatrice*
1907–15		Sir James George Frazer, *The Golden Bough* (3rd edn., in twelve volumes)
1908		G. K. Chesterton, *Orthodoxy* Kenneth Grahame, *The Wind in the Willows*
1909	Edmund Gosse, *The Autumn Garden*.	
1910		Death of Edward VII.
1911	Edmund Gosse, *Collected Poems*.	Scott's unsuccessful journey to the South Pole.
1912		Sinking of *Titanic*.
1913		D. H. Lawrence, *Sons and Lovers* Sigmund Freud, *The Interpretation of Dreams* (trans. A. A. Brill)
1914	Edmund ends work as Librarian at House of Lords.	Beginning of First World War.
1915		James Joyce, *A Portrait of the Artist as a Young Man* D. H. Lawrence, *The Rainbow*

1916		Battle of the Somme.
1917	Edmund Gosse, *The Life of Algernon Charles Swinburne*; (and in British Library: *Confidential Papers on Swinburne's Moral Irregularities*)	Russian October Revolution.
1918		End of the First World War. Sigmund Freud, *Totem and Taboo* (trans. A. A. Brill)
1919	Edmund begins a weekly books column in the *Sunday Times*.	
1921	Edmund Gosse, *Books on the Table*.	
1922		T. S. Eliot, *The Waste Land* James Joyce, *Ulysses*
1924		Sir Henry Howarth Bashford, *Augustus Carp Esq., By Himself*
1925	Edmund is knighted in the New Year Honours List.	Virginia Woolf, *Mrs Dalloway*
1926		General Strike in Britain.
1927	Edmund Gosse, *Leaves and Fruit*.	Lindbergh flies Atlantic.
1928	Edmund Gosse dies on 16 May.	Death of Thomas Hardy.

1857.

PHILIP HENRY GOSSE WITH HIS SON EDMUND IN 1857.

Frontispiece to the first edition of *Father and Son*, 1907.
By permission of the British Library (shelfmark 010827.ee.2).

FATHER AND SON

A STUDY OF TWO TEMPERAMENTS

Der Glaube ist wie die Liebe: er lässt sich nicht erzwingen.

SCHOPENHAUER*

PREFACE

At the present hour, when fiction takes forms so ingenious and so specious, it is perhaps necessary to say that the following narrative, in all its parts, and so far as the punctilious attention of the writer has been able to keep it so, is scrupulously true. If it were not true, in this strict sense, to publish it would be to trifle with all those who may be induced to read it. It is offered to them as a *document*, as a record of educational and religious conditions which, having passed away, will never return. In this respect, as the diagnosis of a dying Puritanism, it is hoped that the narrative will not be altogether without significance.

It offers, too, in a subsidiary sense, a study of the development of moral and intellectual ideas during the progress of infancy. These have been closely and conscientiously noted, and may have some value in consequence of the unusual conditions in which they were produced. The author has observed that those who have written about the facts of their own childhood have usually delayed to note them down until age has dimmed their recollections. Perhaps an even more common fault in such autobiographies is that they are sentimental, and are falsified by self-admiration and self-pity. The writer of these recollections has thought that if the examination of his earliest years was to be undertaken at all, it should be attempted while his memory is still perfectly vivid and while he is still unbiased by the forgetfulness or the sensibility of advancing years.

At one point only has there been any tampering with precise fact. It is believed that, with the exception of the Son, there is but one person mentioned in this book who is still alive. Nevertheless, it has been thought well, in order to avoid any appearance of offence, to alter the majority of the proper names of the private persons spoken of.

As regards the anonymous writer himself, whether the reader does or does not recognise an old acquaintance, occasionally met with in quite other fields, is a matter of no importance. Here no effort has been made to conceal or to identify.*

It is not usual, perhaps, that the narrative of a spiritual struggle should mingle merriment and humour with a discussion of the most solemn subjects. It has, however, been inevitable that they should be so mingled in this narrative. It is true that most funny books try to be funny throughout, while theology is scandalised if it awakens a single smile. But life is not constituted thus, and this book is nothing if it is not a genuine slice of life. There was an extraordinary mixture of comedy and tragedy in the situation which is here described, and those who are affected by the pathos of it will not need to have it explained to them that the comedy was superficial and the tragedy essential.

September 1907.

CHAPTER I

THIS book is the record of a struggle between two temperaments, two consciences and almost two epochs. It ended, as was inevitable, in disruption. Of the two human beings here described, one was born to fly backward, the other could not help being carried forward. There came a time when neither spoke the same language as the other, or encompassed the same hopes, or was fortified by the same desires. But, at least, it is some consolation to the survivor, that neither, to the very last hour, ceased to respect the other, or to regard him with a sad indulgence.

The affection of these two persons was assailed by forces in comparison with which the changes that health or fortune or place introduce are as nothing. It is a mournful satisfaction, but yet a satisfaction, that they were both of them able to obey the law which says that ties of close family relationship must be honoured and sustained. Had it not been so, this story would never have been told.

The struggle began soon, yet of course it did not begin in early infancy. But to familiarise my readers with the conditions of the two persons (which were unusual) and with the outlines of their temperaments (which were, perhaps innately, antagonistic), it is needful to open with some account of all that I can truly and independently recollect, as well as with some statements which are, as will be obvious, due to household tradition.

My parents were poor gentlefolks; not young; solitary, sensitive and, although they did not know it, proud. They both belonged to what is called the Middle Class, and there was this further resemblance between them that they each descended from families which had been more than well-to-do in the eighteenth century, and had gradually sunken in fortune. In both houses there had been a decay of energy which had led to decay in wealth. In the case of my Father's family it had been a slow decline; in that of my Mother's, it had been rapid. My maternal grandfather was born wealthy, and in the opening years of the nineteenth century, immediately after his marriage, he bought a little estate in North Wales, on the slopes of Snowdon.* Here he seems to have lived in a pretentious way, keeping a pack of hounds and entertaining on an extravagant scale. He had a

wife who encouraged him in this vivid life, and three children, my
Mother and her two brothers. His best trait was his devotion to the
education of his children, in which he proclaimed himself a disciple
of Rousseau.* But he can hardly have followed the teaching of 'Émile'
very closely, since he employed tutors to teach his daughter, at an
extremely early age, the very subjects which Rousseau forbade, such
as history, literature and foreign languages.

My Mother was his special favourite, and his vanity did its best to
make a blue-stocking* of her. She read Greek, Latin and even a little
Hebrew, and, what was more important, her mind was trained to be
self-supporting. But she was diametrically opposed in essential matters to her easy-going, luxurious and self-indulgent parents. Review-
ing her life in her thirtieth year, she remarked in some secret notes:
'I cannot recollect the time when I did not love religion.' She used a
still more remarkable expression: 'If I must date my conversion from
my first wish and trial to be holy, I may go back to infancy; if I am to
postpone it till after my last wilful sin, it is scarcely yet begun.' The
irregular pleasures of her parents' life were deeply distasteful to her,
as such were to many young persons in those days of the wide revival
of Conscience,* and when my grandfather, by his reckless expenditure, which he never checked till ruin was upon him, was obliged to
sell his estate, and live in penury, my Mother was the only member
of the family who did not regret the change. For my own part, I
believe I should have liked my reprobate maternal grandfather, but
his conduct was certainly very vexatious. He died, in his eightieth
year, when I was nine months old.

It was a curious coincidence that life had brought both my parents
along similar paths to an almost identical position in respect to
religious belief. She had started from the Anglican stand-point, he
from the Wesleyan,* and each, almost without counsel from others,
and after varied theological experiments, had come to take up precisely the same attitude towards all divisions of the Protestant
Church, that, namely, of detached and unbiased contemplation. So
far as the sects agreed with my Father and my Mother, the sects were
walking in the light; wherever they differed from them, they had
slipped more or less definitely into a penumbra of their own making,
a darkness into which neither of my parents would follow them.
Hence, by a process of selection, my Father and my Mother alike
had gradually, without violence, found themselves shut outside all

Protestant communions, and at last they met only with a few extreme Calvinists* like themselves, on terms of what may almost be called negation—with no priest, no ritual, no festivals, no ornament of any kind, nothing but the Lord's Supper and the exposition of Holy Scripture drawing these austere spirits into any sort of cohesion. They called themselves 'the Brethren', simply; a title enlarged by the world outside into 'Plymouth Brethren'.*

It was accident and similarity which brought my parents together at these meetings of the Brethren. Each was lonely, each was poor, each was accustomed to a strenuous intellectual self-support. He was nearly thirty-eight, she was past forty-two, when they married.* From a suburban lodging, he brought her home to his mother's little house in the north-east of London* without a single day's honeymoon. My Father was a zoologist, and a writer of books on natural history; my Mother also was a writer, author already of two slender volumes of religious verse—the earlier of which, I know not how, must have enjoyed some slight success, since a second edition was printed—afterwards she devoted her pen to popular works of edification.* But how infinitely removed in their aims, their habits, their ambitions from 'literary' people of the present day, words are scarcely adequate to describe. Neither knew nor cared about any manifestation of current literature. For each there had been no poet later than Byron, and neither had read a romance since, in childhood, they had dipped into the Waverley Novels* as they appeared in succession. For each the various forms of imaginative and scientific literature were merely means of improvement and profit, which kept the student 'out of the world', gave him full employment, and enabled him to maintain himself. But pleasure was found nowhere but in the Word of God, and to the endless discussion of the Scriptures each hurried when the day's work was over.

In this strange household the advent of a child was not welcomed, but was borne with resignation. The event was thus recorded in my Father's diary:

'E. delivered of a son. Received green swallow from Jamaica.'

This entry has caused amusement, as showing that he was as much interested in the bird as in the boy. But this does not follow; what the wording exemplifies is my Father's extreme punctilio. The green swallow arrived later in the day than the son, and the earlier visitor was therefore recorded first; my Father was scrupulous in every species of arrangement.

Long afterwards, my Father told me that my Mother suffered much in giving birth to me, and that, uttering no cry, I appeared to be dead. I was laid, with scant care, on another bed in the room, while all anxiety and attention were concentrated on my Mother. An old woman who happened to be there, and who was unemployed, turned her thoughts to me, and tried to awake in me a spark of vitality. She succeeded, and she was afterwards complimented by the doctor on her cleverness. My Father could not—when he told me the story—recollect the name of my preserver. I have often longed to know who she was. For all the rapture of life, for all its turmoils, its anxious desires, its manifold pleasures, and even for its sorrow and suffering, I bless and praise that anonymous old lady from the bottom of my heart.

It was six weeks before my Mother was able to leave her room. The occasion was made a solemn one, and was attended by a species of Churching.* Mr Balfour, an aged minister of the denomination, held a private service in the parlour, and 'prayed for our child, that he may be the Lord's'. This was the opening act of that 'dedication'* which was never henceforward forgotten, and of which the following pages will endeavour to describe the results. Around my tender and unconscious spirit was flung the luminous web, the light and elastic but impermeable veil, which it was hoped would keep me 'unspotted from the world'.

Until this time my Father's mother had lived in the house* and taken the domestic charges of it on her own shoulders. She now consented to leave us to ourselves. There is no question that her exodus was a relief to my Mother, since my paternal grandmother was a strong and masterful woman, buxom, choleric and practical, for whom the interests of the mind did not exist. Her daughter-in-law, gentle as she was, and ethereal in manner and appearance— strangely contrasted (no doubt), in her tinctures of gold hair and white skin, with my grandmother's bold carnations and black tresses—was yet possessed of a will like tempered steel. They were better friends apart, with my Grandmother lodged hard by, in a bright room, her household gods and bits of excellent eighteenth-century furniture around her, her miniatures and sparkling china arranged on shelves.

Left to my Mother's sole care, I became the centre of her solici-tude. But there mingled with those happy animal instincts which sustain the strength and patience of every human mother, and were fully present with her—there mingled with these certain spiritual determinations which can be but rare. They are, in their outline, I suppose, vaguely common to many religious mothers, but there are few indeed who fill up the sketch with so firm a detail as she did. Once again I am indebted to her secret notes, in a little locked volume, seen until now, nearly sixty years later, by no eye save her own. Thus she wrote when I was two months old:

'We have given him to the Lord; and we trust that He will really manifest him to be His own, if he grow up; and if the Lord take him early, we will not doubt that he is taken to Himself. Only, if it please the Lord to take him, I do trust we may be spared seeing him suffering in lingering illness and much pain. But in this as in all things His will is better than what we can choose. Whether his life be prolonged or not, it has already been a blessing to us, and to the saints, in leading us to much prayer, and bringing us into varied need and some trial.'

The last sentence is somewhat obscure to me. How, at that tender age, I contrived to be a blessing 'to the saints' may surprise others and puzzles myself. But 'the saints' was the habitual term by which were indicated the friends who met on Sunday mornings for Holy Communion, and at many other times in the week for prayer and discussion of the Scriptures, in the small hired hall at Hackney,* which my parents attended. I suppose that the solemn dedication of me to the Lord, which was repeated in public in my Mother's arms, being by no means a usual or familiar ceremony even among the Brethren, created a certain curiosity and fervour in the immediate services, or was imagined so to do by the fond, partial heart of my Mother. She, however, who had been so much isolated, now made the care of her child an excuse for retiring still further into silence. With those religious persons who met at the Room, as the modest chapel was called, she had little spiritual and no intellectual sympathy. She noted:

'I do not think it would increase my happiness to be in the midst of the saints at Hackney. I have made up my mind to give myself up to Baby for the winter, and to accept no invitations. To go when I can to the Sunday morning meetings and to see my own Mother.'

The monotony of her existence now became extreme, but she seems to have been happy. Her days were spent in taking care of me, and in directing one young servant. My Father was for ever in his study, writing, drawing, dissecting; sitting, no doubt, as I grew afterwards accustomed to see him, absolutely motionless, with his eye glued to the microscope, for twenty minutes at a time. So the greater part of every week-day was spent, and on Sunday he usually preached one, and sometimes two extempore sermons. His work-day labours were rewarded by the praise of the learned world, to which he was indifferent, but by very little money, which he needed more. For over three years after their marriage, neither of my parents left London for a single day, not being able to afford to travel. They received scarcely any visitors, never ate a meal away from home, never spent an evening in social intercourse abroad. At night they discussed theology, read aloud to one another, or translated scientific brochures from French or German. It sounds a terrible life of pressure and deprivation, and that it was physically unwholesome there can be no shadow of a doubt. But their contentment was complete and unfeigned. In the midst of this, materially, the hardest moment of their lives, when I was one year old, and there was a question of our leaving London, my Mother recorded in her secret notes:—

'We are happy and contented, having all things needful and pleasant, and our present habitation is hallowed by many sweet associations. We have our house to ourselves and enjoy each other's society. If we move we shall no longer be alone. The situation may be more favourable, however, for Baby, as being more in the country. I desire to have no choice in the matter, but as I know not what would be for our good, and God knows, so I desire to leave it with Him, and if it is not His will we should move, He will raise objections and difficulties, and if it is His will He will make Henry [my Father] desirous and anxious to take the step, and then, whatever the result, let us leave all to Him and not regret it.'

No one who is acquainted with the human heart will mistake this attitude of resignation for weakness of purpose. It was not poverty of will, it was abnegation, it was a voluntary act. My Mother, underneath an exquisite amenity of manner, concealed a rigour of spirit which took the form of a constant self-denial. For it to dawn upon her consciousness that she wished for something, was definitely to renounce that wish, or, more exactly, to subject it in every thing to what she conceived to be the will of God.

This is perhaps the right moment for me to say that at this time,

and indeed until the hour of her death, she exercised, without sus-
pecting it, a magnetic power over the will and nature of my Father.
Both were strong, but my Mother was unquestionably the stronger
of the two; it was her mind which gradually drew his to take up a
certain definite position, and this remained permanent although she,
the cause of it, was early removed. Hence, while it was with my
Father that the long struggle which I have to narrate took place,
behind my Father stood the ethereal memory of my Mother's will,
guiding him, pressing him, holding him to the unswerving purpose
which she had formed and defined. And when the inevitable disruption came, what was unspeakably painful was to realise that it was
not from one, but from both parents that the purpose of the child
was separated.

My Mother was a Puritan in grain, and never a word escaped her,
not a phrase exists in her diary, to suggest that she had any privations
to put up with. She seemed strong and well, and so did I; the one of
us who broke down was my Father. With his attack of acute nervous
dyspepsia came an unexpected small accession of money, and we
were able, in my third year, to take a holiday of nearly ten months in
Devonshire.* The extreme seclusion, the unbroken strain, were never
repeated, and when we returned to London, it was to conditions of
greater amenity and to a less rigid practice of 'the world forgetting
by the world forgot'.* That this relaxation was more relative than
positive, and that nothing ever really tempted either of my parents
from their cavern in an intellectual Thebaïd,* my recollections will
amply prove. But each of them was forced by circumstances into a
more or less public position, and neither could any longer quite
ignore the world around.

It is not my business here to re-write the biographies of my
parents. Each of them became, in a certain measure, celebrated, and
each was the subject of a good deal of contemporary discussion.
Each was prominent before the eyes of a public of his or her own,
half a century ago. It is because their minds were vigorous and their
accomplishments distinguished that the contrast between their
spiritual point of view and the aspect of a similar class of persons
to-day is interesting and may, I hope, be instructive. But this is not
another memoir of public individuals, each of whom has had
more than one biographer. My serious duty, as I venture to hold it,
is other;

that's the world's side,
Thus men saw them, praised them, thought they knew
    them!
There, in turn, I stood aside and praised them!
Out of my own self, I dare to phrase it.*

But this is a different inspection, this is a study of

the other side, the novel
Silent silver lights and darks undreamed of,

the record of a state of soul once not uncommon in Protestant Europe,
of which my parents were perhaps the latest consistent exemplars
among people of light and leading.

The peculiarities of a family life, founded upon such principles,
are, in relation to a little child, obvious; but I may be permitted to
recapitulate them. Here was perfect purity, perfect intrepidity, perfect abnegation; yet there was also narrowness, isolation, an absence
of perspective, let it be boldly admitted, an absence of humanity.
And there was a curious mixture of humbleness and arrogance;
entire resignation to the will of God and not less entire disdain of the
judgment and opinion of man. My parents founded every action,
every attitude, upon their interpretation of the Scriptures, and upon
the guidance of the Divine Will as revealed to them by direct answer
to prayer. Their ejaculation in the face of any dilemma was, 'Let us
cast it before the Lord!'

So confident were they of the reality of their intercourse with
God, that they asked for no other guide. They recognised no spiritual authority among men, they subjected themselves to no priest or
minister, they troubled their consciences about no current manifestation of 'religious opinion'. They lived in an intellectual cell,
bounded at its sides by the walls of their own house, but open above
to the very heart of the uttermost heavens.

This, then, was the scene in which the soul of a little child was
planted, not as in an ordinary open flower-border or carefully tended
social parterre, but as on a ledge, split in the granite of some mountain. The ledge was hung between night and the snows on one hand,
and the dizzy depths of the world upon the other; was furnished
with just soil enough for a gentian to struggle skywards and open its
stiff azure stars; and offered no lodgment, no hope of salvation, to
any rootlet which should stray beyond its inexorable limits.

CHAPTER II

OUT of the darkness of my infancy there comes only one flash of memory. I am seated alone, in my baby-chair, at a dinner-table set for several people. Somebody brings in a leg of mutton, puts it down close to me, and goes out. I am again alone, gazing at two low windows, wide open upon a garden. Suddenly, noiselessly, a large, long animal (obviously a greyhound) appears at one window-sill, slips into the room, seizes the leg of mutton and slips out again. When this happened I could not yet talk. The accomplishment of speech came to me very late, doubtless because I never heard young voices. Many years later, when I mentioned this recollection, there was a shout of laughter and surprise:—

'That, then, was what became of the mutton! It was not you, who, as your Uncle A. pretended, ate it up, in the twinkling of an eye, bone and all!'

I suppose that it was the startling intensity of this incident which stamped it upon a memory from which all other impressions of this early date have vanished.

The adventure of the leg of mutton occurred, evidently, at the house of my Mother's brothers, for my parents, at this date, visited no other. My uncles were not religious men,* but they had an almost filial respect for my Mother, who was several years senior to the elder of them. When the catastrophe of my Grandfather's fortune had occurred, they had not yet left school. My Mother, in spite of an extreme dislike of teaching, which was native to her, immediately accepted the situation of a governess in the family of an Irish nobleman.* The mansion was only to be approached, as Miss Edgeworth* would have said, 'through eighteen sloughs, at the imminent peril of one's life', and when one had reached it, the mixture of opulence and squalour, of civility and savagery, was unspeakable. But my Mother was well paid, and she stayed in this distasteful environment, doing the work she hated most, while with the margin of her salary she helped first one of her brothers and then the other through his Cambridge course. They studied hard and did well at the university. At length their sister received, in her *ultima Thule*,* news that her younger brother had taken his degree, and then and there, with a sigh of intense relief, she resigned her situation and came straight back to England.

It is not to be wondered at, then, that my uncles looked up to their sister with feelings of especial devotion. They were not inclined, they were hardly in a position, to criticise her modes of thought. They were easy-going, cultured and kindly gentlemen, rather limited in their views, without a trace of their sister's force of intellect or her strenuous temper. E. resembled her in person; he was tall, fair, with auburn curls; he cultivated a certain tendency to the Byronic type,* fatal and melancholy. A. was short, brown and jocose, with a pretension to common sense; bluff and chatty. As a little child, I adored my Uncle E., who sat silent by the fireside, holding me against his knee, saying nothing, but looking unutterably sad, and occasionally shaking his warm-coloured tresses. With great injustice, on the other hand, I detested my Uncle A., because he used to joke in a manner very displeasing to me, and because he would so far forget himself as to chase, and even, if it will be credited, to tickle me. My uncles, who remained bachelors to the end of their lives, earned a comfortable living, E. by teaching, A. as 'something in the City', and they rented an old rambling house in Clapton,* that same in which I saw the greyhound. Their house had a strange, delicious smell, so unlike anything I smelt anywhere else, that it used to fill my eyes with tears of mysterious pleasure. I know now that this was the odour of cigars, tobacco being a species of incense tabooed at home on the highest religious grounds.

It has been recorded that I was slow in learning to speak. I used to be told that having met all invitations to repeat such words as 'Papa' and 'Mamma' with gravity and indifference, I one day drew towards me a volume, and said 'book' with startling distinctness. I was not at all precocious, but at a rather early age, I think towards the beginning of my fourth year, I learned to read. I cannot recollect a time when a printed page of English was closed to me. But perhaps earlier still my Mother used to repeat to me a poem which I have always taken for granted that she had herself composed, a poem which had a romantic place in my early mental history.* It ran thus, I think:

> O pretty Moon, you shine so bright!
> I'll go to bid Mamma good-night,
> And then I'll lie upon my bed
> And watch you move above my head.

Ah! there, a cloud has hidden you!
But I can see your light shine thro'!
It tries to hide you—quite in vain,
For—there you quickly come again!

It's God, I know, that makes you shine
Upon this little bed of mine;
But I shall all about you know
When I can read and older grow.

Long, long after the last line had become an anachronism, I used to shout this poem from my bed before I went to sleep, whether the night happened to be moon-lit or no.

It must have been my Father who taught me my letters. To my Mother, as I have said, it was distasteful to teach, though she was so prompt and skilful to learn. My Father, on the contrary, taught cheerfully, by fits and starts. In particular, he had a scheme for rationalising geography, which I think was admirable. I was to climb upon a chair, while, standing at my side, with a pencil and a sheet of paper, he was to draw a chart of the markings on the carpet. Then, when I understood the system, another chart on a smaller scale of the furniture in the room, then of a floor of the house, then of the back-garden, then of a section of the street. The result of this was that geography came to me of itself, as a perfectly natural miniature arrangement of objects, and to this day has always been the science which gives me least difficulty. My Father also taught me the simple rules of arithmetic, a little natural history, and the elements of drawing; and he laboured long and unsuccessfully to make me learn by heart hymns, psalms and chapters of Scripture, in which I always failed ignominiously and with tears. This puzzled and vexed him, for he himself had an extremely retentive textual memory. He could not help thinking that I was naughty, and would not learn the chapters, until at last he gave up the effort. All this sketch of an education began, I believe, in my fourth year, and was not advanced or modified during the rest of my Mother's life.

Meanwhile, capable as I was of reading, I found my greatest pleasure in the pages of books. The range of these was limited, for story-books of every description were sternly excluded. No fiction of any kind, religious or secular, was admitted into the house. In this it was to my Mother, not to my Father, that the prohibition was due.

She had a remarkable, I confess to me still somewhat unaccountable impression, that to 'tell a story', that is, to compose fictitious narrative of any kind, was a sin. She carried this conviction to extreme lengths. My Father, in later years, gave me some interesting examples of her firmness. As a young man in America, he had been deeply impressed by 'Salathiel', a pious prose romance of that then popular writer, the Rev. George Croly.* When he first met my Mother, he recommended it to her, but she would not consent to open it. Nor would she read the chivalrous tales in verse of Sir Walter Scott,* obstinately alleging that they were not 'true'. She would read none but lyrical and subjective poetry. Her secret diary reveals the history of this singular aversion to the fictitious, although it cannot be said to explain the cause of it. As a child, however, she had possessed a passion for making up stories, and so considerable a skill in it that she was constantly being begged to indulge others with its exercise. But I will, on so curious a point, leave her to speak for herself:

'When I was a very little child, I used to amuse myself and my brothers with inventing stories, such as I read. Having, as I suppose, naturally a restless mind and busy imagination, this soon became the chief pleasure of my life. Unfortunately, my brothers were always fond of encouraging this propensity, and I found in Taylor, my maid, a still greater tempter. I had not known there was any harm in it, until Miss Shore [a Calvinist governess], finding it out, lectured me severely, and told me it was wicked. From that time forth I considered that to invent a story of any kind was a sin. But the desire to do so was too deeply rooted in my affections to be resisted in my own strength [she was at that time nine years of age], and unfortunately I knew neither my corruption nor my weakness, nor did I know where to gain strength. The longing to invent stories grew with violence; everything I heard or read became food for my distemper. The simplicity of truth was not sufficient for me; I must needs embroider imagination upon it, and the folly, vanity and wickedness which disgraced my heart are more than I am able to express. Even now [at the age of twenty-nine], tho' watched, prayed and striven against, this is still the sin that most easily besets me. It has hindered my prayers and prevented my improvement, and therefore has humbled me very much.'

This is, surely, a very painful instance of the repression of an instinct. There seems to have been, in this case, a vocation such as is rarely heard, and still less often wilfully disregarded and silenced.

Was my Mother intended by nature to be a novelist? I have often thought so, and her talents and vigour of purpose, directed along the line which was ready to form 'the chief pleasure of her life', could hardly have failed to conduct her to great success. She was a little younger than Bulwer Lytton, a little older than Mrs Gaskell,*—but these are vain and trivial speculations!

My own state, however, was, I should think, almost unique among the children of cultivated parents. In consequence of the stern ordinance which I have described, not a single fiction was read or told to me during my infancy. The rapture of the child who delays the process of going to bed by cajoling 'a story' out of his mother or his nurse, as he sits upon her knee, well tucked up, at the corner of the nursery fire,—this was unknown to me. Never, in all my early childhood, did any one address to me the affecting preamble, 'Once upon a time!' I was told about missionaries, but never about pirates; I was familiar with humming-birds, but I had never heard of fairies. Jack the Giant-Killer, Rumpelstiltskin and Robin Hood were not of my acquaintance, and though I understood about wolves, Little Red Ridinghood* was a stranger even by name. So far as my 'dedication' was concerned, I can but think that my parents were in error thus to exclude the imaginary from my outlook upon facts. They desired to make me truthful; the tendency was to make me positive and scep-tical. Had they wrapped me in the soft folds of supernatural fancy, my mind might have been longer content to follow their traditions in an unquestioning spirit.

Having easily said what, in those early years, I did not read, I have great difficulty in saying what I did read. But a queer variety of natural history, some of it quite indigestible by my undeveloped mind; many books of travels, mainly of a scientific character, among them voyages of discovery in the South Seas, by which my brain was dimly filled with splendour; some geography and astronomy, both of them sincerely enjoyed; much theology, which I desired to appreci-ate but could never get my teeth into (if I may venture to say so), and over which my eye and tongue learned to slip without penetrating, so that I would read, and read aloud, and with great propriety of emphasis, page after page without having formed an idea or retained an expression. There was, for instance, a writer on prophecy called Jukes,* of whose works each of my parents was inordinately fond, and I was early set to read Jukes aloud to them. I did it glibly, like a machine, but the sight of Jukes's volumes became an abomination to me, and I never formed the outline of a notion what they were about. Later on, a publication called 'The Penny Cyclopædia'* became my daily, and for a long time almost my sole study; to the subject of this remarkable work I may presently return.

It is difficult to keep anything like chronological order in recording fragments of early recollection, and in speaking of my reading I have been led too far ahead. My memory does not, practically, begin till we returned from certain visits, made with a zoological purpose, to the shores of Devon and Dorset,* and settled, early in my fifth year, in a house at Islington,* in the north of London. Our circumstances were now more easy; my Father had regular and well-paid literary work; and the house was larger and more comfortable than ever before, though still very simple and restricted. My memories, some of which are exactly dated by certain facts, now become clear and almost abundant. What I do not remember, except from having it very often repeated to me, is what may be considered the only 'clever' thing that I said during an otherwise unillustrious childhood. It was not startlingly 'clever', but it may pass. A lady—when I was just four—rather injudiciously showed me a large print of a human skeleton, saying 'There! you don't know what that is, do you?' Upon which, immediately and very archly, I replied, 'Isn't it a man with the meat off?' This was thought wonderful, and, as it is supposed that I had never had the phenomenon explained to me, it certainly displays some quickness in seizing an analogy. I had often watched my Father, while he soaked the flesh off the bones of fishes and small mammals. If I venture to repeat this trifle, it is only to point out that the system on which I was being educated deprived all things, human life among the rest, of their mystery. The 'bare-grinning skeleton of death' was to me merely a prepared specimen of that featherless plantigrade vertebrate, *homo sapiens*.*

As I have said that this anecdote was thought worth repeating, I ought to proceed to say that there was, so far as I can recollect, none of that flattery of childhood which is so often merely a backhanded way of indulging the vanity of parents. My Mother, indeed, would hardly have been human if she had not occasionally entertained herself with the delusion that her solitary duckling was a cygnet. This my Father did not encourage, remarking, with great affection, and chucking me under the chin, that I was 'a nice little ordinary boy'.

My Mother, stung by this want of appreciation, would proceed so far
as to declare that she believed that in future times the F.R.S. would
be chiefly known as his son's father!* (This is a pleasantry frequent in
professional families.)

To this my Father, whether convinced or not, would make no
demur, and the couple would begin to discuss, in my presence, the
direction which my shining talents would take. In consequence of
my dedication to 'the Lord's Service', the range of possibilities was
much restricted. My Father, who had lived long in the Tropics, and
who nursed a perpetual nostalgia for 'the little lazy isles where the
trumpet-orchids blow',* leaned towards the field of missionary
labour. My Mother, who was cold about foreign missions, preferred
to believe that I should be the Charles Wesley of my age, 'or perhaps,' she had the candour to admit, 'merely the George Whitefield'.*
I cannot recollect the time when I did not understand that I was
going to be a minister of the Gospel.

It is so generally taken for granted that a life strictly dedicated to
religion is stiff and dreary, that I may have some difficulty in persuading my readers that, as a matter of fact, in these early days of
my childhood, before disease and death had penetrated to our slender society, we were always cheerful and often gay. My parents were
playful with one another, and there were certain stock family jests
which seldom failed to enliven the breakfast table. My Father and
Mother lived so completely in the atmosphere of faith, and were so
utterly convinced of their intercourse with God, that, so long as that
intercourse was not clouded by sin, to which they were delicately
sensitive, they could afford to take the passing hour very lightly.
They would even, to a certain extent, treat the surroundings of their
religion as a subject of jest, joking very mildly and gently about such
things as an attitude at prayer or the nature of a supplication. They
were absolutely indifferent to forms. They prayed, seated in their
chairs, as willingly as, reversed, upon their knees; no ritual having
any significance for them. My Mother was sometimes extremely gay,
laughing with a soft, merry sound. What I have since been told of the
guileless mirth of nuns in a convent has reminded me of the gaiety of
my parents during my early childhood.

So long as I was a mere part of them, without individual existence,
and swept on, a satellite, in their atmosphere, I was mirthful when
they were mirthful, and grave when they were grave. The mere fact

that I had no young companions, no story books, no outdoor amusements, none of the thousand and one employments provided for
other children in more conventional surroundings, did not make me
discontented or fretful, because I did not know of the existence of
such entertainments. In exchange, I became keenly attentive to the
limited circle of interests open to me. Oddly enough, I have no
recollection of any curiosity about other children, nor of any desire
to speak to them or play with them. They did not enter into my
dreams, which were occupied entirely with grown-up people and
animals. I had three dolls, to whom my attitude was not very intelligible. Two of these were female, one with a shapeless face of rags, the
other in wax. But, in my fifth year, when the Crimean War broke out,*
I was given a third doll, a soldier, dressed very smartly in a scarlet
cloth tunic. I used to put the dolls on three chairs, and harangue
them aloud, but my sentiment to them was never confidential, until
our maid-servant one day, intruding on my audience, and misunderstanding the occasion of it, said: 'What? a boy, and playing with a
soldier when he's got two lady-dolls to play with?' I had never
thought of my dolls as confidants before, but from that time forth I
paid a special attention to the soldier, in order to make up to him for
Lizzie's unwarrantable insult.

The declaration of war with Russia brought the first breath of
outside life into our Calvinist cloister. My parents took in a daily
newspaper, which they had never done before, and events in picturesque places, which my Father and I looked out on the map, were
eagerly discussed. One of my vividest early memories can be dated
exactly. I was playing about the house, and suddenly burst into the
breakfast-room, where, close to the door, sat an amazing figure, a
very tall young man, as stiff as my doll, in a gorgeous scarlet tunic.
Quite far away from him, at her writing-table, my Mother sat with
her Bible open before her, and was urging the gospel plan of salvation on his acceptance. She promptly told me to run away and play,
but I had seen a great sight. This guardsman was in the act of leaving
for the Crimea, and his adventures,—he was converted in consequence of my Mother's instruction,—were afterwards told by her
in a tract, called 'The Guardsman of the Alma',* of which I believe
that more than half a million of copies were circulated. He was killed
in that battle, and this added an extraordinary lustre to my dream of
him. I see him still in my mind's eye, large, stiff, and unspeakably

brilliant, seated, from respect, as near as possible to our parlour door. This apparition gave reality to my subsequent conversations with the soldier doll.

That same victory of the Alma, which was reported in London on my fifth birthday, is also marked very clearly in my memory by a family circumstance. We were seated at breakfast, at our small round table drawn close up to the window, my Father with his back to the light. Suddenly, he gave a sort of cry, and read out the opening sentences from the *Times* announcing a battle in the valley of the Alma. No doubt the strain of national anxiety had been very great, for both he and my Mother seemed deeply excited. He broke off his reading when the fact of the decisive victory was assured, and he and my Mother sank simultaneously on their knees in front of their tea and bread-and-butter, while in a loud voice my Father gave thanks to the God of Battles. This patriotism was the more remarkable, in that he had schooled himself, as he believed, to put his 'heavenly citizenship' above all earthly duties. To those who said: 'Because you are a Christian, surely you are not less an Englishman?' he would reply by shaking his head, and by saying: 'I am a citizen of no earthly State.' He did not realise that, in reality, and to use a cant phrase not yet coined in 1854, there existed in Great Britain no more thorough 'Jingo'* than he.

Another instance of the remarkable way in which the interests of daily life were mingled, in our strange household, with the practice of religion, made an impression upon my memory. We had all three been much excited by a report that a certain dark geometer-moth,* generated in underground stables, had been met with in Islington. Its name, I think is *boletobia fuliginaria*, and I believe that it is excessively rare in England. We were sitting at family prayers, on a summer morning, I think in 1855, when through the open window a brown moth came sailing. My Mother immediately interrupted the reading of the Bible by saying to my Father, 'O! Henry, do you think that can be *boletobia?*' My Father rose up from the sacred book, examined the insect, which had now perched, and replied: 'No! it is only the common Vapourer, *orgygia antiqua!*',* resuming his seat, and the exposition of the Word, without any apology or embarrassment.

In the course of this, my sixth year, there happened a series of minute and soundless incidents which, elementary as they may seem when told, were second in real importance to none in my mental

history. The recollection of them confirms me in the opinion that
certain leading features in each human soul are inherent to it, and
cannot be accounted for by suggestion or training. In my own case, I
was most carefully withdrawn, like Princess Blanchefleur* in her
marble fortress, from every outside influence whatever, yet to me the
instinctive life came as unexpectedly as her lover came to her in the
basket of roses. What came to me was the consciousness of self, as a
force and as a companion, and it came as the result of one or two
shocks, which I will relate.

In consequence of hearing so much about an Omniscient God, a
being of supernatural wisdom and penetration who was always with
us, who made, in fact, a fourth in our company, I had come to think
of Him, not without awe, but with absolute confidence. My Father
and Mother, in their serene discipline of me, never argued with one
another, never even differed; their wills seemed absolutely one. My
Mother always deferred to my Father, and in his absence spoke of
him to me, as if he were all-wise. I confused him in some sense with
God; at all events I believed that my Father knew everything and saw
everything. One morning in my sixth year, my Mother and I were
alone in the morning-room, when my Father came in and announced
some fact to us. I was standing on the rug, gazing at him, and when
he made this statement, I remember turning quickly, in embarrassment, and looking into the fire. The shock to me was as that of a
thunderbolt, for what my Father had said *was not true*. My Mother
and I, who had been present at the trifling incident, were aware that
it had not happened exactly as it had been reported to him. My
Mother gently told him so, and he accepted the correction. Nothing
could possibly have been more trifling to my parents, but to me it
meant an epoch. Here was the appalling discovery, never suspected
before, that my Father was not as God, and did not know everything.
The shock was not caused by any suspicion that he was not telling
the truth, as it appeared to him, but by the awful proof that he was
not, as I had supposed, omniscient.

This experience was followed by another, which confirmed the
first, but carried me a great deal further. In our little back-garden,
my Father had built up a rockery for ferns and mosses, and from the
water-supply of the house he had drawn a leaden pipe so that it
pierced upwards through the rockery and produced, when a tap was
turned, a pretty silvery parasol of water. The pipe was exposed

somewhere near the foot of the rockery. One day, two workmen, who were doing some repairs, left their tools during the dinner-hour in the back-garden, and as I was marching about I suddenly thought that to see whether one of these tools could make a hole in the pipe would be attractive. It did make such a hole, quite easily, and then the matter escaped my mind. But a day or two afterwards, when my Father came in to dinner, he was very angry. He had turned the tap, and instead of the fountain arching at the summit, there had been a rush of water through a hole at the foot. The rockery was absolutely ruined.

Of course I realised in a moment what I had done, and I sat frozen with alarm, waiting to be denounced. But my Mother remarked on the visit of the plumbers two or three days before, and my Father instantly took up the suggestion. No doubt that was it; the mischievous fellows had thought it amusing to stab the pipe and spoil the fountain. No suspicion fell on me; no question was asked of me. I sat there, turned to stone within, but outwardly sympathetic and with unchecked appetite.

We attribute, I believe, too many moral ideas to little children. It is obvious that in this tremendous juncture, I ought to have been urged forward by good instincts, or held back by naughty ones. But I am sure that the fear which I experienced for a short time, and which so unexpectedly melted away, was a purely physical one. It had nothing to do with the motions of a contrite heart. As to the destruction of the fountain, I was sorry about that, for my own sake, since I admired the skipping water extremely, and had had no idea that I was spoiling its display. But the emotions which now thronged within me, and which led me with an almost unwise alacrity, to seek solitude in the back-garden, were not moral at all, they were intellectual. I was not ashamed of having successfully—and so surprisingly—deceived my parents by my crafty silence; I looked upon that as a providential escape, and dismissed all further thought of it. I had other things to think of.

In the first place, the theory that my Father was omniscient or infallible was now dead and buried. He probably knew very little; in this case he had not known a fact of such importance that if you did not know that, it could hardly matter what you knew. My Father, as a deity, as a natural force of immense prestige, fell in my eyes to a human level. In future, his statements about things in general need not be accepted implicitly. But of all the thoughts which rushed upon my savage and undeveloped little brain at this crisis, the most curious was that I had found a companion and a confidant in myself. There was a secret in this world and it belonged to me and to a somebody who lived in the same body with me. There were two of us, and we could talk with one another. It is difficult to define impressions so rudimentary, but it is certain that it was in this dual form that the sense of my individuality now suddenly descended upon me, and it is equally certain that it was a great solace to me to find a sympathiser in my own breast.

About this time, my Mother, carried away by the current of her literary and her philanthropic work, left me more and more to my own devices. She was seized with a great enthusiasm; as one of her admirers and disciples has written, 'she went on her way, sowing beside all waters'.* I would not for a moment let it be supposed that I regard her as a Mrs Jellyby,* or that I think she neglected me. But a remarkable work had opened up before her; after her long years in a mental hermitage, she was drawn forth into the clamorous harvest-field of souls. She developed an unexpected gift of persuasion over strangers whom she met in the omnibus or in the train, and with whom she courageously grappled. This began by her noting, with deep humility and joy, that 'I have reason to judge the sound conversion to God of three young persons within a few weeks, by the instrumentality of my conversations with them'. At the same time, as another of her biographers has said, 'those testimonies to the Blood of Christ, the fruits of her pen, began to be spread very widely, even to the most distant parts of the globe'.* My Father, too, was at this time at the height of his activity. After breakfast, each of them was amply occupied, perhaps until night-fall; our evenings we still always spent together. Sometimes my Mother took me with her on her 'unknown day's employ';* I recollect pleasant rambles through the City by her side, and the act of looking up at her figure soaring above me. But when all was done, I had hours and hours of complete solitude, in my Father's study, in the back-garden, above all in the garret.

The garret was a fairy place. It was a low lean-to, lighted from the roof. It was wholly unfurnished, except for two objects, an ancient hat-box and a still more ancient skin-trunk. The hat-box puzzled me extremely, till one day, asking my Father what it was, I got a distracted answer which led me to believe that it was itself a sort of hat, and I made a laborious but repeated effort to wear it. The skin-trunk was absolutely empty, but the inside of the lid of it was lined with sheets of what I now know to have been a sensational novel.* It was, of course, a fragment, but I read it, kneeling on the bare floor, with indescribable rapture. It will be recollected that the idea of fiction, of a deliberately invented story, had been kept from me with entire success. I therefore implicitly believed the tale in the lid of the trunk to be a true account of the sorrows of a lady of title, who had to flee the country, and who was pursued into foreign lands by enemies bent upon her ruin. Somebody had an interview with a 'minion' in a 'mask'; I went downstairs and looked up these words in Bailey's 'English Dictionary',* but was left in darkness as to what they had to do with the lady of title. This ridiculous fragment filled me with delicious fears; I fancied that my Mother, who was out so much, might be threatened by dangers of the same sort; and the fact that the narrative came abruptly to an end, in the middle of one of its most thrilling sentences, wound me up almost to a disorder of wonder and romance.

The preoccupation of my parents threw me more and more upon my own resources. But what are the resources of a solitary child of six? I was never inclined to make friends with servants, nor did our successive maids proffer, so far as I recollect, any advances. Perhaps, with my 'dedication' and my grown-up ways of talking, I did not seem to them at all an attractive little boy. I continued to have no companions, or even acquaintances of my own age. I am unable to recollect exchanging two words with another child till after my Mother's death.

The abundant energy which my Mother now threw into her pub-lic work did not affect the quietude of our private life. We had some visitors in the day-time, people who came to consult one parent or the other. But they never stayed to a meal, and we never returned their visits. I do not quite know how it was that neither of my parents took me to any of the sights of London, although I am sure it was a question of principle with them. Notwithstanding all our study of natural history, I was never introduced to live wild beasts at the Zoo, nor to dead ones at the British Museum. I can understand better why we never visited a picture-gallery or a concert-room. So far as I can recollect, the only time I was ever taken to any place of

entertainment was when my Father and I paid a visit, long anticipated, to the Great Globe in Leicester Square.* This was a
huge structure, the interior of which one ascended by means of a
spiral staircase. It was a poor affair; that was concave in it which
should have been convex, and my imagination was deeply affronted.
I could invent a far better Great Globe than that in my mind's eye in
the garret.

   Being so restricted, then, and yet so active, my mind took refuge
in an infantile species of natural magic. This contended with the
definite ideas of religion which my parents were continuing, with too
mechanical a persistency, to force into my nature, and it ran parallel
with them. I formed strange superstitions, which I can only render
intelligible by naming some concrete examples. I persuaded myself
that, if I could only discover the proper words to say or the proper
passes to make, I could induce the gorgeous birds and butterflies in
my Father's illustrated manuals to come to life, and fly out of the
book, leaving holes behind them. I believed that, when, at the
Chapel, we sang, drearily and slowly, loud hymns of experience and
humiliation, I could boom forth with a sound equal to that of dozens
of singers, if I could only hit upon the formula. During morning and
evening prayers, which were extremely lengthy and fatiguing, I fancied that one of my two selves could flit up, and sit clinging to the
cornice, and look down on my other self and the rest of us, if I could
only find the key. I laboured for hours in search of these formulas,
thinking to compass my ends by means absolutely irrational. For
example, I was convinced that if I could only count consecutive
numbers long enough, without losing one, I should suddenly, on
reaching some far-distant figure, find myself in possession of the
great secret. I feel quite sure that nothing external suggested these
ideas of magic, and I think it probable that they approached the ideas
of savages at a very early stage of development.*

   All this ferment of mind was entirely unobserved by my parents.
But when I formed the belief that it was necessary, for the success of
my practical magic, that I should hurt myself, and when, as a matter
of fact, I began, in extreme secrecy, to run pins into my flesh and
bang my joints with books, no one will be surprised to hear that my
Mother's attention was drawn to the fact that I was looking 'delicate'. The notice nowadays universally given to the hygienic rules of
life was rare fifty years ago, and among deeply religious people, in

particular, fatalistic views of disease prevailed. If any one was ill, it showed that 'the Lord's hand was extended in chastisement', and much prayer was poured forth in order that it might be explained to the sufferer, or to his relations, in what he or they had sinned. People would, for instance, go on living over a cess-pool, working themselves up into an agony to discover how they had incurred the displeasure of the Lord, but never moving away. As I became very pale and nervous, and slept badly at nights, with visions and loud screams in my sleep, I was taken to a physician, who stripped me and tapped me all over (this gave me some valuable hints for my magical practices), but could find nothing the matter. He recommended,—whatever physicians in such cases always recommend,—but nothing was done. If I was feeble it was the Lord's Will, and we must acquiesce.

It culminated in a sort of fit of hysterics, when I lost all self-control, and sobbed with tears, and banged my head on the table. While this was proceeding, I was conscious of that dual individuality of which I have already spoken, since while one part of me gave way, and could not resist, the other part in some extraordinary sense seemed standing aloof, much impressed. I was alone with my Father when this crisis suddenly occurred, and I was interested to see that he was greatly alarmed. It was a very long time since we had spent a day out of London, and I said, on being coaxed back to calmness, that I wanted 'to go into the country'. Like the dying Falstaff, I babbled of green fields.* My Father, after a little reflection, proposed to take me to Primrose Hill.* I had never heard of the place, and names have always appealed directly to my imagination. I was in the highest degree delighted, and could hardly restrain my impatience. As soon as possible we set forth westward, my hand in my Father's, with the liveliest anticipations. I expected to see a mountain absolutely carpeted with primroses, a terrestrial galaxy like that which covered the hill that led up to Montgomery Castle in Donne's poem.* But at length, as we walked from the Chalk Farm direction,* a miserable acclivity stole into view—surrounded, even in those days, on most sides by houses, with its grass worn to the buff by millions of boots, and resembling what I meant by 'the country' about as much as Poplar resembles Paradise.* We sat down on a bench at its inglorious summit, whereupon I burst into tears, and in a heart-rending whisper sobbed, 'Oh! Papa, let us go home!'

This was the lachrymose epoch in a career not otherwise given to weeping, for I must tell one more tale of tears. About this time,—the autumn of 1855,—my parents were disturbed more than once in the twilight, after I had been put to bed, by shrieks from my crib. They would rush up to my side, and find me in great distress, but would be unable to discover the cause of it. The fact was that I was half beside myself with ghostly fears, increased and pointed by the fact that there had been some daring burglaries in our street. Our servant-maid, who slept at the top of the house, had seen, or thought she saw, upon a moonlight night, the figure of a crouching man, silhouetted against the sky, slip down from the roof and leap into her room. She screamed, and he fled away. Moreover, as if this were not enough for my tender nerves, there had been committed a horrid murder, at a baker's shop just round the corner in the Caledonian Road,* to which murder actuality was given to us by the fact that my Mother had been 'just thinking' of getting her bread from this shop. Children, I think, were not spared the details of these affairs fifty years ago; at least, I was not, and my nerves were a packet of spilikins.*

But what made me scream o' nights, was that when my Mother had tucked me up in bed, and had heard me say my prayer, and had prayed aloud on her knees at my side, and had stolen downstairs, noises immediately began in the room. There was a rustling of clothes, and a slapping of hands, and a gurgling, and a sniffing, and a trotting. These horrible muffled sounds would go on, and die away, and be resumed; I would pray very fervently to God to save me from my enemies; and sometimes I would go to sleep. But on other occasions, my faith and fortitude alike gave way, and I screamed 'Mama! Mama!' Then would my parents come bounding up the stairs, and comfort me, and kiss me, and assure me it was nothing. And nothing it was while they were there, but no sooner had they gone than the ghostly riot recommenced. It was at last discovered by my Mother that the whole mischief was due to a card of framed texts, fastened by one nail to the wall; this did nothing when the bed-room door was shut, but when it was left open (in order that my parents might hear me call), the card began to gallop in the draught, and made the most intolerable noises.

Several things tended at this time to alienate my conscience from the line which my Father had so rigidly traced for it. The question of the efficacy of prayer, which has puzzled wiser heads than mine was, began to trouble me. It was insisted on in our household that if anything was desired, you should not, as my Mother said, 'lose any time in seeking for it, but ask God to guide you to it'. In many junctures of life, this is precisely what, in sober fact, they did. I will not dwell here on their theories, which my Mother put forth, with unflinching directness, in her published writings. But I found that a difference was made between my privileges in this matter and theirs, and this led to many discussions. My parents said: 'Whatever you need, tell Him and He will grant it, if it is His will.' Very well; I had need of a large painted humming-top which I had seen in a shop-window in the Caledonian Road. Accordingly, I introduced a suppli-cation for this object into my evening prayer, carefully adding the words: 'If it is Thy will.' This, I recollect, placed my Mother in a dilemma, and she consulted my Father. Taken, I suppose, at a dis-advantage, my Father told me I must not pray for 'things like that'. To which I answered by another query, 'Why?' And I added that he said we ought to pray for things we needed, and that I needed the humming-top a great deal more than I did the conversion of the heathen or the restitution of Jerusalem to the Jews, two objects of my nightly supplication which left me very cold.

I have reason to believe, looking back upon this scene, conducted by candle-light in the front parlour, that my Mother was much baffled by the logic of my argument. She had gone so far as to say publicly that no 'things or circumstances are too insignificant to bring before the God of the whole earth'. I persisted that this covered the case of the humming-top, which was extremely signifi-cant to me. I noticed that she held aloof from the discussion, which was carried on with some show of annoyance by my Father. He had never gone quite so far as she did in regard to this question of praying for material things. I am not sure that she was convinced that I ought to have been checked; but he could not help seeing that it reduced their favourite theory to an absurdity for a small child to exercise the privilege. He ceased to argue, and told me peremptorily that it was not right for me to pray for things like humming-tops, and that I must do it no more. His authority, of course, was para-mount, and I yielded; but my faith in the efficacy of prayer was a good deal shaken. The fatal suspicion had crossed my mind that the reason why I was not to pray for the top was because it was too expensive for my parents to buy, that being the usual excuse for not getting things I wished for.

It was about the date of my sixth birthday that I did something very naughty, some act of direct disobedience, for which my Father, after a solemn sermon, chastised me, sacrificially, by giving me several cuts with a cane.* This action was justified, as everything he did was justified, by reference to Scripture—'Spare the rod and spoil the child.'* I suppose that there are some children, of a sullen and lymphatic temperament, who are smartened up and made more wide-awake by a whipping. It is largely a matter of convention, the exercise being endured (I am told) with pride by the infants of our aristocracy, but not tolerated by the lower classes. I am afraid that I proved my inherent vulgarity by being made, not contrite or humble, but furiously angry by this caning. I cannot account for the flame of rage which it awakened in my bosom. My dear, excellent Father had beaten me, not very severely, without ill-temper, and with the most genuine desire to improve me. But he was not well-advised, especially so far as the 'dedication to the Lord's service' was concerned. This same 'dedication' had ministered to my vanity, and there are some natures which are not improved by being humiliated. I have to confess with shame that I went about the house for some days with a murderous hatred of my Father locked within my bosom. He did not suspect that the chastisement had not been wholly efficacious, and he bore me no malice; so that after a while, I forgot and thus forgave him. But I do not regard physical punishment as a wise element in the education of proud and sensitive children.

My theological misdeeds culminated, however, in an act so puerile and preposterous that I should not venture to record it if it did not throw some glimmering of light on the subject which I have proposed to myself in writing these pages. My mind continued to dwell on the mysterious question of prayer. It puzzled me greatly to know why, if we were God's children, and if he was watching over us by night and day, we might not supplicate for toys and sweets and smart clothes as well as for the conversion of the heathen. Just at this juncture, we had a special service at the Room, at which our attention was particularly called to what we always spoke of as 'the field of missionary labour'. The East was represented among 'the saints' by an excellent Irish peer, who had, in his early youth, converted and married a lady of colour; this Asiatic shared in our Sunday morning meetings, and was an object of helpless terror to me; I shrank from her amiable caresses, and vaguely identified her with a personage much spoken of in our family circle, the 'Personal Devil'.

All these matters drew my thoughts to the subject of idolatry, which was severely censured at the missionary meeting. I cross-examined my Father very closely as to the nature of this sin, and pinned him down to the categorical statement that idolatry consisted in praying to any one or anything but God himself. Wood and stone, in the words of the hymn, were peculiarly liable to be bowed down to by the heathen in their blindness. I pressed my Father further on this subject, and he assured me that God would be very angry, and would signify His anger, if any one, in a Christian country, bowed down to wood and stone. I cannot recall why I was so pertinacious on this subject, but I remember that my Father became a little restive under my cross-examination. I determined, however, to test the matter for myself, and one morning, when both my parents were safely out of the house, I prepared for the great act of heresy. I was in the morning-room on the ground-floor, where, with much labour, I hoisted a small chair on to the table close to the window. My heart was now beating as if it would leap out of my side, but I pursued my experiment. I knelt down on the carpet in front of the table and looking up I said my daily prayer in a loud voice, only substituting the address 'O Chair!' for the habitual one.

Having carried this act of idolatry safely through, I waited to see what would happen. It was a fine day, and I gazed up at the slip of white sky above the houses opposite, and expected something to appear in it. God would certainly exhibit his anger in some terrible form, and would chastise my impious and wilful action. I was very much alarmed, but still more excited; I breathed the high, sharp air of defiance. But nothing happened; there was not a cloud in the sky, not an unusual sound in the street. Presently I was quite sure that nothing would happen. I had committed idolatry, flagrantly and deliberately, and God did not care.

The result of this ridiculous act was not to make me question the existence and power of God; those were forces which I did not dream of ignoring. But what it did was to lessen still further my confidence in my Father's knowledge of the Divine mind. My Father had said, positively, that if I worshipped a thing made of wood, God would manifest his anger. I had then worshipped a chair, made (or partly made) of wood, and God had made no sign whatever. My Father, therefore, was not really acquainted with the Divine practice in cases of idolatry. And with that, dismissing the subject, I dived again into the unplumbed depths of the 'Penny Cyclopædia'.

CHAPTER III

THAT I might die in my early childhood was a thought which frequently recurred to the mind of my Mother. She endeavoured, with a Roman fortitude, to face it without apprehension. Soon after I had completed my fifth year she had written as follows in her secret journal:

'Should we be called on to weep over the early grave of the dear one whom now we are endeavouring to train for heaven, may we be able to remember that we never ceased to pray for and watch over him. It is easy, comparatively, to watch over an infant. Yet shall I be sufficient for these things? I am not. But God is sufficient. In his strength I have begun the warfare, in his strength I will persevere, and I will faint not till either I myself or my little one is beyond the reach of earthly solicitude.'

That either she or I would be called away from earth, and that our physical separation was at hand, seems to have been always vaguely present in my Mother's dreams, as an obstinate conviction to be carefully recognised and jealously guarded against.

It was not, however, until the course of my seventh year, that the tragedy occurred, which altered the whole course of our family existence. My Mother had hitherto seemed strong and in good health; she had even made the remark to my Father, that 'sorrow and pain, the badges of Christian discipleship', appeared to be withheld from her. On her birthday, which was to be her last, she had written these ejaculations in her locked diary:

'Lord, forgive the sins of the past, and help me to be faithful in future! May this be a year of much blessing, a year of jubilee! May I be kept lowly, trusting, loving! May I have more blessing than in all former years combined! May I be happier as a wife, mother, sister, writer, mistress, friend!'

But a symptom began to alarm her and in the beginning of May, having consulted a local physician without being satisfied, she went to see a specialist* in a northern suburb in whose judgment she had great confidence. This occasion I recollect with extreme vividness. I had been put to bed by my Father, in itself a noteworthy event. My crib stood near a window overlooking the street; my parents' ancient four-poster, a relic of the eighteenth century, hid me from the door, but I could see the rest of the room. After falling asleep on this particular evening, I awoke silently, surprised to see two lighted candles on the table, and my Father seated writing by them. I also saw a little meal arranged.

While I was wondering at all this, the door opened, and my Mother entered the room; she emerged from behind the bed-curtains, with her bonnet on, having returned from her expedition. My Father rose hurriedly, pushing back his chair, and greeted her by exclaiming: 'Well, what does he say?' There was a pause, while my Mother seemed to be steadying her voice, and then she replied, loudly and distinctly, 'He says it is—' and she mentioned one of the most cruel maladies* by which our poor mortal nature can be tormented. Then I saw them fold one another in a silent long embrace, and presently sink together out of sight on their knees, at the further side of the bed, whereupon my Father lifted up his voice in prayer. Neither of them had noticed me, and now I lay back on my pillow and fell asleep.

Next morning, when we three sat at breakfast, my mind reverted to the scene of the previous night. With my eyes on my plate, as I was cutting up my food, I asked, casually, 'What is—?' mentioning the disease whose unfamiliar name I had heard from my bed. Receiving no reply, I looked up to discover why my question was not answered, and I saw my parents gazing at each other with lamentable eyes. In some way, I know not how, I was conscious of the presence of an incommunicable mystery, and I kept silence, though tortured with curiosity, nor did I ever repeat my inquiry.

About a fortnight later, my Mother began to go three times a week all the long way from Islington to Pimlico, in order to visit a certain practitioner,* who undertook to apply a special treatment to her case. This involved great fatigue and distress to her, but so far as I was personally concerned it did me a great deal of good. I invariably accompanied her, and when she was very tired and weak, I enjoyed the pride of believing that I protected her. The movement, the exercise, the occupation, lifted my morbid fears and superstitions like a cloud. The medical treatment to which my poor Mother was subjected was very painful, and she had a peculiar sensitiveness to pain. She carried on her evangelical work as long as she possibly could, continuing to converse with her fellow passengers on spiritual matters. It was wonderful that a woman, so reserved and proud as she by nature was, could conquer so completely her natural timidity. In those last months, she scarcely ever got into a railway carriage or into an omnibus, without presently offering tracts to the persons sitting within reach of her, or endeavouring to begin a conversation with some one on the sufficiency of the Blood of Jesus to cleanse the human heart from sin. Her manners were so gentle and persuasive, she looked so innocent, her small, sparkling features were lighted up with so much benevolence, that I do not think she ever met with discourtesy or roughness. Imitative imp that I was, I sometimes took part in these strange conversations, and was mightily puffed up by compliments paid, in whispers, to my infant piety. But my Mother very properly discouraged this, as tending in me to spiritual pride.

If my parents, in their desire to separate themselves from the world, had regretted that through their happiness they seemed to have forfeited the Christian privilege of affliction, they could not continue to complain of any absence of temporal adversity. Everything seemed to combine, in the course of this fatal year 1856, to harass and alarm them. Just at a moment when illness created a special drain upon their resources, their slender income, instead of being increased, was seriously diminished. There is little sympathy felt in this world of rhetoric for the silent sufferings of the genteel poor, yet there is no class that deserves a more charitable commiseration.

At the best of times, the money which my parents had to spend was an exiguous and an inelastic sum. Strictly economical, proud—in an old-fashioned mode now quite out of fashion—to conceal the fact of their poverty, painfully scrupulous to avoid giving inconvenience to shop-people, tradesmen or servants, their whole financial career had to be carried on with the adroitness of a campaign through a hostile country. But now, at the moment when fresh pressing claims were made on their resources, my Mother's small capital suddenly disappeared. It had been placed, on bad advice (they were as children in such matters), in a Cornish mine, the grotesque name of which, Wheal Maria, became familiar to my ears. One day the river Tamar,* in a playful mood, broke into Wheal Maria, and not a penny more was ever lifted from that unfortunate enterprise. About the same time, a small annuity which my Mother had inherited also ceased to be paid.

On my Father's books and lectures, therefore, the whole weight now rested, and that at a moment when he was depressed and unnerved by anxiety. It was contrary to his principles to borrow money, so that it became necessary to pay doctor's and chemist's bills punctually, and yet to carry on the little household with the very small margin. Each artifice of economy was now exercised to enable this to be done without falling into debt, and every branch of expenditure was cut down; clothes, books, the little garden which was my Father's pride, all felt the pressure of new poverty.* Even our food, which had always been simple, now became Spartan indeed, and I am sure that my Mother often pretended to have no appetite that there might remain enough to satisfy my hunger. Fortunately my Father was able to take us away in the autumn for six weeks by the sea in Wales, the expenses of this tour being paid for by a professional engagement, so that my seventh birthday was spent in an ecstasy of happiness, on golden sands, under a brilliant sky, and in sight of the glorious azure ocean beating in from an infinitude of melting horizons. Here, too, my Mother, perched in a nook of the high rocks, surveyed the west, and forgot for a little while her weakness and the gnawing, grinding pain.

But in October, our sorrows seemed to close in upon us. We went back to London, and for the first time in their married life, my parents were divided. My Mother was now so seriously weaker that the omnibus-journeys to Pimlico became impossible. My Father could not leave his work, and so my Mother and I had to take a gloomy lodging close to the doctor's house. The experiences upon which I presently entered were of a nature in which childhood rarely takes a part. I was now my Mother's sole and ceaseless companion; the silent witness of her suffering, of her patience, of her vain and delusive attempts to obtain alleviation of her anguish. For nearly three months I breathed the atmosphere of pain, saw no other light, heard no other sounds, thought no other thoughts, than those which accompany physical suffering and weariness. To my memory these weeks seem years; I have no measure of their monotony. The lodgings were bare and yet tawdry; out of dingy windows we looked from a second storey upon a dull small street, drowned in autumnal fog. My Father came to see us when he could, but otherwise, save when we made our morning expedition to the doctor, or when a slatternly girl waited upon us with our distasteful meals, we were alone,—without any other occupation than to look forward to that occasional abatement of suffering which was what we hoped for most.

It is difficult for me to recollect how these interminable hours were spent. But I read aloud in a great part of them. I have now in my mind's cabinet a picture of my chair turned towards the window, partly that I might see the book more distinctly, partly not to see quite so distinctly that dear patient figure rocking on her sofa, or leaning, like a funeral statue, like a muse upon a monument, with her head on her arms against the mantelpiece. I read the Bible every day, and at much length, also,—with I cannot but think some praiseworthy patience,—a book of incommunicable dreariness, called Newton's 'Thoughts on the Apocalypse'.* Newton bore a great resemblance to my old aversion, Jukes, and I made a sort of playful compact with my Mother that if I read aloud a certain number of pages out of 'Thoughts on the Apocalypse', as a reward I should be allowed to recite 'my own favourite hymns'. Among these there was one which united her suffrages with mine. Both of us extremely admired the piece by Toplady* which begins:—

> What though my frail eyelids refuse
>   Continual watchings to keep,
> And, punctual as midnight renews,
>   Demand the refreshment of sleep.

To this day, I cannot repeat this hymn without a sense of poignant emotion, nor can I pretend to decide how much of this is due to its merit and how much to the peculiar nature of the memories it recalls. But it might be as rude as I genuinely think it to be skilful, and I should continue to regard it as a sacred poem. Among all my childish memories none is clearer than my looking up,—after reading, in my high treble,

> Kind Author and Ground of my hope,
>   Thee, Thee for my God I avow;
> My glad Ebenezer set up,
>   And own Thou hast help'd me till now;
>
> I muse on the years that are past,
>   Wherein my defence Thou hast prov'd,
> Nor wilt Thou relinquish at last
>   A sinner so signally lov'd,—

and hearing my Mother, her eyes brimming with tears and her

alabastrine fingers tightly locked together, murmur in unconscious repetition:

> Nor wilt Thou relinquish at last
> A sinner so signally lov'd.

In our lodgings at Pimlico I came across a piece of verse which exercised a lasting influence on my taste. It was called 'The Cameronian's Dream', and it had been written by a certain James Hyslop,* a schoolmaster on a man-of-war. I do not know how it came into my possession, but I remember it was adorned by an extremely dim and ill-executed wood-cut of a lake surrounded by mountains, with tombstones in the foreground. This lugubrious frontispiece positively fascinated me, and lent a further gloomy charm to the ballad itself. It was in this copy of mediocre verses that the sense of romance first appealed to me, the kind of nature-romance which is connected with hills, and lakes, and the picturesque costumes of old times. The following stanza, for instance, brought a revelation to me:

> 'Twas a dream of those ages of darkness and blood,
> When the minister's home was the mountain and wood;
> When in Wellwood's dark valley the standard of Zion,
> All bloody and torn, 'mong the heather was lying.

I persuaded my Mother to explain to me what it was all about, and she told me of the affliction of the Scottish saints, their flight to the waters and the wilderness, their cruel murder while they were singing 'their last song to the God of Salvation'.* I was greatly fired, and the following stanza, in particular, reached my ideal of the Sublime:

> The muskets were flashing, the blue swords were
>   gleaming,
> The helmets were cleft, and the red blood was streaming,
> The heavens grew dark, and the thunder was rolling,
> When in Wellwood's dark muirlands the mighty were
>   falling.

Twenty years later I met with the only other person whom I have ever encountered who had even heard of 'The Cameronian's Dream'. This was Robert Louis Stevenson,* who had been greatly struck by it when he was about my age. Probably the same ephemeral edition of it reached, at the same time, each of our pious households. As my Mother's illness progressed, she could neither sleep, save by the use of opiates, nor rest, except in a sloping posture, propped up by many pillows. It was my great joy, and a pleasant diversion, to be allowed to shift, beat up, and rearrange these pillows, a task which I learned to accomplish not too awkwardly. Her sufferings, I believe, were principally caused by the violence of the medicaments to which her doctor, who was trying a new and fantastic 'cure', thought it proper to subject her. Let those who take a pessimistic view of our social progress ask themselves whether such tortures could to-day be inflicted on a delicate patient, or whether that patient would be allowed to exist, in the greatest misery, in a lodging with no professional nurse to wait upon her, and with no companion but a little helpless boy of seven years of age. Time passes smoothly and swiftly, and we do not perceive the mitigations which he brings in his hands. Everywhere, in the whole system of human life, improvements, alleviations, ingenious appliances and humane inventions are being introduced to lessen the great burden of suffering.

If we were suddenly transplanted into the world of only fifty years ago, we should be startled and even horror-stricken by the wretchedness to which the step backwards would re-introduce us. It was in the very year of which I am speaking, a year of which my personal memories are still vivid, that Sir James Simpson received the Monthyon prize* as a recognition of his discovery of the use of anæsthetics. Can our thoughts embrace the mitigation of human torment which the application of chloroform alone has caused? My early experiences, I confess, made me singularly conscious, at an age when one should know nothing about these things, of that torrent of sorrow and anguish and terror which flows under all the footsteps of man. Within my childish conscience, already, some dim inquiry was awake as to the meaning of this mystery of pain—

> The floods of the tears meet and gather;
>   The sound of them all grows like thunder;
>   O into what bosom, I wonder,
>   Is poured the whole sorrow of years?
>   For Eternity only seems keeping
>   Account of the great human weeping;
> May God then, the Maker and Father,
>   May He find a place for the tears!*

In my Mother's case, the savage treatment did no good; it had to be abandoned, and a day or two before Christmas, while the fruits were piled in the shop-fronts and the butchers were shouting outside their forests of carcases, my Father brought us back in a cab through the streets to Islington, a feeble and languishing company. Our invalid bore the journey fairly well, enjoying the air, and pointing out to me the glittering evidences of the season, but we paid heavily for her little entertainment, since, at her earnest wish the window of the cab having been kept open, she caught a cold, which became, indeed, the technical cause of a death that no applications could now have long delayed.

Yet she lingered with us six weeks more, and during this time I again relapsed, very naturally, into solitude. She now had the care of a practised woman, one of the 'saints' from the Chapel, and I was only permitted to pay brief visits to her bedside. That I might not be kept indoors all day and every day, a man, also connected with the meeting-house, was paid a trifle to take me out for a walk each morning. This person, who was by turns familiar and truculent, was the object of my intense dislike. Our relations became, in the truest sense, 'forced'; I was obliged to walk by his side, but I held that I had no further responsibility to be agreeable, and after a while I ceased to speak to him, or to answer his remarks. On one occasion, poor dreary man, he met a friend and stopped to chat with him. I considered this act to have dissolved the bond; I skipped lightly from his side, examined several shop-windows which I had been forbidden to look into, made several darts down courts and up passages, and finally, after a delightful morning, returned home, having known my directions perfectly. My official conductor, in a shocking condition of fear, was crouching by the area-rails looking up and down the street. He darted upon me, in a great rage, to know 'what I meant by it?' I drew myself up as tall as I could, hissed 'Blind leader of the blind!' at him, and, with this inappropriate (but very effective) Parthian shot,* slipped into the house.

When it was quite certain that no alleviations and no medical care could prevent, or even any longer postpone, the departure of my Mother, I believe that my future conduct became the object of her greatest and her most painful solicitude. She said to my Father that the worst trial of her faith came from the feeling that she was called upon to leave that child whom she had so carefully trained from his earliest infancy for the peculiar service of the Lord, without any

knowledge of what his further course would be. In many conversations, she most tenderly and closely urged my Father, who, however,
needed no urging, to watch with unceasing care over my spiritual
welfare. As she grew nearer her end, it was observed that she became
calmer, and less troubled by fears about me. The intensity of her
prayers and hopes seemed to have a prevailing force; it would have
been a sin to doubt that such supplications, such confidence and
devotion, such an emphasis of will, should not be rewarded by an
answer from above in the affirmative. She was able, she said, to leave
me 'in the hands of her loving Lord', or, on another occasion, 'to the
care of her covenant God'.

Although her faith was so strong and simple, my Mother possessed no quality of the mystic. She never pretended to any visionary
gifts, believed not at all in dreams or portents, and encouraged nothing in herself or others which was superstitious or fantastic. In order
to realise her condition of mind, it is necessary, I think, to accept the
view that she had formed a definite conception of the absolute,
unmodified and historical veracity, in its direct and obvious sense, of
every statement contained within the covers of the Bible. For her,
and for my Father, nothing was symbolic, nothing allegorical or
allusive in any part of Scripture, except what was, in so many words,
proffered as a parable or a picture. Pushing this to its extreme limit,
and allowing nothing for the changes of scene or time or race, my
parents read injunctions to the Corinthian converts without any suspicion that what was apposite in dealing with half-breed Achaian
colonists of the first century might not exactly apply to respectable
English men and women of the nineteenth.* They took it, text by
text, as if no sort of difference existed between the surroundings of
Trimalchion's feast and those of a City dinner.* Both of my parents, I
think, were devoid of sympathetic imagination; in my Father, I am
sure, it was singularly absent. Hence, although their faith was so
strenuous that many persons might have called it fanatical, there was
no mysticism about them. They went rather to the opposite extreme,
to the cultivation of a rigid and iconoclastic literalness.

This was curiously exemplified in the very lively interest which
they both took in what is called 'the interpretation of prophecy', and
particularly in unwrapping the dark sayings bound up in the Book of
Revelation. In their impartial survey of the Bible, they came to this
collection of solemn and splendid visions, sinister and obscure, and

they had no intention of allowing these to be merely stimulating to the fancy, or vaguely doctrinal in symbol. When they read of seals broken and of vials poured forth, of the star which was called Wormwood that fell from Heaven, and of men whose hair was as the hair of women and their teeth as the teeth of lions,* they did not admit for a moment that these vivid mental pictures were of a poetic character, but they regarded them as positive statements, in guarded language, describing events which were to happen, and could be recognised when they did happen. It was the explanation, the perfectly prosaic and positive explanation, of all these wonders which drew them to study the Jukeses and the Newtons whose books they so much enjoyed. They were helped by these guides to recognise in wild Oriental visions direct statements regarding Napoleon III and Pope Pius IX and the King of Piedmont,* historic figures which they conceived as foreshadowed, in language which admitted of plain interpretation, under the names of denizens of Babylon and companions of the Wild Beast.*

My Father was in the habit of saying, in later years, that no small element in his wedded happiness had been the fact that my Mother and he were of one mind in the interpretation of Sacred Prophecy. Looking back, it appears to me that this unusual mental exercise was almost their only relaxation, and that in their economy it took the place which is taken, in profaner families, by cards or the piano. It was a distraction; it took them completely out of themselves. During those melancholy weeks at Pimlico, I read aloud another work of the same nature as those of Newton and Jukes,* the 'Horæ Apocalypticæ' of a Mr Elliott.* This was written, I think, in a less disagreeable style, and certainly it was less opaquely obscure to me. My recollection distinctly is that when my Mother could endure nothing else, the arguments of this book took her thoughts away from her pain and lifted her spirits. Elliott saw 'the queenly arrogance of Popery' everywhere, and believed that the very last days of Babylon the Great* were come. Lest I say what may be thought extravagant, let me quote what my Father wrote in his diary at the time of my Mother's death. He said that the thought that Rome was doomed (as seemed not impossible in 1857) so affected my Mother that it 'irradiated her dying hours with an assurance that was like the light of the Morning Star, the harbinger of the rising sun'.*

After our return to Islington, there was a complete change in my relation to my Mother. At Pimlico, I had been all-important, her only companion, her friend, her confidant. But now that she was at home again, people and things combined to separate me from her. Now, and for the first time in my life, I no longer slept in her room, no longer sank to sleep under her kiss, no longer saw her mild eyes smile on me with the earliest sunshine. Twice a day, after breakfast and before I went to rest, I was brought to her bedside; but we were never alone, other people, sometimes strange people, were there. We had no cosy talk; often she was too weak to do more than pat my hand: her loud and almost constant cough terrified and harassed me. I felt, as I stood, awkwardly and shyly, by her high bed, that I had shrunken into a very small and insignificant figure, that she was floating out of my reach, that all things, but I knew not what nor how, were coming to an end. She herself was not herself; her head, that used to be held so erect, now rolled or sank upon the pillow; the sparkle was all extinguished from those bright, dear eyes. I could not understand it; I meditated long, long upon it all in my infantile darkness, in the garret, or in the little slip of a cold room where my bed was now placed; and a great, blind anger against I knew not what awakened in my soul.

The two retreats which I have mentioned were now all that were left to me. In the back-parlour some one from outside gave me occasional lessons, of a desultory character. The breakfast-room was often haunted by visitors, unknown to me by face or name,—ladies, who used to pity me and even to pet me, until I became nimble in escaping from their caresses. Everything seemed to be unfixed, uncertain; it was like being on the platform of a railway-station waiting for a train. In all this time, the agitated, nervous presence of my Father, whose pale face was permanently drawn with anxiety, added to my perturbation, and I became miserable, stupid, as if I had lost my way in a cold fog.

Had I been older and more intelligent, of course, it might have been of him and not of myself that I should have been thinking. As I now look back upon that tragic time, it is for him that my heart bleeds,—for them both, so singularly fitted as they were to support and cheer one another in an existence which their own innate and cultivated characteristics had made little hospitable to other sources of comfort. This is not to be dwelt on here. But what must be recorded was the extraordinary tranquillity, the serene and sensible resignation, with which at length my parents faced the awful hour. Language cannot utter what they suffered, but there was no rebellion, no repining; in their case even an atheist might admit that the overpowering miracle of grace was mightily efficient.

It seems almost cruel to the memory of their opinions that the only words which rise to my mind, the only ones which seem in the least degree adequate to describe the attitude of my parents, had fallen from the pen of one whom, in their want of imaginative sympathy, they had regarded as anathema. But John Henry Newman* might have come from the contemplation of my Mother's death-bed when he wrote: 'All the trouble which the world inflicts upon us, and which flesh cannot but feel,—sorrow, pain, care, bereavement,— these avail not to disturb the tranquillity and the intensity with which faith gazes at the Divine Majesty.'* It was 'tranquillity', it was not the rapture of the mystic. Almost in the last hour of her life, urged to confess her 'joy' in the Lord, my Mother, rigidly honest, meticulous in self-analysis, as ever, replied: 'I have peace, but not *joy*. It would not do to go into eternity with a lie in my mouth.'

When the very end approached, and her mind was growing clouded, she gathered her strength together to say to my Father, 'I shall walk with Him in white. Won't you take your lamb and walk with me?' Confused with sorrow and alarm, my Father failed to understand her meaning. She became agitated, and she repeated two or three times: 'Take our lamb, and walk with me!' Then my Father comprehended, and pressed me forward; her hand fell softly upon mine and she seemed content. Thus was my dedication, that had begun in my cradle, sealed with the most solemn, the most poignant and irresistible insistence, at the death-bed of the holiest and purest of women. But what a weight, intolerable as the burden of Atlas,* to lay on the shoulders of a little fragile child!

CHAPTER IV

CERTAINLY the preceding year, the seventh of my life, had been weighted for us with comprehensive disaster. I have not yet mentioned that, at the beginning of my Mother's fatal illness, misfortune came upon her brothers. I have never known the particulars of their ruin, but, I believe in consequence of A.'s unsuccessful speculations, and of the fact that E. had allowed the use of his name as a surety, both my uncles were obliged to fly from their creditors, and take refuge in Paris. This happened just when our need was the sorest, and this, together with the poignancy of knowing that their sister's devoted labours for them had been all in vain, added to their unhappiness. It was doubtless also the reason why, having left England, they wrote to us no more, carefully concealing from us even their address, so that when my Mother died, my Father was unable to communicate with them. I fear that they fell into dire distress; before very long we learned that A. had died, but it was fifteen years more before we heard anything of E., whose life had at length been preserved by the kindness of an old servant, but whose mind was now so clouded that he could recollect little or nothing of the past; and soon he also died. Amiable, gentle, without any species of practical ability, they were quite unfitted to struggle with the world, which had touched them only to wreck them.

The flight of my uncles at this particular juncture left me without a relative on my Mother's side at the time of her death. This isolation threw my Father into a sad perplexity. His only obvious source of income—but it happened to be a remarkably hopeful one—was an engagement to deliver a long series of lectures on marine natural history throughout the north and centre of England. These lectures were an entire novelty; nothing like them had been offered to the provincial public before; and the fact that the newly-invented marine aquarium* was the fashionable toy of the moment added to their attraction. My Father was bowed down by sorrow and care, but he was not broken. His intellectual forces were at their height, and so was his popularity as an author. The lectures were to begin in March; my Mother was buried on the 13th of February. It seemed at first, in the inertia of bereavement, to be all beyond his powers to make the supreme effort, but the wholesome prick of need urged him on. It was a question of paying for food and clothes, of keeping a roof above our heads. The captain of a vessel in a storm must navigate his ship, although his wife lies dead in the cabin. That was my Father's position in the spring of 1857; he had to stimulate, instruct, amuse large audiences of strangers, and seem gay, although affliction and loneliness had settled in his heart. He had to do this, or starve.

But the difficulty still remained. During these months what was to become of me? My Father could not take me with him from hotel to hotel and from lecture-hall to lecture-hall. Nor could he leave me, as people leave the domestic cat, in an empty house for the neighbours to feed at intervals. The dilemma threatened to be insurmountable, when suddenly there descended upon us a kind, but little-known, paternal cousin from the west of England,* who had heard of our calamities. This lady had a large family of her own at Bristol; she offered to find room in it for me so long as ever my Father should be away in the north, and when my Father, bewildered by so much goodness, hesitated, she came up to London and carried me forcibly away in a whirlwind of good-nature. Her benevolence was quite spontaneous; and I am not sure that she had not added to it already by helping to nurse our beloved sufferer through part of her illness. Of that I am not positive, but I recollect very clearly her snatching me from our cold and desolate hearthstone, and carrying me off to her cheerful house at Clifton.*

Here, for the first time, when half through my eighth year, I was thrown into the society of young people. My cousins were none of them, I believe, any longer children, but they were youths and maidens busily engaged in various personal interests, all collected in a hive of wholesome family energy. Everybody was very kind to me, and I sank back, after the strain of so many months, into mere childhood again. This long visit to my cousins at Clifton must have been very delightful: I am dimly aware that it was: yet I remember but few of its incidents. My memory, so clear and vivid about earlier solitary times, now in all this society becomes blurred and vague. I recollect certain pleasures; being taken, for instance, to a menagerie,* and having a practical joke, in the worst taste, played upon me by the pelican. One of my cousins, who was a medical student, showed me a pistol, and helped me to fire it; he smoked a pipe, and I was oddly conscious that both the firearm and the tobacco were definitely hostile to my 'dedication'. My girl-cousins took turns in putting me to bed, and on cold nights, or when they were in a hurry, allowed me to say my prayer under the bed-clothes instead of kneeling at a chair. The result of this was further spiritual laxity, because I could not help going to sleep before the prayer was ended.

The visit to Clifton was, in fact, a blessed interval in my strenuous childhood. It probably prevented my nerves from breaking down under the pressure of the previous months. The Clifton family was God-fearing, in a quiet, sensible way, but there was a total absence of all the intensity and compulsion of our religious life at Islington. I was not encouraged—I even remember that I was gently snubbed— when I rattled forth, parrot-fashion, the conventional phraseology of 'the saints'. For a short, enchanting period of respite, I lived the life of an ordinary little boy, relapsing, to a degree which would have filled my Father with despair, into childish thoughts and childish language. The result was that of this little happy breathing-space I have nothing to report. Vague, half-blind remembrances of walks, with my tall cousins waving like trees above me,* pleasant noisy even- ings in a great room on the ground-floor, faint silver-points of excur- sions into the country, all this is the very pale and shadowy testimony to a brief interval of healthy, happy child-life, when my hard-driven soul was allowed to have, for a little while, no history.

The life of a child is so brief, its impressions are so illusory and fugitive, that it is as difficult to record its history as it would be to design a morning cloud sailing before the wind. It is short, as we count shortness in after years, when the drag of lead pulls down to earth the foot that used to flutter with a winged impetuosity, and to float with the pulse of Hermes.* But in memory, my childhood was long, long with interminable hours, hours with the pale cheek pressed against the window pane, hours of mechanical and repeated lonely 'games', which had lost their savour, and were kept going by sheer inertness. Not unhappy, not fretful, but long,—long, long. It seems to me, as I look back to the life in the motherless Islington house, as I resumed it in that slow eighth year of my life, that time had ceased to move. There was a whole age between one tick of the eight-day clock* in the hall, and the next tick. When the milkman went his rounds in our grey street, with his eldritch scream* over the top of each set of area railings, it seemed as though he would never disappear again. There was no past and no future for me, and the

present felt as though it were sealed up in a Leyden jar.* Even my
dreams were interminable, and hung stationary from the nightly sky.

At this time, the street was my theatre, and I spent long periods, as
I have said, leaning against the window. I feel now the coldness of the
pane, and the feverish heat that was produced, by contrast, in
the orbit round the eye. Now and then amusing things happened.
The onion-man was a joy long waited for. This worthy was a tall and
bony Jersey protestant* with a raucous voice, who strode up our
street several times a week, carrying a yoke across his shoulders,
from the ends of which hung ropes of onions. He used to shout, at
abrupt intervals, in a tone which might wake the dead:

> Here's your rope. . . .
> To hang the Pope. . . .
> And a penn'orth of cheese to choke him.*

The cheese appeared to be legendary; he sold only onions. My
Father did not eat onions, but he encouraged this terrible fellow,
with his wild eyes and long strips of hair, because of his 'godly
attitude towards the Papacy', and I used to watch him dart out of the
front door, present his penny, and retire, graciously waving back the
proffered onion. On the other hand, my Father did not approve of a
fat sailor, who was a constant passer-by. This man, who was probably
crazed, used to walk very slowly up the centre of our street, vocifer-
ating with the voice of a bull,

> Wa-a-atch and pray-hay!
> Night and day-hay!

This melancholy admonition was the entire business of his life. He
did nothing at all but walk up and down the streets of Islington
exhorting the inhabitants to watch and pray. I do not recollect that
this sailor-man stopped to collect pennies, and my impression is that
he was, after his fashion, a volunteer evangelist.

The tragedy of Mr Punch* was another, and a still greater delight.
I was never allowed to go out into the street to mingle with the little
crowd which gathered under the stage, and as I was extremely near-
sighted, the impression I received was vague. But when, by happy
chance, the show stopped opposite our door, I saw enough of that
ancient drama to be thrilled with terror and delight. I was much
affected by the internal troubles of the Punch family; I thought that
with a little more tact on the part of Mrs Punch and some restraint

held over a temper, naturally violent, by Mr Punch, a great deal of this sad misunderstanding might have been prevented.

The momentous close, when a figure of shapeless horror appears on the stage, and quells the hitherto undaunted Mr Punch, was to me the bouquet of the entire performance. When Mr Punch, losing his nerve, points to this shape and says in an awestruck, squeaking whisper, 'Who's that? Is it the butcher?' and the stern answer comes, 'No, Mr Punch!' And then, 'Is it the baker?' 'No, Mr Punch!' 'Who is it then?' (this in a squeak trembling with emotion and terror); and then the full, loud reply, booming like a judgment-bell, 'It is the Devil come to take you down to Hell', and the form of Punch, with kicking legs, sunken in epilepsy on the floor,—all this was solemn and exquisite to me beyond words. I was not amused—I was deeply moved and exhilarated, 'purged', as the old phrase hath it, 'with pity and terror'.*

Another joy, in a lighter key, was watching a fantastic old man who came slowly up the street, hung about with drums and flutes and kites and coloured balls, and bearing over his shoulders a great sack. Children and servant-girls used to bolt up out of areas, and chaffer with this gaudy person, who would presently trudge on, always repeating the same set of words—

> Here's your toys
> For girls and boys,
> For bits of brass
> And broken glass,

(these four lines being spoken in a breathless hurry)

A penny or a vial-bottèll . . .

(this being drawled out in an endless wail).

I was not allowed to go forth and trade with this old person, but sometimes our servant-maid did, thereby making me feel that if I did not hold the rose of merchandise, I was very near it. My experiences with my cousins at Clifton had given me the habit of looking out into the world,—even though it was only into the pale world of our quiet street.

My Father and I were now great friends. I do not doubt that he felt his responsibility to fill as far as might be the gap which the death of my Mother had made in my existence. I spent a large portion of my time in his study, while he was writing or drawing, and though very little conversation passed between us, I think that each enjoyed the companionship of the other. There were two, and some-times three aquaria in the room, tanks of sea-water, with glass sides, inside which all sorts of creatures crawled and swam; these were sources of endless pleasure to me, and at this time began to be laid upon me the occasional task of watching and afterwards reporting the habits of animals.

At other times, I dragged a folio volume of the 'Penny Cyclopædia' up to the study with me, and sat there reading successive articles on such subjects as Parrots, Parthians, Passion-flowers, Passover and Pastry, without any invidious preferences, all information being equally welcome, and equally fugitive. That something of all this loose stream of knowledge clung to odd cells of the back of my brain seems to be shown by the fact that to this day, I occasionally find myself aware of some stray useless fact about peonies or pemmican or pepper, which I can only trace back to the 'Penny Cyclopædia' of my infancy.

It will be asked what the attitude of my Father's mind was to me, and of mine to his, as regards religion, at this time, when we were thrown together alone so much. It is difficult to reply with exacti-tude. But so far as the former is concerned, I think that the extreme violence of the spiritual emotions to which my Father had been subjected, had now been followed by a certain reaction. He had not changed his views in any respect, and he was prepared to work out the results of them with greater zeal than ever, but just at present his religious nature, like his physical nature, was tired out with anxiety and sorrow. He accepted the supposition that I was entirely with him in all respects, so far, that is to say, as a being so rudimentary and feeble as a little child could be. My Mother, in her last hours, had dwelt on our unity in God; we were drawn together, she said, elect from the world, in a triplicity of faith and joy. She had constantly repeated the words: 'We shall be one family, one song. One Song! one Family!' My Father, I think, accepted this as a prophecy, he felt no doubt of our triple unity; my Mother had now merely passed before us, through a door, into a world of light,* where we should presently join her, where all things would be radiant and blissful, but where we three would, in some unknown way, be particularly drawn together in a tie of inexpressible benediction. He fretted at the delay;

he would fain have taken me by the hand, and have joined her in the realms of holiness and light, at once, without this dreary dalliance with earthly cares.

He held this confidence and vision steadily before him, but nothing availed against the melancholy of his natural state. He was conscious of his dull and solitary condition, and he saw, too, that it enveloped me. I think his heart was, at this time, drawn out towards me in an immense tenderness. Sometimes, when the early twilight descended upon us in the study, and he could no longer peer with advantage into the depths of his microscope, he would beckon me to him silently, and fold me closely in his arms. I used to turn my face up to his, patiently and wonderingly, while the large, unwilling tears gathered in the corners of his eyelids. My training had given me a preternatural faculty of stillness and we would stay so, without a word or a movement, until the darkness filled the room. And then, with my little hand in his, we would walk sedately downstairs, to the parlour, where we would find that the lamp was lighted, and that our melancholy vigil was ended. I do not think that at any part of our lives my Father and I were drawn so close to one another as we were in that summer of 1857. Yet we seldom spoke of what lay so warm and fragrant between us, the flower-like thought of our Departed.

The visit to my cousins had made one considerable change in me. Under the old solitary discipline, my intelligence had grown at the expense of my sentiment. I was innocent, but inhuman. The long suffering and the death of my Mother had awakened my heart, had taught me what pain was, but had left me savage and morose. I had still no idea of the relations of human beings to one another; I had learned no word of that philosophy which comes to the children of the poor in the struggle of the street and to the children of the well-to-do in the clash of the nursery. In other words, I had no humanity; I had been carefully shielded from the chance of 'catching' it, as though it were the most dangerous of microbes.* But now that I had enjoyed a little of the common experience of childhood, a great change had come upon me. Before I went to Clifton, my mental life was all interior, a rack of baseless dream upon dream. But, now, I was eager to look out of window, to go out in the streets; I was taken with a curiosity about human life. Even, from my vantage of the window-pane, I watched boys and girls go by with an interest which began to be almost wistful.

Still I continued to have no young companions. But on summer evenings I used to drag my Father out, taking the initiative myself, stamping in playful impatience at his irresolution, fetching his hat and stick, and waiting. We used to sally forth at last together, hand in hand, descending the Caledonian Road, with all its shops, as far as Mother Shipton, or else winding among the semi-genteel squares and terraces westward by Copenhagen Street, or, best of all, mounting to the Regent's Canal,* where we paused to lean over the bridge and watch flotillas of ducks steer under us, or little white dogs dash, impotently furious, from stem to stern of the great, lazy barges painted in a crude vehemence of vermilion and azure. These were happy hours, when the spectre of Religion ceased to overshadow us for a little while, when my Father forgot the Apocalypse and dropped his austere phraseology, and when our bass and treble voices used to ring out together over some foolish little jest or some mirthful recollection of his past experiences. Little soft oases these, in the hard desert of our sandy spiritual life at home.

There was an unbending, too, when we used to sing together, in my case very tunelessly. I had inherited a plentiful lack of musical genius from my Mother, who had neither ear nor voice, and who had said, in the course of her last illness, 'I shall sing His praise, *at length*, in strains I never could master here below'. My Father, on the other hand, had some knowledge of the principles of vocal music, although not, I am afraid, much taste. He had at least great fondness for singing hymns, in the manner then popular with the Evangelicals, very loudly, and so slowly that I used to count how many words I could read, silently, between one syllable of the singing and another. My lack of skill did not prevent me from being zealous at these vocal exercises, and my Father and I used to sing lustily together. The Wesleys, Charlotte Elliott ('Just as I am without one plea') and James Montgomery* ('For ever with the Lord') represented his predilection in hymnology. I acquiesced, but that would not have been my independent choice. These represented the devotional verse which made its direct appeal to the evangelical mind, and served in those 'Puseyite' days to counteract the High Church poetry founded on 'The Christian Year'.* Of that famous volume I never met with a copy until I was grown up, and equally unknown in our circle were the hymns of Newman, Faber and Neale.*

It was my Father's plan from the first to keep me entirely ignorant of the poetry of the High Church, which deeply offended his Calvinism; he thought that religious truth could be sucked in, like mother's milk, from hymns which were godly and sound, and yet correctly versified; and I was therefore carefully trained in this direction from an early date. But my spirit had rebelled against some of these hymns, especially against those written—a mighty multitude—by Horatio Bonar;* naughtily refusing to read Bonar's 'I heard the voice of Jesus say' to my Mother in our Pimlico lodgings. A secret hostility to this particular form of effusion was already, at the age of seven, beginning to define itself in my brain, side by side with an unctuous infantile conformity.

I find a difficulty in recalling the precise nature of the religious instruction which my Father gave me at this time. It was incessant, and it was founded on the close inspection of the Bible, particularly of the epistles of the New Testament. This summer, as my eighth year advanced, we read the 'Epistle to the Hebrews',* with very great deliberation, stopping every moment, that my Father might expound it, verse by verse. The extraordinary beauty of the language,—for instance, the matchless cadences and images of the first chapter,—made a certain impression upon my imagination, and were (I think) my earliest initiation into the magic of literature. I was incapable of defining what I felt, but I certainly had a grip in the throat, which was in its essence a purely aesthetic emotion, when my Father read, in his pure, large, ringing voice, such passages as 'The heavens are the works of Thy hands. They shall perish, but Thou remainest, and they all shall wax old as doth a garment, and as a vesture shalt Thou fold them up, and they shall be changed; but Thou art the same, and Thy years shall not fail.'* But the dialectic parts of the Epistle puzzled and confused me. Such metaphysical ideas as 'laying again the foundation of repentance from dead works' and 'crucifying the Son of God afresh'* were not successfully brought down to the level of my understanding.

My Father's religious teaching to me was almost exclusively doctrinal. He did not observe the value of negative education, that is to say, of leaving nature alone to fill up the gaps which it is her design to deal with at a later and riper date. He did not, even, satisfy himself with those moral injunctions which should form the basis of infantile discipline. He was in a tremendous hurry to push on my spiritual growth, and he fed me with theological meat which it was impossible for me to digest. Some glimmer of a suspicion that he was sailing on the wrong tack must, I should suppose, have broken in upon him when we had reached the eighth and ninth chapters of Hebrews, where, addressing readers who had been brought up under the Jewish dispensation, and had the formalities of the Law of Moses in their very blood, the apostle battles with their dangerous conservatism.* It is a very noble piece of spiritual casuistry,* but it is signally unfitted for the comprehension of a child. Suddenly, by my flushing up with anger and saying, 'O how I do hate that Law', my Father perceived, and paused in amazement to perceive, that I took the Law to be a person of malignant temper from whose cruel bondage, and from whose intolerable tyranny and unfairness, some excellent person was crying out to be delivered. I wished to hit Law with my fist, for being so mean and unreasonable.

Upon this, of course, it was necessary to reopen the whole line of exposition. My Father, without realising it, had been talking on his own level, not on mine, and now he condescended to me. But without very great success. The melodious language, the divine forensic audacities, the magnificent ebb and flow of argument which make the 'Epistle to the Hebrews' such a miracle, were far and away beyond my reach, and they only bewildered me. Some evangelical children of my generation, I understand, were brought up on a work called 'Line upon Line: Here a Little, and there a Little'.* My Father's ambition would not submit to anything suggested by such a title as that, and he committed, from his own point of view, a fatal mistake when he sought to build spires and battlements without having been at the pains to settle a foundation beneath them.

We were not always reading the 'Epistle to the Hebrews', however; not always was my flesh being made to creep by having it insisted upon that 'almost all things are by the Law purged with blood, and without blood is no remission of sin'.* In our lighter moods, we turned to the 'Book of Revelation', and chased the phantom of Popery through its fuliginous pages.* My Father, I think, missed my Mother's company almost more acutely in his researches into prophecy than in anything else. This had been their unceasing recreation, and no third person could possibly follow the curious path which they had hewn for themselves through this jungle of symbols. But, more and more, my Father persuaded himself that I, too, was initiated, and by degrees I was made to share in all his speculations and interpretations.

Hand in hand we investigated the number of the Beast,* which number is six hundred three score and six. Hand in hand we inspected the nations, to see whether they had the mark of Babylon in their foreheads. Hand in hand we watched the spirits of devils gathering the kings of the earth into the place which is called in the Hebrew tongue Armageddon.* Our unity in these excursions was so delightful, that my Father was lulled in any suspicion he might have formed that I did not quite understand what it was all about. Nor could he have desired a pupil more docile or more ardent than I was in my flaming denunciations of the Papacy.

If there was one institution more than another which, at this early stage of my history, I loathed and feared, it was what we invariably spoke of as 'the so-called Church of Rome'. In later years, I have met with stout Protestants, gallant 'Down-with-the-Pope' men from County Antrim,* and ladies who see the hand of the Jesuits in every public and private misfortune. It is the habit of a loose and indifferent age to consider this dwindling body of enthusiasts with suspicion, and to regard their attitude towards Rome as illiberal. But my own feeling is that they are all too mild, that their denunciations err on the side of the anodyne. I have no longer the slightest wish myself to denounce the Roman communion, but, if it is to be done, I have an idea that the latter-day Protestants do not know how to do it. In Lord Beaconsfield's phrase, these anti-Pope men 'don't understand their own silly business'.* They make concessions and allowances, they put on gloves to touch the accursed thing.

Not thus did we approach the Scarlet Woman* in the 'fifties. We palliated nothing, we believed in no good intentions, we used (I myself used, in my tender innocency) language of the seventeenth century* such as is now no longer introduced into any species of controversy. As a little boy, when I thought, with intense vagueness, of the Pope, I used to shut my eyes tight and clench my fists. We welcomed any social disorder in any part of Italy, as likely to be annoying to the Papacy. If there was a custom-house officer stabbed in a *fracas* at Sassari,* we gave loud thanks that liberty and light were breaking in upon Sardinia. If there was an unsuccessful attempt to murder the Grand Duke, we lifted up our voices to celebrate the faith and sufferings of the dear persecuted Tuscans, and the record of some apocryphal monstrosity in Naples* would only reveal to us a glorious opening for Gospel energy. My Father celebrated the announcement in the newspapers of a considerable emigration from the Papal Dominions, by rejoicing at 'this out-crowding of many, throughout the harlot's domain, from her sins and her plagues'.

No, the Protestant League may consider itself to be an earnest and active body, but I can never look upon its efforts as anything but lukewarm, standing, as I do, with the light of other days around me. As a child, whatever I might question, I never doubted the turpitude of Rome. I do not think I had formed any idea whatever of the character or pretensions or practices of the Catholic Church, or indeed of what it consisted, or its nature, but I regarded it with a vague terror as a wild beast, the only good point about it being that it was very old and was soon to die. When I turned to Jukes or Newton for further detail, I could not understand what they said. Perhaps, on the whole, there was no disadvantage in that.

It is possible that some one may have observed to my Father that the conditions of our life were unfavourable to our health, although I hardly think that he would have encouraged any such advice. As I look back upon this far-away time, I am surprised at the absence in it of any figures but our own. He and I together, now in the study among the sea-anemones and star-fishes; now on the canal-bridge, looking down at the ducks; now at our hard little meals, served up as those of a dreamy widower are likely to be when one maid-of-all-work provides them, now under the lamp at the maps we both loved so much, this is what I see:—no third presence is ever with us. Whether it occurred to himself that such a solitude *à deux* was excellent, in the long run, for neither of us, or whether any chance visitor or one of the 'Saints', who used to see me at the Room every Sunday morning, suggested that a female influence might put a little rose-colour into my pasty cheeks, I know not. All I am sure of is that one day, towards the close of the summer, as I was gazing into the street, I saw a four-wheeled cab stop outside our door, and deposit, with several packages, a strange lady, who was shown up into my Father's study and was presently brought down and introduced to me.

Miss Marks,* as I shall take the liberty of calling this person, was so long a part of my life that I must pause to describe her. She was tall, rather gaunt, with high cheek-bones; her teeth were prominent and very white; her eyes were china-blue, and were always absolutely fixed, wide open, on the person she spoke to; her nose was inclined to be red at the tip. She had a kind, hearty, sharp mode of talking, but did not exercise it much, being on the whole taciturn. She was bustling and nervous, not particularly refined, not quite, I imagine, what is called 'a lady'. I supposed her, if I thought of the matter at all, to be very old, but perhaps she may have seen, when we knew her first, some forty-five summers. Miss Marks was an orphan, depending upon her work for her living; she would not, in these days of examinations, have come up to the necessary educational standards, but she had enjoyed experience in teaching, and was prepared to be a conscientious and careful governess, up to her lights. I was now informed by my Father that it was in this capacity that she would in future take her place in our household. I was not informed, what I gradually learned by observation, that she would also act in it as housekeeper.

Miss Marks was a somewhat grotesque personage, and might easily be painted as a kind of eccentric Dickens character, a mixture of Mrs Pipchin and Miss Sally Brass.* I will confess that when, in years to come, I read 'Dombey and Son', certain features of Mrs Pipchin did irresistibly remind me of my excellent past governess. I can imagine Miss Marks saying, but with a facetious intent, that children who sniffed would not go to heaven. But I was instantly ashamed of the parallel, because my gaunt old friend was a thoroughly good and honest woman, not intelligent and not graceful, but desirous in every way to do her duty. Her duty to me she certainly did, and I am afraid I hardly rewarded her with the devotion she deserved. From the first, I was indifferent to her wishes, and, as much as was convenient, I ignored her existence. She held no power over my attention, and if I accepted her guidance along the path of instruction, it was because, odd as it may sound, I really loved knowledge. I accepted her company without objection, and though there were occasional outbreaks of tantrums on both sides, we got on very well together for several years. I did not, however, at any time surrender my inward will to the wishes of Miss Marks.

In the circle of our life the religious element took so preponderating a place, that it is impossible to avoid mentioning, what might otherwise seem unimportant, the theological views of Miss Marks. How my Father had discovered her, or from what field of educational enterprise he plucked her in her prime, I never knew, but she used to mention that my Father's ministrations had 'opened her eyes', from which 'scales' had fallen. She had accepted, on their presentation to her, the entire gamut of his principles. Miss Marks was accustomed, while putting me to bed, to dwell darkly on the incidents of her past, which had, I fear, been an afflicted one. I believe I do her rather limited intelligence no injury when I say that it was prepared to swallow, at one mouthful, whatever my Father presented to it, so delighted was its way-worn possessor to find herself in a comfortable, or, at least, an independent position. She soon bowed, if there was indeed any resistance from the first, very contentedly in the House of Rimmon, learning to repeat, with marked fluency, the customary formulas and shibboleths.* On my own religious development she had no great influence. Any such guttering theological rushlight as Miss Marks might dutifully exhibit faded for me in the blaze of my Father's glaring beacon-lamp of faith.

Hardly was Miss Marks settled in the family, than my Father left us on an expedition about which my curiosity was exercised, but not, until later, satisfied. He had gone, as we afterwards found, to South Devon, to a point on the coast which he had known of old. Here he had hired a horse, and had ridden about until he saw a spot he liked, where a villa was being built on speculation. Nothing equals the courage of these recluse men; my Father got off his horse, and tied it to the gate, and then he went in and bought the house on a ninety-nine years' lease. I need hardly say that he had made the matter a subject of the most earnest prayer, and had entreated the Lord for guidance. When he felt attracted to this particular villa, he did not doubt that he was directed to it in answer to his supplication, and he wasted no time in further balancing or inquiring. On my eighth birthday, with bag and baggage complete, we all made the toilful journey down into Devonshire, and I was a town-child no longer.

CHAPTER V

A NEW element now entered into my life, a fresh rival arose to compete for me with my Father's dogmatic theology. This rival was the Sea. When Wordsworth was a little child, the presence of the mountains and the clouds lighted up his spirit with gleams that were like the flashing of a shield.* He has described, in the marvellous pages of the 'Prelude', the impact of nature upon the infant soul, but he has described it vaguely and faintly, with some 'infirmity of love for days disowned by memory',*—I think because he was brought up in the midst of spectacular beauty, and could name no moment, mark no 'here' or 'now', when the wonder broke upon him. At the age of twice five summers, he thought it was, that he began to hold unconscious intercourse with nature, 'drinking in a pure organic pleasure'* from the floating mists and winding waters. Perhaps, in his anxiety to be truthful, and in the absence of any record, he put the date of this conscious rapture too late rather than too early. Certainly my own impregnation with the obscurely-defined but keenly-felt loveliness of the open sea dates from the first week of my ninth year.

The village, on the outskirts of which we had taken up our abode, was built parallel to the cliff-line above the shore, but half a mile inland.* For a long time after the date I have now reached, no other form of natural scenery than the sea had any effect upon me at all. The tors of the distant moor might be drawn in deep blue against the pallor of our morning or our evening sky, but I never looked at them. It was the Sea, always the sea, nothing but the sea. From our house, or from the field at the back of our house, or from any part of the village itself, there was no appearance to suggest that there could lie anything in an easterly direction to break the infinitude of red ploughed fields. But on that earliest morning, how my heart remembers! we hastened,—Miss Marks, the maid, and I between them,— along a couple of high-walled lanes, when suddenly, far below us, in an immense arc of light, there stretched the enormous plain of waters. We had but to cross a step or two of downs, when the hollow sides of the great limestone cove yawned at our feet, descending, like a broken cup, down, down to the moon of snow-white shingle and the expanse of blue-green sea.

In these twentieth-century days, a careful municipality has studded the down with rustic seats and has shut its dangers out with railings, has cut a winding carriage-drive round the curves of the cove down to the shore, and has planted sausage-laurels at intervals in clearings made for that æsthetic purpose. When last I saw the place, thus smartened and secured, with its hair in curl-papers and its feet in patent-leathers, I turned from it in anger and disgust, and could almost have wept. I suppose that to those who knew it in no other guise, it may still have beauty. No parish councils, beneficent and shrewd, can obscure the lustre of the waters or compress the vastness of the sky. But what man could do to make wild beauty ineffectual, tame and empty, has amply been performed at Oddicombe.*

Very different was it fifty years ago, in its uncouth majesty. No road, save the merest goat-path, led down its concave wilderness, in which loose furze-bushes and untrimmed brambles wantoned into the likeness of trees, each draped in audacious tissue of wild clematis. Through this fantastic maze the traveller wound his way, led by little other clue than by the instinct of descent. For me, as a child, it meant the labour of a long, an endless morning, to descend to the snow-white pebbles, to sport at the edge of the cold, sharp sea, and then to climb up home again, slipping in the sticky red mud, clutching at the smooth boughs of the wild ash, toiling, toiling upwards into flat land out of that hollow world of rocks.

On the first occasion, I recollect, our Cockney housemaid, enthusiastic young creature that she was, flung herself down upon her knees, and drank of the salt waters. Miss Marks, more instructed in phenomena, refrained, but I, although I was perfectly aware what the taste would be, insisted on sipping a few drops from the palm of my hand. This was a slight recurrence of what I have called my 'natural magic' practices, which had passed into the background of my mind, but had not quite disappeared. I recollect that I thought I might secure some power of walking on the sea, if I drank of it—a perfectly irrational movement of mind, like those of savages.*

My great desire was to walk out over the sea as far as I could, and then lie flat on it, face downwards, and peer into the depths. I was tormented with this ambition, and, like many grown-up people, was so fully occupied by these vain and ridiculous desires that I neglected the actual natural pleasures around me. The idea was not quite so demented as it may seem, because we were in the habit of singing, as well as reading, of those enraptured beings who spend their days in 'flinging down their golden crowns upon the jasper sea'.* Why, I argued, should I not be able to fling down my straw hat upon the tides of Oddicombe? And, without question, a majestic scene upon the Lake of Gennesaret* had also inflamed my fancy. Of all these things, of course, I was careful to speak to no one.

It was not with Miss Marks, however, but with my Father, that I became accustomed to make the laborious and exquisite journeys down to the sea and back again. His work as a naturalist eventually took him, laden with implements, to the rock-pools on the shore, and I was in attendance as an acolyte. But our earliest winter in South Devon was darkened for us both by disappointments, the cause of which lay, at the time, far out of my reach. In the spirit of my Father were then running, with furious velocity, two hostile streams of influence. I was standing, just now, thinking of these things, where the Cascine ends in the wooded point which is carved out sharply by the lion-coloured swirl of the Arno on the one side and by the pure flow of the Mugnone* on the other. The rivers meet, and run parallel, but there comes a moment when the one or the other must conquer, and it is the yellow vehemence that drowns the purer tide.

So, through my Father's brain, in that year of scientific crisis, 1857, there rushed two kinds of thought, each absorbing, each convincing, yet totally irreconcilable. There is a peculiar agony in the paradox that truth has two forms, each of them indisputable, yet each antagonistic to the other. It was this discovery, that there were two theories of physical life, each of which was true, but the truth of each incompatible with the truth of the other, which shook the spirit of my Father with perturbation. It was not, really, a paradox, it was a fallacy, if he could only have known it, but he allowed the turbid volume of superstition to drown the delicate stream of reason. He took one step in the service of truth, and then he drew back in an agony, and accepted the servitude of error.

This was the great moment in the history of thought when the theory of the mutability of species was preparing to throw a flood of light upon all departments of human speculation and action. It was becoming necessary to stand emphatically in one army or the other. Lyell* was surrounding himself with disciples, who were making strides in the direction of discovery. Darwin* had long been collecting facts with regard to the variation of animals and plants. Hooker and Wallace, Asa Gray and even Agassiz,* each in his own sphere, were coming closer and closer to a perception of that secret which was first to reveal itself clearly to the patient and humble genius of Darwin. In the year before, in 1856, Darwin, under pressure from Lyell, had begun that modest statement of the new revelation, that 'abstract of an essay', which developed so mightily into 'The Origin of Species'.* Wollaston's 'Variation of Species'* had just appeared, and had been a nine days' wonder in the wilderness.

On the other side, the reactionaries, although never dreaming of the fate which hung over them, had not been idle. In 1857 the astounding question had for the first time been propounded with contumely, 'What, then, did we come from an orang-outang?'* The famous 'Vestiges of Creation'* had been supplying a sugar-and-water panacea for those who could not escape from the trend of evidence, and who yet clung to revelation. Owen* was encouraging reaction by resisting, with all the strength of his prestige, the theory of the mutability of species.

In this period of intellectual ferment, as when a great political revolution is being planned, many possible adherents were confidentially tested with hints and encouraged to reveal their bias in a whisper. It was the notion of Lyell, himself a great mover of men, that before the doctrine of natural selection was given to a world which would be sure to lift up at it a howl of execration, a certain bodyguard of sound and experienced naturalists, expert in the description of species, should be privately made aware of its tenour. Among those who were thus initiated, or approached with a view towards possible illumination, was my Father. He was spoken to by Hooker, and later on by Darwin, after meetings of the Royal Society* in the summer of 1857.

My Father's attitude towards the theory of natural selection was critical in his career, and, oddly enough, it exercised an immense influence on my own experience as a child. Let it be admitted at once, mournful as the admission is, that every instinct in his intelligence went out at first to greet the new light. It had hardly done so, when a recollection of the opening chapter of Genesis checked it at the outset. He consulted with Carpenter,* a great investigator, but one who was fully as incapable as himself of remodelling his ideas with regard to the old, accepted hypotheses. They both determined, on various grounds, to have nothing to do with the terrible theory, but to hold steadily to the law of the fixity of species. It was exactly at this juncture that we left London, and the slight and occasional, but always extremely salutary personal intercourse with men of scientific leading which my Father had enjoyed at the British Museum and at the Royal Society came to an end. His next act was to burn his ships, down to the last beam and log out of which a raft could have been made. By a strange act of wilfulness, he closed the doors upon himself for ever.

My Father had never admired Sir Charles Lyell. I think that the famous 'Lord Chancellor manner' of the geologist intimidated him, and we undervalue the intelligence of those whose conversation puts us at a disadvantage. For Darwin and Hooker, on the other hand, he had a profound esteem, and I know not whether this had anything to do with the fact that he chose, for his impetuous experiment in reaction, the field of geology, rather than that of zoology or botany. Lyell had been threatening to publish a book on the geological history of Man, which was to be a bomb-shell flung into the camp of the catastrophists.* My Father, after long reflection, prepared a theory of his own, which, as he fondly hoped, would take the wind out of Lyell's sails, and justify geology to godly readers of 'Genesis'. It was, very briefly, that there had been no gradual modification of the surface of the earth, or slow development of organic forms, but, that when the catastrophic act of creation took place, the world presented, instantly, the structural appearance of a planet on which life had long existed.

The theory, coarsely enough, and to my Father's great indignation, was defined by a hasty press as being this—that God hid the fossils in the rocks in order to tempt geologists into infidelity. In truth, it was the logical and inevitable conclusion of accepting, literally, the doctrine of a sudden act of creation; it emphasised the fact that any breach in the circular course of nature could be conceived only on the supposition that the object created bore false witness to past processes, which had never taken place. For instance, Adam would certainly possess hair and teeth and bones in a condition which it must have taken many years to accomplish, yet he was created full-grown yesterday. He would certainly—though Sir Thomas Browne* denied it—display an *omphalos*,* yet no umbilical cord had ever attached him to a mother.

Never was a book cast upon the waters with greater anticipations of success than was this curious, this obstinate, this fanatical volume. My Father lived in a fever of suspense, waiting for the tremendous issue. This 'Omphalos' of his, he thought, was to bring all the turmoil of scientific speculation to a close, fling geology into the arms of Scripture, and make the lion eat grass with the lamb.* It was not surprising, he admitted, that there had been experienced an ever-increasing discord between the facts which geology brings to light and the direct statements of the early chapters of 'Genesis'. Nobody was to blame for that. My Father, and my Father alone, possessed the secret of the enigma; he alone held the key which could smoothly open the lock of geological mystery. He offered it, with a glowing gesture, to atheists and Christians alike. This was to be the universal panacea; this the system of intellectual therapeutics which could not but heal all the maladies of the age. But, alas! atheists and Christians alike looked at it and laughed, and threw it away.

In the course of that dismal winter, as the post began to bring in private letters, few and chilly, and public reviews, many and scornful, my Father looked in vain for the approval of the churches, and in vain for the acquiescence of the scientific societies, and in vain for the gratitude of those 'thousands of thinking persons', which he had rashly assured himself of receiving. As his reconciliation of Scripture statements and geological deductions was welcomed nowhere; as Darwin continued silent, and the youthful Huxley was scornful, and even Charles Kingsley,* from whom my Father had expected the most instant appreciation, wrote that he could not 'give up the painful and slow conclusion of five and twenty years' study of geology, and believe that God has written on the rocks one enormous and superfluous lie',—as all this happened or failed to happen, a gloom, cold and dismal, descended upon our morning tea cups. It was what the poets mean by an 'inspissated'* gloom; it thickened day by day, as hope and self-confidence evaporated in thin clouds of disappointment. My Father was not prepared for such a fate. He had been the spoiled darling of the public, the constant favourite of the press, and now, like the dark angels of old,

> so huge a rout
> Encumbered him with ruin.*

He could not recover from amazement at having offended

everybody by an enterprise which had been undertaken in the cause of universal reconciliation.

During that grim season, my Father was no lively companion, and circumstance after circumstance combined to drive him further from humanity. He missed more than ever the sympathetic ear of my Mother; there was present to support him nothing of that artful, female casuistry which insinuates into the wounded consciousness of a man the conviction that, after all, he is right and all the rest of the world is wrong. My Father used to tramp in solitude round and round the red ploughed field which was going to be his lawn, or, sheltering himself from the thin Devonian rain, pace up and down the still-naked verandah, where blossoming creepers were to be. And I think that there was added to his chagrin with all his fellow mortals a first tincture of that heresy which was to attack him later on. It was now that, I fancy, he began, in his depression, to be angry with God. How much devotion had he given, how many sacrifices had he made, only to be left storming round this red morass with no one in all the world to care for him except one pale-faced child with its cheek pressed to the window!

After one or two brilliant excursions to the sea, winter, in its dampest, muddiest, most languid form, had fallen upon us and shut us in. It was a dreary winter for the wifeless man and the motherless boy. We had come into the house, in precipitate abandonment to that supposed answer to prayer, a great deal too soon. In order to rake together the lump sum for buying it, my Father had denuded himself of almost everything, and our sticks of chairs and tables filled but two or three rooms. Half the little house, or 'villa' as we called it, was not papered, two-thirds were not furnished. The workmen were still finishing the outside when we arrived, and in that connection I recall a little incident which exhibits my Father's morbid delicacy of conscience. He was accustomed, in his brighter moments—and this was before the publication of his 'Omphalos'—occasionally to sing loud Dorsetshire songs of his early days, in a strange, broad Wessex lingo that I loved. One October afternoon he and I were sitting on the verandah, and my father was singing; just round the corner, out of sight, two carpenters were putting up the framework of a green-house. In a pause, one of them said to his fellow: 'He can zing a zong, zo well's another, though he be a minister.'* My Father, who was holding my hand loosely, clutched it, and looking up, I saw his eyes darken. He never sang a secular song again during the whole of his life.

Later in the year, and after his literary misfortune, his conscience became more troublesome than ever. I think he considered the failure of his attempt at the reconciliation of science with religion to have been intended by God as a punishment for something he had done or left undone. In those brooding tramps round and round the garden, his soul was on its knees searching the corners of his conscience for some sin of omission or commission, and one by one every pleasure, every recreation, every trifle scraped out of the dust of past experience, was magnified into a huge offence. He thought that the smallest evidence of levity, the least unbending to human instinct, might be seized by those around him as evidence of inconsistency, and might lead the weaker brethren into offence. The incident of the carpenters and the comic song is typical of a condition of mind which now possessed my Father, in which act after act became taboo, not because each was sinful in itself, but because it might lead others into sin.

I have the conviction that Miss Marks was now mightily afraid of my Father. Whenever she could, she withdrew to the room she called her 'boudoir', a small, chilly apartment, sparsely furnished, looking over what was in process of becoming the vegetable garden. Very properly, that she might have some sanctuary, Miss Marks forbade me to enter this virginal bower, which, of course, became to me an object of harrowing curiosity. Through the key-hole I could see practically nothing; one day I contrived to slip inside, and discovered that there was nothing to see but a plain bedstead and a toilet-table, void of all attraction. In this 'boudoir', on winter afternoons, a fire would be lighted, and Miss Marks would withdraw to it, not seen by us any more between high-tea and the apocalyptic exercise known as 'worship'—in less strenuous households much less austerely practised under the name of 'family prayers'. Left meanwhile to our own devices, my Father would mainly be reading, his book or paper held close up to the candle, while his lips and heavy eyebrows occasionally quivered and palpitated, with literary ardour, in a manner strangely exciting to me. Miss Marks, in a very high cap, and her large teeth shining, would occasionally appear in the doorway, desiring, with spurious geniality, to know how we were 'getting on'. But on these occasions neither of us replied to Miss Marks.

Sometimes, in the course of this winter, my Father and I had long cosy talks together over the fire. Our favourite subject was murders. I wonder whether little boys of eight, soon to go up-stairs alone at night, often discuss violent crime with a widower-papa? The practice, I cannot help thinking, is unusual; it, was, however, consecutive with us. We tried other secular subjects, but we were sure to come round at last to 'what do you suppose they really did with the body?' I was told, a thrilled listener, the adventure of Mrs Manning, who killed a gentleman on the stairs and buried him in quick-lime in the back-kitchen, and it was at this time that I learned the useful historical fact, which abides with me after half a century, that Mrs Manning was hanged in black satin, which thereupon went wholly out of fashion in England. I also heard about Burke and Hare,* whose story nearly froze me into stone with horror.

These were crimes which appear in the chronicles. But who will tell me what 'the Carpet-bag Mystery'* was, which my Father and I discussed evening after evening? I have never come across a whisper of it since, and I suspect it of having been a hoax. As I recall the details, people in a boat, passing down the Thames, saw a carpet-bag hung high in air, on one of the projections of a pier of Waterloo Bridge. Being with difficulty dragged down—or perhaps up—this bag was found to be full of human remains, dreadful butcher's business of joints and fragments. Persons were missed, were identified, were again denied—the whole is a vapour in my memory which shifts as I try to define it. But clear enough is the picture I hold of myself, in a high chair, on the left-hand side of the sitting-room fireplace, the leaping flames reflected in the glass-case of tropical insects on the opposite wall, and my Father, leaning anxiously forward, with uplifted finger, emphasising to me the pros and cons of the horrible carpet-bag evidence.

I suppose that my interest in these discussions—and Heaven knows I was animated enough—amused and distracted my Father, whose idea of a suitable theme for childhood's ear now seems to me surprising. I soon found that these subjects were not welcome to everybody, for, starting the Carpet-bag Mystery one morning with Miss Marks, in the hope of delaying my arithmetic lesson, she fairly threw her apron over her ears, and told me, from that vantage, that if I did not desist at once, she should scream.

Occasionally we took winter walks together, my Father and I,

down some lane that led to a sight of the sea, or over the rolling
downs. We tried to recapture the charm of those delightful strolls in
London, when we used to lean over the bridges and watch the ducks.
But we could not recover this pleasure. My Father was deeply
enwoven in the chain of his own thoughts, and would stalk on,
without a word, buried in angry reverie. If he spoke to me, on these
excursions, it was a pain to me to answer him. I could talk on easy
terms with him indoors, seated in my high chair, with our heads on a
level, but it was intolerably laborious to look up into the firmament
and converse with a dark face against the sky. The actual exercise of
walking, too, was very exhausting to me; the bright red mud, to the
strange colour of which I could not for a long while get accustomed,
becoming caked about my little shoes, and wearying me extremely. I
would grow petulant and cross, contradict my Father, and oppose his
whims. These walks were distressing to us both, yet he did not like to
walk alone, and he had no other friend. However, as the winter
advanced, they had to be abandoned, and the habit of our taking a
'constitutional' together was never resumed.

I look back upon myself at this time as upon a cantankerous, ill-
tempered and unobliging child. The only excuse I can offer is that I
really was not well. The change to Devonshire had not suited me; my
health gave the excellent Miss Marks some anxiety, but she was not
ready in resource. The dampness of the house was terrible; indoors
and out, the atmosphere seemed soaked in chilly vapours. Under my
bed-clothes at night I shook like a jelly, unable to sleep for cold,
though I was heaped with coverings, while my skin was all puckered
with goose-flesh. I could eat nothing solid, without suffering
immediately from violent hiccough, so that much of my time was
spent lying prone on my back upon the hearth-rug, awakening the
echoes like a cuckoo. Miss Marks, therefore, cut off all food but
milk-sop, a loathly bowl of which appeared at every meal. In consequence the hiccough lessened, but my strength declined with it. I
languished in a perpetual catarrh. I was roused to a consciousness
that I was not considered well by the fact that my Father prayed
publicly at morning and evening 'worship' that if it was the Lord's
will to take me to himself there might be no doubt whatever
about my being a sealed child of God and an inheritor of glory. I was
partly disconcerted by, partly vain of, this open advertisement of my
ailments.

Of our dealings with the 'Saints', a fresh assortment of whom met us on our arrival in Devonshire, I shall speak presently. My Father's austerity of behaviour was, I think, perpetually accentuated by his fear of doing anything to offend the consciences of these persons, whom he supposed, no doubt, to be more sensitive than they really were. He was fond of saying that 'a very little stain upon the conscience makes a wide breach in our communion with God', and he counted possible errors of conduct by hundreds and by thousands. It was in this winter that his attention was particularly drawn to the festival of Christmas, which, apparently, he had scarcely noticed in London.

On the subject of all feasts of the Church he held views of an almost grotesque peculiarity. He looked upon each of them as nugatory and worthless, but the keeping of Christmas appeared to him by far the most hateful, and nothing less than an act of idolatry. 'The very word is Popish,' he used to exclaim, 'Christ's Mass!' pursing up his lips with the gesture of one who tastes assafœtida* by accident. Then he would adduce the antiquity of the so-called feast, adapted from horrible heathen rites, and itself a soiled relic of the abominable Yule-Tide.* He would denounce the horrors of Christmas until it almost made me blush to look at a holly-berry.

On Christmas Day of this year 1857 our villa saw a very unusual sight. My Father had given strictest charge that no difference whatever was to be made in our meals on that day; the dinner was to be neither more copious than usual nor less so. He was obeyed, but the servants, secretly rebellious, made a small plum-pudding for themselves. (I discovered afterwards, with pain, that Miss Marks received a slice of it in her boudoir.) Early in the afternoon, the maids,—of whom we were now advanced to keeping two,—kindly remarked that 'the poor dear child ought to have a bit, anyhow', and wheedled me into the kitchen, where I ate a slice of plum-pudding. Shortly I began to feel that pain inside which in my frail state was inevitable, and my conscience smote me violently. At length I could bear my spiritual anguish no longer, and bursting into the study I called out: 'Oh! Papa, Papa, I have eaten of flesh offered to idols!'* It took some time, between my sobs, to explain what had happened. Then my Father sternly said: 'Where is the accursed thing?' I explained that as much as was left of it was still on the kitchen table. He took me by the hand, and ran with me into the midst of the startled servants, seized what remained of the pudding, and with the plate in one hand and me still tight in the other, ran till we reached the dust-heap, when he flung the idolatrous confectionery on to the middle of the ashes, and then raked it deep down into the mass. The suddenness, the violence, the velocity of this extraordinary act made an impression on my memory which nothing will ever efface.

The key is lost by which I might unlock the perverse malady from which my Father's conscience seemed to suffer during the whole of this melancholy winter. But I think that a dislocation of his intellectual system had a great deal to do with it. Up to this point in his career, he had, as we have seen, nourished the delusion that science and revelation could be mutually justified, that some sort of compromise was possible. With great and ever greater distinctness, his investigations had shown him that in all departments of organic nature there are visible the evidences of slow modification of forms, of the type developed by the pressure and practice of æons. This conviction had been borne in upon him until it was positively irresistible. Where was his place, then, as a sincere and accurate observer? Manifestly, it was with the pioneers of the new truth, it was with Darwin, Wallace and Hooker. But did not the second chapter of 'Genesis' say that in six days the heavens and earth were finished, and the host of them, and that on the seventh day God ended his work which he had made?

Here was a dilemma! Geology certainly *seemed* to be true, but the Bible, which was God's word, *was* true. If the Bible said that all things in Heaven and Earth were created in six days, created in six days they were,—in six literal days of twenty-four hours each. The evidences of spontaneous variation of form, acting, over an immense space of time, upon ever-modifying organic structures, *seemed* overwhelming, but they must either be brought into line with the six-day labour of creation, or they must be rejected. I have already shown how my Father worked out the ingenious 'Omphalos' theory in order to justify himself as a strictly scientific observer who was also a humble slave of revelation. But the old convention and the new rebellion would alike have none of his compromise.

To a mind so acute and at the same time so narrow as that of my Father—a mind which is all logical and positive without breadth, without suppleness and without imagination—to be subjected to a check of this kind is agony. It has not the relief of a smaller nature, which escapes from the dilemma by some foggy formula; nor the resolution of a larger nature to take to it wings and surmount the obstacle. My Father, although half suffocated by the emotion of being lifted, as it were, on the great biological wave, never dreamed of letting go his clutch of the ancient tradition, but hung there, strained and buffeted. It is extraordinary that he—an 'honest hodman of science', as Huxley once called him—should not have been content to allow others, whose horizons were wider than his could be, to pursue those purely intellectual surveys for which he had no species of aptitude. As a collector of facts and marshaller of observations, he had not a rival in that age; his very absence of imagination aided him in this work. But he was more an attorney than a philosopher, and he lacked that sublime humility which is the crown of genius. For, this obstinate persuasion that he alone knew the mind of God, that he alone could interpret the designs of the Creator, what did it result from if not from a congenital lack of that highest modesty which replies 'I do not know' even to the questions which Faith, with menacing finger, insists on having most positively answered?

CHAPTER VI

DURING the first year of our life in Devonshire, the ninth year of my age, my Father's existence, and therefore mine, was almost entirely divided between attending to the little community of 'Saints' in the village and collecting, examining and describing marine creatures from the sea-shore. In the course of these twelve months, we had scarcely any social distractions of any kind, and I never once crossed the bounds of the parish. After the worst of the winter was over, my Father recovered much of his spirits and his power of work, and the earliest sunshine soothed and refreshed us both. I was still almost always with him, but we had now some curious companions.

The village, at the southern end of which our villa stood, was not pretty. It had no rural picturesqueness of any kind. The only pleasant feature of it, the handsome and ancient parish church, with its umbrageous churchyard, was then almost entirely concealed by a congeries of mean shops, which were ultimately, before the close of my childhood, removed. The village consisted of two parallel lines of contiguous houses, all whitewashed and most of them fronted by trifling shop-windows; for half a mile this street ascended to the church, and then it descended for another half-mile, ending suddenly in fields, the hedges of which displayed, at intervals, the inevitable pollard elm-tree. The walk through the village, which we seemed to make incessantly, was very wearisome to me. I dreaded the rudeness of the children, and there was nothing in the shops to amuse me. Walking on the inch or two of broken pavement in front of the houses was disagreeable and tiresome, and the fœtor* which breathed on close days from the open doors and windows made me feel faint. But this walk was obligatory, since the 'Public Room', as our little chapel was called, lay at the further extremity of the dreary street.

We attended this place of worship immediately on our arrival, and my Father, uninvited but unresisted, immediately assumed the administration of it. It was a square, empty room, built, for I know not what purpose, over a stable. Ammoniac odours used to rise through the floor as we sat there at our long devotions. Before our coming, a little flock of persons met in the Room, a community of the indefinite sort just then becoming frequent in the West of

England, pious rustics connected with no other recognised body of Christians, and depending directly on the independent study of the Bible. They were largely women, but there was more than a sprinkling of men, poor, simple and generally sickly. In later days, under my Father's ministration, the body increased and positively flourished. It came to include retired professional men, an admiral, nay, even the brother of a peer. But in those earliest years the 'brethren' and 'sisters' were all of them ordinary peasants. They were jobbing gardeners and journeymen carpenters, masons and tailors, washerwomen and domestic servants. I wish that I could paint, in colours so vivid that my readers could perceive what their little society consisted of, this quaint collection of humble, conscientious, ignorant and gentle persons. In chronicle or fiction, I have never been fortunate enough to meet with anything which resembled them. The caricatures of enmity and worldly scorn are as crude, to my memory, as the unction of religious conventionality is featureless.

The origin of the meeting had been odd. A few years before we came, a crew of Cornish fishermen, quite unknown to the villagers, were driven by stress of weather into the haven under the cliff. They landed, and, instead of going to a public-house, they looked about for a room where they could hold a prayer-meeting. They were devout Wesleyans; they had come from the open sea, they were far from home, and they had been starved by lack of their customary religious privileges. As they stood about in the street before their meeting, they challenged the respectable girls who came out to stare at them, with the question, 'Do you love the Lord Jesus, my maid?' Receiving dubious answers, they pressed the inhabitants to come in and pray with them, which several did. Ann Burmington, who long afterwards told me about it, was one of those girls, and she repeated that the fishermen said, 'What a dreadful thing it will be, at the Last Day, when the Lord says, "Come, ye blessed", and says it not to you, and then, "Depart, ye cursed", and you maidens have to depart.' They were finely-built young men, with black beards and shining eyes, and I do not question that some flash of sex unconsciously mingled with the curious episode, although their behaviour was in all respects discreet. It was, perhaps, not wholly a coincidence that almost all those particular girls remained unmarried to the end of their lives. After two or three days, the fishermen went off to sea again. They prayed and sailed away, and the girls, who had not even asked their names, never heard of them again. But several of the young women were definitely converted, and they formed the nucleus of our little gathering.

My Father preached, standing at a desk; or celebrated the communion in front of a deal table, with a white napkin spread over it. Sometimes the audience was so small, generally so unexhilarating, that he was discouraged, but he never flagged in energy and zeal. Only those who had given evidence of intelligent acceptance of the theory of simple faith in their atonement through the Blood of Jesus were admitted to the communion, or, as it was called 'the Breaking of Bread'. It was made a very strong point that no one should 'break bread',—unless for good reason shown—until he or she had been baptized, that is to say, totally immersed, in solemn conclave, by the ministering brother. This rite used, in our earliest days, to be performed, with picturesque simplicity, in the sea on the Oddicombe beach, but to this there were, even in those quiet years, extreme objections. A jeering crowd could scarcely be avoided, and women, in particular, shrank from the ordeal. This used to be a practical difficulty, and my Father, when communicants confessed that they had not yet been baptized, would shake his head and say gravely, 'Ah! ah! you shun the Cross of Christ!' But that baptism in the sea on the open beach *was* a 'cross', he would not deny, and when we built our own little chapel, a sort of font, planked over, was arranged in the room itself.

Among these quiet, taciturn people, there were several whom I recall with affection. In this remote corner of Devonshire, on the road nowhither, they had preserved much of the air of that eighteenth century which the elders among them perfectly remembered. There was one old man, born before the French Revolution,* whose figure often recurs to me. This was James Petherbridge, the Nestor of our meeting,* extremely tall and attenuated; he came on Sundays in a full, white smock-frock, smartly embroidered down the front, and when he settled himself to listen, he would raise this smock like a skirt, and reveal a pair of immensely long thin legs, cased in tight leggings, and ending in shoes with buckles. As the sacred message fell from my Father's lips, the lantern jaws of Mr Petherbridge slowly fell apart, while his knees sloped to so immense a distance from one another that it seemed as though they never could meet again. He had been pious all his life, and he used to tell us, in some modest pride, that when he was a lad, the farmer's wife who was his mistress used to say, 'I think our Jem is going to be a Methody,* he do so hanker after godly discoursings.' Mr Petherbridge was accustomed to pray orally, at our prayer-meetings, in a funny old voice like wind in a hollow tree, and he seldom failed to express a hope that 'the Lord would support Miss Lafoy'—who was the village schoolmistress, and one of our congregation,—'in her labour of teaching the young idea how to shoot'.* I, not understanding this literary allusion, long believed the school to be addicted to some species of pistol-practice.

The key of the Room was kept by Richard Moxhay, the mason, who was of a generation younger than Mr Petherbridge, but yet 'getting on in years'. Moxhay, I cannot tell why, was always dressed in white corduroy, on which any stain of Devonshire scarlet mud was painfully conspicuous; when he was smartened up, his appearance suggested that somebody had given him a coating of that rich Western whitewash which looks like Devonshire cream. His locks were long and sparse, and as deadly black as his clothes were white. He was a modest, gentle man, with a wife even more meek and gracious than himself. They never, to my recollection, spoke unless they were spoken to, and their melancholy impassiveness used to vex my Father, who once, referring to the Moxhays, described them, sententiously but justly, as being 'laborious, but it would be an exaggeration to say happy, Christians'. Indeed, my memory pictures almost all the 'saints' of that early time as sad and humble souls, lacking vitality, yet not complaining of anything definite. A quite surprising number of them, it is true, male and female, suffered from different forms of consumption, so that the Room rang in winter evenings with a discord of hacking coughs. But it seems to me that, when I was quite young, half the inhabitants of our rural district were affected with phthisis.* No doubt, our peculiar religious community was more likely to attract the feeble members of a population, than to tempt the flush and the fair.

Miss Marks, patient pilgrim that she was, accepted this quaint society without a murmur, although I do not think it was much to her taste. But in a very short time it was sweetened to her by the formation of a devoted and romantic friendship for one of the 'sisters', who was, indeed, if my childish recollection does not fail me, a very charming person. The consequence of this enthusiastic alliance was that I was carried into the bosom of the family to which Miss Marks' new friend belonged, and of these excellent people I must give what picture I can. Almost opposite the Room, therefore at the far end of the village, across one of the rare small gardens, (in which this first winter I discovered with rapture the magenta stars of a new flower, hepatica)*—a shop-window displayed a thin row of plates and dishes, cups and saucers; above it was painted the name of Burmington. This china-shop was the property of three orphan sisters, Ann, Mary Grace, and Bess, the latter lately married to a carpenter, who was 'elder' at our meeting; the other two, resolute old maids. Ann, whom I have already mentioned, had been one of the girls converted by the Cornish fishermen. She was about ten years older than Bess, and Mary Grace came half-way between them. Ann was a very worthy woman, but masterful and passionate, suffering from an ungovernable temper, which, at calmer moments she used to refer to, not without complacency, as 'the sin which doth most easily beset me'. Bess was insignificant, and vulgarised by domestic cares. But Mary Grace was a delightful creature.

The Burmingtons lived in what was almost the only old house surviving in the village. It was an extraordinary construction of two storeys, with vast rooms, and winding passages, and surprising changes of level. The sisters were poor, but very industrious, and never in anything like want; they sold, as I have said, crockery, and they took in washing, and did a little fine needlework, and sold the produce of a great, vague garden at the back. In process of time, the elder sisters took a young woman, whose name was Drusilla Elliott, to live with them as servant and companion; she was a converted person,* worshipping with a kindred sect, the Bible Christians. I remember being much interested in hearing how Bess, before her marriage, became converted. Mary Grace, on account of her infirm health, slept alone in one room; in another, of vast size, stood a family four-poster, where Ann slept with Drusilla Elliott, and another bed in the same room took Bess. The sisters and their friend had been constantly praying that Bess might 'find peace', for she was still a stranger to salvation. One night, she suddenly called out, rather crossly, 'What are you two whispering about? Do go to sleep,' to which Ann replied: 'We are praying for you.' 'How do you know', answered Bess, 'that I don't believe?' And then she told them that, that very night, when she was sitting in the shop, she had closed with

God's offer of redemption. Late in the night as it was, Ann and Drusilla could do no less than go in and waken Mary Grace, whom, however, they found awake, praying, she too, for the conversion of Bess. They told her the good news, and all four, kneeling in the darkness, gave thanks aloud to God for his infinite mercy.

It was Mary Grace Burmington who now became the romantic friend of Miss Marks, and a sort of second benevolence to me. She must have been under thirty years of age; she was very small, and she was distressingly deformed in the spine, but she had an animated, almost a sparkling countenance. When we first arrived in the village, Mary Grace was only just recovering from a gastric fever which had taken her close to the grave. I remember hearing that the vicar, a stout and pompous man at whom we always glared defiance, went, in Mary Grace's supposed extremity, to the Burmingtons' shop-door, and shouted: 'Peace be to this house', intending to offer his ministrations, but that Ann, who was in one of her tantrums, positively hounded him from the doorstep and down the garden, in her passionate nonconformity. Mary Grace, however, recovered, and soon became, not merely Miss Marks' inseparable friend, but my Father's spiritual factotum.* He found it irksome to visit the 'saints' from house to house, and Mary Grace Burmington gladly assumed this labour. She proved a most efficient coadjutor; searched out, cherished and confirmed any of those, especially the young, who were attracted by my Father's preaching, and for several years was a great joy and comfort to us all. Even when her illness so increased that she could no longer rise from her bed, she was a centre of usefulness and cheerfulness from that retreat, where she 'received', in a kind of rustic state, under a patchwork coverlid that was like a basket of flowers.

My Father, ever reflecting on what could be done to confirm my spiritual vocation, to pin me down, as it were, beyond any possibility of escape, bethought him that it would accustom me to what he called 'pastoral work in the Lord's service', if I accompanied Mary Grace on her visits from house to house. If it is remembered that I was only eight and a half when this scheme was carried into practice, it will surprise no one to hear that it was not crowned with success. I disliked extremely this visitation of the poor. I felt shy, I had nothing to say, with difficulty could I understand their soft Devonian *patois*,* and most of all—a signal perhaps of my neurotic condition*—I dreaded and loathed the smells of their cottages. One had to run over the whole gamut of odours, some so faint that they embraced the nostril with a fairy kiss, others bluntly gross, of the 'knock-you-down' order; some sweet, with a dreadful sourness; some bitter, with a smack of rancid hair-oil. There were fine manly smells of the pigsty and the open drain, and these prided themselves on being all they seemed to be; but there were also feminine odours, masquerading as you knew not what, in which penny whiffs, vials of balm and opoponax,* seemed to have become tainted, vaguely, with the residue of the slop-pail. It was not, I think, that the villagers were particularly dirty, but those were days before the invention of sanitary science, and my poor young nose was morbidly, nay ridiculously sensitive. I often came home from 'visiting the saints' absolutely incapable of eating the milk-sop, with brown sugar strewn over it, which was my evening meal.

There was one exception to my unwillingness to join in the pastoral labours of Mary Grace. When she announced, on a fine afternoon, that we were going to Pavor and Barton, I was always agog to start. These were two hamlets in our parish, and, I should suppose, the original home of its population. Pavor was, even then, decayed almost to extinction, but Barton preserved its desultory street of ancient, detached cottages. Each, however poor, had a wild garden round it, and, where the inhabitants possessed some pride in their surroundings, the roses and the jasmines and that distinguished creeper,—which one sees nowhere at its best, but in Devonshire cottage-gardens,—the stately cotoniaster,* made the whole place a bower. Barton was in vivid contrast to our own harsh, open, squalid village, with its mean modern houses, its absence of all vegetation. The ancient thatched cottages of Barton were shut in by moist hills, and canopied by ancient trees; they were approached along a deep lane which was all a wonder and a revelation to me that spring, since, in the very words of Shelley:*

> There in the warm hedge grew lush eglantine,
>   Green cow-bind and the moonlight-coloured May,
> And cherry blossoms, and white cups, whose wine
>   Was the bright dew yet drained not by the day;
> And wild roses, and ivy serpentine
>   With its dark buds and leaves, wandering astray.

Around and beyond Barton there lay fairyland. All was mysterious, unexplored, rich with infinite possibilities. I should one day
enter it, the sword of make-believe in my hand, the cap of courage on
my head, 'when you are a big boy', said the oracle of Mary Grace.
For the present, we had to content ourselves with being an
unadventurous couple—a little woman, bent half double, and a pre-
ternaturally sedate small boy—as we walked very slowly, side by
side, conversing on terms of high familiarity, in which Biblical and
colloquial phrases were quaintly jumbled, through the sticky red
mud of the Pavor lanes with Barton as a bourne before us.

When we came home, my Father would sometimes ask me for
particulars. Where had we been, whom had we found at home, what
testimony had those visited been able to give of the Lord's goodness
to them, what had Mary Grace replied in the way of exhortation,
reproof or condolence? These questions I hated at the time, but they
were very useful to me, since they gave me the habit of concentrating
my attention on what was going on in the course of our visits, in case
I might be called upon to give a report. My Father was very kind in
the matter; he cultivated my powers of expression, he did not snub
me when I failed to be intelligent. But I overheard Miss Marks and
Mary Grace discussing the whole question under the guise of referring to 'you know whom, not a hundred miles hence', fancying that I
could not recognise their little ostrich because its head was in a bag
of metaphor. I understood perfectly, and gathered that they both of
them thought this business of my going into undrained cottages
injudicious. Accordingly, I was by degrees taken 'visiting' only when
Mary Grace was going into the country-hamlets, and then I was
usually left outside, to skip among the flowers and stalk the
butterflies.

I must not, however, underestimate the very prominent part taken
all through this spring and summer of 1858 by the collection of
specimens on the sea-shore. My Father had returned, the chagrin of
his failure in theorising now being mitigated, to what was his real
work in life, the practical study of animal forms in detail. He was not
a biologist, in the true sense of the term.* That luminous indication
which Flaubert gives of what the action of the scientific mind should
be, 'affranchissant l'esprit et pesant les mondes, sans haine, sans
peur, sans pitié, sans amour et sans Dieu',* was opposed in every
segment to the attitude of my Father, who, nevertheless, was a man

of very high scientific attainment. But, again I repeat, he was not a philosopher; he was incapable, by temperament and education, of forming broad generalisations and of escaping in a vast survey from the troublesome pettiness of detail. He saw everything through a lens, nothing in the immensity of nature. Certain senses were absent in him; I think that, with all his justice, he had no conception of the importance of liberty; with all his intelligence, the boundaries of the atmosphere in which his mind could think at all were always close about him; with all his faith in the Word of God, he had no confidence in the Divine Benevolence; and with all his passionate piety, he habitually mistook fear for love.

It was down on the shore, tramping along the pebbled terraces of the beach, clambering over the great blocks of fallen conglomerate which broke the white curve with rufous promontories* that jutted into the sea, or, finally, bending over those shallow tidal pools in the limestone rocks which were our proper hunting-ground,—it was in such circumstances as these that my Father became most easy, most happy, most human. That hard look across his brows, which it wearied me to see, the look that came from sleepless anxiety of conscience, faded away, and left the dark countenance still always stern indeed, but serene and unupbraiding. Those pools were our mirrors, in which, reflected in the dark hyaline and framed by the sleek and shining fronds of oar-weed,* there used to appear the shapes of a middle-aged man and a funny little boy, equally eager, and, I almost find the presumption to say, equally well prepared for business.

If any one goes down to those shores now, if man or boy seeks to follow in our traces, let him realise at once, before he takes the trouble to roll up his sleeves, that his zeal will end in labour lost. There is nothing, now, where in our days there was so much. Then the rocks between tide and tide were submarine gardens of a beauty that seemed often to be fabulous, and was positively delusive, since, if we delicately lifted the weed-curtains of a windless pool, though we might for a moment see its sides and floor paven with living blossoms, ivory-white, rosy-red, orange and amethyst, yet all that panoply would melt away, furled into the hollow rock, if we so much as dropped a pebble in to disturb the magic dream.

Half a century ago, in many parts of the coast of Devonshire and Cornwall, where the limestone at the water's edge is wrought into crevices and hollows, the tide-line was, like Keats' Grecian vase, 'a still unravished bride of quietness'.* These cups and basins were always full, whether the tide was high or low, and the only way in which they were affected was that twice in the twenty-four hours they were replenished by cold streams from the great sea, and then twice were left brimming to be vivified by the temperate movement of the upper air. They were living flower-beds, so exquisite in their perfection, that my Father, in spite of his scientific requirements, used not seldom to pause before he began to rifle them, ejaculating that it was indeed a pity to disturb such congregated beauty. The antiquity of these rock-pools, and the infinite succession of the soft and radiant forms, sea-anemones, sea-weeds, shells, fishes, which had inhabited them, undisturbed since the creation of the world, used to occupy my Father's fancy. We burst in, he used to say, where no one had ever thought of intruding before; and if the Garden of Eden had been situate in Devonshire, Adam and Eve, stepping lightly down to bathe in the rainbow-coloured spray, would have seen the identical sights that we now saw,—the great prawns gliding like transparent launches, *anthea* waving in the twilight its thick white waxen tentacles, and the fronds of the dulse* faintly streaming on the water, like huge red banners in some reverted atmosphere.

All this is long over, and done with. The ring of living beauty drawn about our shores was a very thin and fragile one. It had existed all those centuries solely in consequence of the indifference, the blissful ignorance of man. These rock-basins, fringed by corallines,* filled with still water almost as pellucid as the upper air itself, thronged with beautiful sensitive forms of life,—they exist no longer, they are all profaned, and emptied, and vulgarised. An army of 'collectors' has passed over them, and ravaged every corner of them. The fairy paradise has been violated, the exquisite product of centuries of natural selection has been crushed under the rough paw of well-meaning, idle-minded curiosity. That my Father, himself so reverent, so conservative, had by the popularity of his books acquired the direct responsibility for a calamity that he had never anticipated, became clear enough to himself before many years had passed, and cost him great chagrin. No one will see again on the shore of England what I saw in my early childhood, the submarine vision of dark rocks, speckled and starred with an infinite variety of colour, and streamed over by silken flags of royal crimson and purple.

In reviving these impressions, I am unable to give any exact chronological sequence to them. These particular adventures began early in 1858, they reached their greatest intensity in the summer of 1859, and they did not altogether cease, so far as my Father was concerned, until nearly twenty years later. But it was while he was composing what, as I am told by scientific men of to-day, continues to be his most valuable contribution to knowledge, his 'History of the British Sea-Anemones and Corals',* that we worked together on the shore for a definite purpose, and the last instalment of that still-classic volume was ready for press by the close of 1859.

The way in which my Father worked, in his most desperate escapades, was to wade breast-high into one of the huge pools, and examine the worm-eaten surface of the rock above and below the brim. In such remote places—spots where I could never venture, being left, a slightly timorous Andromeda,* chained to a safer level of the cliff—in these extreme basins, there used often to lurk a marvellous profusion of animal and vegetable forms. My Father would search for the roughest and most corroded points of rock, those offering the best refuge for a variety of creatures, and would then chisel off fragments as low down in the water as he could. These pieces of rock were instantly plunged in the salt water of jars which we had brought with us for the purpose. When as much had been collected as we could carry away—my Father always dragged about an immense square basket, the creak of whose handles I can still fancy that I hear—we turned to trudge up the long climb home. Then all our prizes were spread out, face upward, in shallow pans of clean sea-water.

In a few hours, when all dirt had subsided, and what living creatures we had brought seemed to have recovered their composure, my work began. My eyes were extremely keen and powerful, though they were vexatiously near-sighted. Of no use in examining objects at any distance, in investigating a minute surface my vision was trained to be invaluable. The shallow pan, with our spoils, would rest on a table near the window, and I, kneeling on a chair opposite the light, would lean over the surface till everything was within an inch or two of my eyes. Often I bent, in my zeal, so far forward that the water touched the tip of my nose and gave me a little icy shock. In this attitude—an idle spectator might have formed the impression that I was trying to wash my head and could not quite summon up resolution enough to plunge—in this odd pose I would remain for a

long time, holding my breath, and examining with extreme care
every atom of rock, every swirl of detritus. This was a task which my
Father could only perform by the help of a lens, with which, of
course, he took care to supplement my examination. But that my
survey was of use, he has himself most handsomely testified in his
'Actinologia Britannica',* where he expresses his debt to the 'keen
and well-practised eye of my little son'. Nor, if boasting is not to be
excluded, is it every eminent biologist, every proud and masterful
F.R.S., who can lay his hand on his heart and swear that, before
reaching the age of ten years, he had added, not merely a new species, but a new genus to the British *fauna*. That, however, the author
of these pages can do, who on June 29, 1859, discovered a tiny
atom,—and ran in the greatest agitation to announce the discovery
of that object 'as a form with which he was unacquainted',—which
figures since then on all lists of sea-anemones as *phellia murocincta*,
or the walled corklet. Alas! that so fair a swallow should have made
no biological summer in after-life.

   These delicious agitations by the edge of the salt sea wave must
have greatly improved my health, which however was still looked
upon as fragile. I was loaded with coats and comforters, and strolled
out between Miss Marks and Mary Grace Burmington, a muffled
ball of flannel. This alone was enough to give me a look of delicacy,
which the 'saints', in their blunt way, made no scruple of comment-
ing upon to my face. I was greatly impressed by a conversation held
over my bed one evening by the servants. Our cook, Susan, a person
of enormous size, and Kate,* the tattling, tiresome parlour-maid who
waited upon us, on the summer evening I speak of were standing—I
cannot tell why—on each side of my bed. I shut my eyes, and lay
quite still, in order to escape conversing with them, and they spoke
to one another. 'Ah, poor lamb,' Kate said trivially, '*he's* not long
for this world; going home to Jesus, he is,—in a jiffy, I should say by
the look of 'un.' But Susan answered: 'Not so. I dreamed about 'un,
and I know for sure that he is to be spared for missionary service.'
'Missionary service?' repeated Kate, impressed. 'Yes,' Susan went
on, with solemn emphasis, 'he'll bleed for his Lord in heathen parts,
that's what the future have in store for '*im*.' When they were gone, I
beat upon the coverlid with my fists, and I determined that whatever
happened, I would not, not, *not*, go out to preach the Gospel among
horrid, tropical niggers.*

CHAPTER VII

IN the history of an infancy so cloistered and uniform as mine, such a real adventure as my being publicly and successfully kidnapped cannot be overlooked. There were several 'innocents' in our village, harmless eccentrics who had more or less unquestionably crossed the barrier which divides the sane from the insane. They were not discouraged by public opinion; indeed, several of them were favoured beings, suspected by my Father of exaggerating their mental density in order to escape having to work, like dogs, who, as we all know, could speak as well as we do, were they not afraid of being made to fetch and carry. Miss Mary Flaw was not one of these imbeciles. She was what the French call a *detraquée*;* she had enjoyed a good intelligence and an active mind, but her wits had left the rails and were careering about the country. Miss Flaw was the daughter of a retired Baptist minister, and she lived, with I remember not what relations, in a little solitary house high up at Barton Cross, whither Mary Grace and I would sometimes struggle when our pastoral duties were over. In later years, when I met with those celebrated verses in which the philosopher expresses the hope

> In the downhill of life, when I find I'm declining,
>> May my lot no less fortunate be
> Than a snug elbow-chair can afford for reclining,
>> And a cot that o'erlooks the wide sea,*

my thoughts returned instinctively, and they still return, to the high abode of Miss Flaw. There was a porch at her door, both for shelter and shade, and it was covered with jasmine; but the charm of the place was a summer-house close by, containing a table, encrusted with cowry-shells,* and seats from which one saw the distant waters of the bay. At the entrance to this grot there was always set a 'snug elbow-chair', destined, I suppose, for the Rev. Mr Flaw, or else left there in pious memory of him, since I cannot recollect whether he was alive or dead.

I delighted in these visits to Mary Flaw. She always received us with effusion, tripping forward to meet us, and leading us, each by a hand held high, with a dancing movement which I thought infinitely graceful, to the cowry-shell bower, where she would regale us with Devonshire cream and with small hard biscuits that were like pebbles. The conversation of Mary Flaw was a great treat to me. I enjoyed its irregularities, its waywardness; it was like a tune that wandered into several keys. As Mary Grace Burmington put it, one never knew what dear Mary Flaw would say next, and that she did not herself know added to the charm. She had become crazed, poor thing, in consequence of a disappointment in love, but of course I did not know that, nor that she was crazed at all. I thought her brilliant and original, and I liked her very much. In the light of coming events, it would be affectation were I to pretend that she did not feel a similar partiality for me.

Miss Flaw was, from the first, devoted to my Father's ministrations, and it was part of our odd village indulgence that no one ever dreamed of preventing her from coming to the Room. On Sunday evenings the bulk of the audience was arranged on forms, with backs to them, set in the middle of the floor, with a passage round them, while other forms were placed against the walls. My Father preached from a lectern, facing the audience. If darkness came on in the course of the service, Richard Moxhay, glimmering in his cream-white corduroys, used to go slowly round, lighting groups of tallow candles by the help of a box of lucifers. Mary Flaw always assumed the place of honour, on the left extremity of the front bench, immediately opposite my Father. Miss Marks and Mary Grace, with me ensconced and almost buried between them, occupied the right of the same bench. While the lighting proceeded, Miss Flaw used to direct it from her seat, silently, by pointing out to Moxhay, who took no notice, what groups of candles he should light next. She did this just as the clown in the circus directs the grooms how to move the furniture, and Moxhay paid no more attention to her than the grooms do to the clown. Miss Flaw had another peculiarity: she silently went through a service exactly similar to ours, but much briefer. The course of our evening service was this. My Father prayed, and we all knelt down; then he gave out a hymn, and most of us stood up to sing; then he preached for about an hour, while we sat and listened; then a hymn again, then prayer and the valediction.

Mary Flaw went through this ritual, but on a smaller scale. We all knelt down together, but when we rose from our knees, Miss Flaw was already standing up, and was pretending, without a sound, to sing a hymn; in the midst of our hymn, she sat down, opened her Bible, found a text, and then leaned back, her eyes fixed in space, listening to an imaginary sermon, which our own real one soon caught up, and coincided with for about three-quarters of an hour. Then, while our sermon went peacefully on, Miss Flaw would rise, and sing in silence (if I am permitted to use such an expression) her own visionary hymn; then she would kneel down and pray, then rise, collect her belongings, and sweep, in fairy majesty, out of the chapel, my Father still rounding his periods from the pulpit. Nobody ever thought of preventing these movements, or of checking the poor creature in her innocent flightiness, until the evening of the great event.

It was all my own fault. Mary Flaw had finished her imaginary service earlier than usual. She had stood up alone with her hymn-book before her; she had flung herself on her knees alone, in the attitude of devotion; she had risen; she had seated herself for a moment to put on her gloves, and to collect her Bible, her hymn-book and her pocket-handkerchief in her reticule.* She was ready to start, and she looked around her with a pleasant air; my Father, all undisturbed, booming away meanwhile over our heads. I know not why the manœuvres of Miss Flaw especially attracted me that evening, but I leaned out across Miss Marks and I caught Miss Flaw's eye. She nodded, I nodded; and the amazing deed was done, I hardly know how. Miss Flaw, with incredible swiftness, flew along the line, plucked me by the coat-collar from between my paralysed pro-tectresses, darted with me down the chapel and out into the dark, before any one had time to say 'Jack Robinson'.*

My Father gazed from the pulpit and the stream of exhortation withered on his lips. No one in the body of the audience stirred; no one but himself had clearly seen what had happened. Vague rows of 'saints' with gaping countenances stared up at him, while he shouted, 'Will nobody stop them?' as we whisked out through the doorway. Forth into the moist night we went, and up the lampless village, where, a few minutes later, the swiftest of the congregation, with my Father at their head, found us sitting on the door-step of the butcher's shop. My captor was now quite quiet, and made no objec-tion to my quitting her,—'without a single kiss or a good-bye', as the poet says.*

Although I had scarcely felt frightened at the time, doubtless my nerves were shaken by this escapade, and it may have had something to do with the recurrence of the distressing visions from which I had suffered as a very little child. These came back, with a force and expansion due to my increased maturity. I had hardly laid my head down on the pillow, than, as it seemed to me, I was taking part in a mad gallop through space. Some force, which had tight hold of me, so that I felt myself an atom in its grasp, was hurrying me on, over an endless slender bridge, under which on either side a loud torrent rushed at a vertiginous depth below. At first our helpless flight,—for I was bound hand and foot like Mazeppa,*—proceeded in a straight line, but presently it began to curve, and we raced and roared along, in what gradually became a monstrous vortex, reverberant with noises, loud with light, while, as we proceeded, enormous concentric circles engulfed us, and wheeled above and about us. It seemed as if we,—I, that is, and the undefined force which carried me,—were pushing feverishly on towards a goal which our whole concentrated energies were bent on reaching, but which a frenzied despair in my heart told me we never could reach, yet the attainment of which alone could save us from destruction. Far away, in the pulsation of the great luminous whorls, I could just see that goal, a ruby-coloured point waxing and waning, and it bore, or to be exact it consisted of, the letters of the word CARMINE.*

This agitating vision recurred night after night, and filled me with inexpressible distress. The details of it altered very little, and I knew what I had to expect when I crept into bed. I knew that for a few minutes I should be battling with the chill of the linen sheets, and trying to keep awake, but that then, without a pause, I should slip into that terrible realm of storm and stress in which I was bound hand and foot, and sent galloping through infinity. Often have I wakened, with unutterable joy, to find my Father and Miss Marks, whom my screams had disturbed, standing one on each side of my bed. They could release me from my nightmare, which seldom assailed me twice a night, but how to preserve me from its original attack passed their understanding. My Father, in his tenderness, thought to exorcise the demon by prayer. He would appear in the bed-room, just as I was first slipping into bed, and he would kneel at my side. The light from a candle on the mantel-shelf streamed down upon his dark head of hair while his face was buried in the coverlid, from which a loud voice came up, a little muffled, begging that I might be preserved against all the evil spirits that walk in darkness and that the deep might not swallow me up.

This little ceremony gave a distraction to my thoughts, and may have been useful in that way. But it led to an unfortunate circumstance. My Father began to enjoy these orisons at my bed-side, and to prolong them. Perhaps they lasted a little too long, but I contrived to keep awake through them, sometimes by a great effort. On one unhappy night, however, I gave even worse offence than slumber would have given. My Father was praying aloud, in the attitude I have described, and I was half sitting, half lying in bed, with the clothes sloping from my chin. Suddenly a rather large insect, dark and flat, with more legs than a self-respecting insect ought to need, appeared at the bottom of the counterpane, and slowly advanced. I think it was nothing worse than a beetle. It walked successfully past my Father's sleek black ball of a head, and climbed straight up at me, nearer, nearer, till it seemed all a twinkle of horns and joints. I bore it in silent fascination till it almost tickled my chin, and then I screamed 'Papa! Papa!' My Father rose in great dudgeon, removed the insect (what were insects to him!) and then gave me a tremendous lecture.

The sense of desperation which this incident produced I shall not easily forget. Life seemed really to be very harassing when to visions within and beetles without there was joined the consciousness of having grievously offended God by an act of disrespect. It is difficult for me to justify to myself the violent jobation* which my Father gave me in consequence of my scream, except by attributing to him something of the human weakness of vanity. I cannot help thinking that he liked to hear himself speak to God in the presence of an admiring listener. He prayed with fervour and animation, in pure Johnsonian English,* and I hope I am not undutiful if I add my impression that he was not displeased with the sound of his own devotions. My cry for help had needlessly, as he thought, broken in upon this holy and seemly performance. 'You, the child of a naturalist,' he remarked in awesome tones, '*you* to pretend to feel terror at the advance of an insect?' It could but be a pretext, he declared, for avoiding the testimony of faith in prayer. 'If your heart were fixed, if it panted after the Lord, it would take more than the movements of a beetle to make you disturb oral supplication at His footstool. Beware! for God is a jealous God and He consumes them in wrath who make a noise like a dog.'

My Father took at all times a singular pleasure in repeating that 'our God is a jealous God'. He liked the word, which I suppose he used in an antiquated sense. He was accustomed to tell the 'saints' at the room,—in a very genial manner, and smiling at them as he said it,—'I am jealous over you, my beloved brothers and sisters, with a godly jealousy.' I know that this was interpreted by some of the saints,—for I heard Mary Grace say so to Miss Marks,—as meaning that my Father was resentful because some of them attended the service at the Wesleyan chapel on Thursday evenings. But my Father was utterly incapable of such littleness as this, and when he talked of 'jealousy' he meant a lofty solicitude, a careful watchfulness. He meant that their spiritual honour was a matter of anxiety to him. No doubt when he used to tell me to remember that our God is a jealous God, he meant that my sins and short-comings were not matters of indifference to the Divine Being. But I think, looking back, that it was very extraordinary for a man, so instructed and so intelligent as he, to dwell so much on the possible anger of the Lord, rather than on his pity and love. The theory of extreme Puritanism can surely offer no quainter example of its fallacy than this idea that the omnipotent Jehovah could be seriously offended, and could stoop to revenge, because a little, nervous child of nine had disturbed a prayer by being frightened at an insect.

The fact that the word 'Carmine' appeared as the goal of my visionary pursuits is not so inexplicable as it may seem. My Father was at this time producing numerous water-colour drawings of minute and even of microscopic forms of life. These he executed in the manner of miniature, with an amazing fidelity of form and with a brilliancy of colour which remains unfaded after fifty years. By far the most costly of his pigments was the intense crimson which is manufactured out of the very spirit and essence of cochineal.* I had lately become a fervent imitator of his works of art, and I was allowed to use all of his colours, except one; I was strictly forbidden to let a hair of my paint-brush touch the little broken mass of carmine which was all that he possessed. We believed, but I do not know whether this could be the fact, that carmine of this superlative quality was sold at a guinea a cake. 'Carmine', therefore, became my shibboleth of self-indulgence;* it was a symbol of all that taste and art and wealth could combine to produce. I imagined, for instance, that at Belshazzar's feast, the loftiest épergne of gold,* surrounded by flowers and jewels, carried the monarch's proudest possession, a cake of carmine. I knew of no object in the world of luxury more desirable than this, and its obsession in my waking hours is quite enough, I think, to account for 'carmine' having been the torment of my dreams.

The little incident of the beetle displays my Father's mood at this period in its worst light. His severity was not very creditable, perhaps, to his good sense, but without a word of explanation it may seem even more unreasonable than it was. My Father might have been less stern to my lapses from high conduct, and my own mind at the same time less armoured against his arrows, if our relations had been those which exist in an ordinary religious family. He would have been more indulgent, and my own affections might nevertheless have been more easily alienated, if I had been treated by him as a commonplace child, standing as yet outside the pale of conscious Christianity. But he had formed the idea, and cultivated it assiduously, that I was an *âme d'élite*,* a being to whom the mysteries of salvation had been divinely revealed and by whom they had been accepted. I was, to his partial fancy, one in whom the Holy Ghost had already performed a real and permanent work. Hence, I was inside the pale; I had attained that inner position which divided, as we used to say, the Sheep from the Goats.* Another little boy might be very well-behaved, but if he had not consciously 'laid hold on Christ', his good deeds, so far, were absolutely useless. Whereas I might be a very naughty boy, and require much chastisement from God and man, but nothing—so my Father thought—could invalidate my election,* and sooner or later, perhaps even after many stripes, I must inevitably be brought back to a state of grace.

The paradox between this unquestionable sanctification by faith and my equally unquestionable naughtiness, occupied my Father greatly at this time. He made it a frequent subject of intercession at family prayers, not caring to hide from the servants misdemeanours of mine, which he spread out with a melancholy unction before the Lord. He cultivated the belief that all my little ailments, all my aches and pains, were sent to correct my faults. He carried this persuasion very far, even putting this exhortation before, instead of after, an instant relief of my sufferings. If I burned my finger with a sulphur match, or pinched the end of my nose in the door (to mention but two sorrows that recur to my memory), my Father would solemnly ejaculate: 'O may these afflictions be much sanctified to him!' before offering any remedy for my pain. So that I almost longed, under the pressure of these pangs, to be a godless child, who had never known the privileges of saving grace, since I argued that such a child would be subjected to none of the sufferings which seemed to assail my path.

What the ideas or conduct of 'another child' might be I had, however, at this time no idea, for, strange as it may sound, I had not, until my tenth year was far advanced, made acquaintance with any such creature. The 'saints' had children, but I was not called upon to cultivate their company, and I had not the slightest wish to do so. But early in 1859 I was allowed, at last, to associate with a child of my own age. I do not recall that this permission gave me any rapture; I accepted it philosophically, but without that delighted eagerness which I might have been expected to show. My earliest companion, then, was a little boy of almost exactly my own age. His name was Benny, which no doubt was short for Benjamin. His surname I have forgotten,* but his mother—I think he had no father—was a solemn and shadowy lady of means who lived in a villa, which was older and much larger than ours, on the opposite side of the road. Going to 'play with Benny' involved a small public excursion, and this I was now allowed to make by myself—an immense source of self-respect.

Everything in my little memories seems to run askew; obviously I ought to have been extremely stirred and broadened by this earliest association with a boy of my own age! Yet I cannot truly say that it was so. Benny's mother possessed what seemed to me a vast domain, with lawns winding among broad shrubberies, and a kitchen-garden, with aged fruit-trees in it. The ripeness of this place, mossed and leafy, was gratifying to my senses, on which the rawness of our own bald garden jarred. There was an old brick wall between the two divisions, upon which it was possible for us to climb up, and from this we gained Pisgah-views* which were a prodigious pleasure. But I had not the faintest idea how to 'play'; I had never learned, had never heard of any 'games'. I think Benny must have lacked initiative almost as much as I did. We walked about, and shook the bushes, and climbed along the wall; I think that was almost all we ever did do. And, sadly enough, I cannot recover a phrase from Benny's lips, nor an action, nor a gesture although I remember quite clearly how some grown-up people of that time looked, and the very words they said.

For example, I recollect Miss Wilkes very distinctly, since I studied her with great deliberation, and with a suspicious watchfulness
that was above my years. In Miss Wilkes a type that had hitherto
been absolutely unfamiliar to us obtruded upon our experience. In
our Eveless Eden, Woman, if not exactly *hirsuta et horrida*,* had
always been 'of a certain age'. But Miss Wilkes was a comparatively
young thing, and she advanced not by any means unconscious of her
charms. All was feminine, all was impulsive, about Miss Wilkes;
every gesture seemed eloquent with girlish innocence and the playful
dawn of life. In actual years I fancy she was not so extremely youthful, since she was the responsible and trusted head-mistress of a
large boarding-school for girls, but in her heart the joy of life ran
high. Miss Wilkes had a small, round face, with melting eyes, and
when she lifted her head, her ringlets seemed to vibrate and shiver
like the bells of a pagoda. She had a charming way of clasping her
hands, and holding them against her bodice, while she said, 'O,
but—really now?' in a manner inexpressibly engaging. She was very
earnest, and she had a pleading way of calling out: 'O but aren't you
teasing me?' which would have brought a tiger fawning to her
crinoline.

After we had spent a full year without any social distractions, it
seems that our circle of acquaintances had now begun to extend, in
spite of my Father's unwillingness to visit his neighbours. He was a
fortress that required to be stormed, but there was considerable local
curiosity about him, so that by-and-by escalading* parties were
formed, some of which were partly successful. In the first place,
Charles Kingsley* had never hesitated to come, from the beginning,
ever since our arrival. He had reason to visit our neighbouring town
rather frequently, and on such occasions he always marched up and
attacked us. It was extraordinary how persistent he was, for my
Father must have been a very trying friend. I vividly recollect that a
sort of cross-examination of would-be communicants was going on
in our half-furnished drawing-room one week-day morning, when
Mr Kingsley was announced; my Father, in stentorian tones,* replied:
'Tell Mr Kingsley that I am engaged in examining Scripture with
certain of the Lord's children.' And I, a little later, kneeling at the
window, while the candidates were being dismissed with prayer,
watched the author of 'Hypatia'* nervously careering about the garden, very restless and impatient, yet preferring this ignominy to the

chance of losing my Father's company altogether. Kingsley, a daring spirit, used sometimes to drag us out trawling with him in Torbay, and although his hawk's beak and rattling voice frightened me a little, his was always a jolly presence that brought some refreshment to our seriousness.

But the other visitors who came in Kingsley's wake and without his excuse, how they disturbed us! We used to be seated, my Father at his microscope, I with my map or book, in the down-stairs room we called the study. There would be a hush around us in which you could hear a sea-anemone sigh. Then, abruptly, would come a ring at the front door; my Father would bend at me a corrugated brow, and murmur, under his breath, 'What's that?' and then, at the sound of foot-steps, would bolt into the verandah, and round the garden into the potting-shed. If it was no visitor more serious than the postman or the tax-gatherer, I used to go forth and coax the timid wanderer home. If it was a caller, above all a female caller, it was my privilege to prevaricate, remarking innocently that 'Papa is out!'

Into a paradise so carefully guarded, I know not how that serpent Miss Wilkes could penetrate, but there she was. She 'broke bread' with the Brethren at the adjacent town, from which she carried on strategical movements, which were, up to a certain point, highly successful. She professed herself deeply interested in microscopy, and desired that some of her young ladies should study it also. She came attended by an unimportant mamma, and by pupils to whom I had sometimes, very unwillingly, to show our 'natural objects'. They would invade us, and fill our quietness with chattering noise; I could bear none of them, and I was singularly drawn to Miss Marks by finding that she disliked them too.

By whatever arts she worked, Miss Wilkes certainly achieved a certain ascendency. When the knocks came at the front door, I was now instructed to see whether the visitor were not she, before my Father bolted to the potting-shed. She was an untiring listener, and my Father had a genius for instruction. Miss Wilkes was never weary of expressing what a revelation of the wonderful works of God in creation her acquaintance with us had been. She would gaze through the microscope at awful forms, and would persevere until the silver rim which marked the confines of the drop of water under inspection would ripple inwards with a flash of light and vanish, because the drop itself had evaporated. 'Well, I can only say, how marvellous are Thy doings!' was a frequent ejaculation of Miss Wilkes, and one that was very well received. She learned the Latin names of many of the species, and it seems quite pathetic to me, looking back, to realise how much trouble the poor woman took. She 'hung', as the expression is, upon my Father's every word, and one instance of this led to a certain revelation.

My Father, who had an extraordinary way of saying anything that came up into his mind, stated one day,—the fashions, I must suppose, being under discussion,—that he thought white the only becoming colour for a lady's stockings. The stockings of Miss Wilkes had up to that hour been of a deep violet, but she wore white ones in future whenever she came to our house. This delicacy would have been beyond my unaided infant observation, but I heard Miss Marks mention the matter, in terms which they supposed to be secret, to her confidante, and I verified it at the ancles of the lady. Miss Marks continued by saying, in confidence, and 'quite as between you and me, dear Mary Grace', that Miss Wilkes was a 'minx'. I had the greatest curiosity about words, and as this was a new one, I looked it up in our large English Dictionary. But there the definition of the term was this:—'Minx: the female of minnock;* a pert wanton.'* I was as much in the dark as ever.

Whether she was the female of a minnock (whatever that may be) or whether she was only a very well-meaning schoolmistress desirous of enlivening a monotonous existence, Miss Wilkes certainly took us out of ourselves a good deal. Did my Father know what danger he ran? It was the opinion of Miss Marks and of Mary Grace that he did not, and in the back-kitchen, a room which served those ladies as a private oratory in the summer-time, much prayer was offered up that his eyes might be opened ere it was too late. But I am inclined to think that they were open all the time, that, at all events, they were what the French call *entr'ouvert*,* that enough light for practical purposes came sifted in through his eyelashes. At a later time, being reminded of Miss Wilkes, he said with a certain complaisance, 'Ah, yes! she proffered much entertainment during my widowed years!' He used to go down to her boarding-school, the garden of which had been the scene of a murder, and was romantically situated on the edge of a quarried cliff; he always took me with him, and kept me at his side all through these visits, notwithstanding Miss Wilkes' solicitude that the fatigue and excitement would be too much for the dear child's strength, unless I rested a little on the parlour sofa.

About this time, the question of my education came up for discussion in the household, as indeed it well might. Miss Marks had long proved practically inadequate in this respect, her slender acquirements evaporating, I suppose, like the drops of water under the microscope, while the field of her general duties became wider. The subjects in which I took pleasure, and upon which I possessed books, I sedulously taught myself; the other subjects, which formed the vast majority, I did not learn at all. Like Aurora Leigh,*

> I brushed with extreme flounce
> The circle of the universe,

especially zoology, botany and astronomy, but with the explicit exception of geology, which my Father regarded as tending directly to the encouragement of infidelity. I copied a great quantity of maps, and read all the books of travels that I could find. But I acquired no mathematics, no languages, no history, so that I was in danger of gross illiteracy in these important departments.

My Father grudged the time, but he felt it a duty to do something to fill up these deficiencies, and we now started Latin, in a little eighteenth-century reading-book, out of which my Grandfather* had been taught. It consisted of strings of words, and of grim arrangements of conjuction and declension, presented in a manner appallingly unattractive. I used to be set down in the study, under my Father's eye, to learn a solid page of this compilation, while he wrote or painted. The window would be open in summer, and my seat was close to it. Outside, a bee was shaking the clematis-blossom, or a red-admiral butterfly was opening and shutting his wings on the hot concrete of the verandah, or a blackbird was racing across the lawn. It was almost more than human nature could bear to have to sit holding up to my face the dreary little Latin book, with its sheep-skin cover that smelt of mildewed paste.

But out of this strength there came an unexpected sudden sweetness. The exercise of hearing me repeat my strings of nouns and verbs had revived in my Father his memories of the classics. In the old solitary years, a long time ago, by the shores of Canadian rapids, on the edge of West Indian swamps, his Virgil* had been an inestimable solace to him. To extremely devout persons, there is something

objectionable in most of the great writers of antiquity. Horace,
Lucretius, Terence, Catullus, Juvenal,*—in each there is one quality
or another definitely repulsive to a reader who is determined to know
nothing but Christ and him crucified. From time immemorial, however, it has been recognised in the Christian church that this objection does not apply to Virgil. He is the most evangelical of the
classics; he is the one who can be enjoyed with least to explain away
and least to excuse. One evening my Father took down his Virgil
from an upper shelf, and his thoughts wandered away from surrounding things; he travelled in the past again. The book was a
Delphin edition of 1798,* which had followed him in all his wander-
ings; there was a great scratch on the sheep-skin cover that a thorn
had made in a forest of Alabama. And then, in the twilight, as he
shut the volume at last, oblivious of my presence, he began to murmur and to chant the adorable verses by memory.

> Tityre, tu patulae recubans sub tegmine fagi,*

he warbled; and I stopped my play, and listened as if to a nightingale,
till he reached

> tu, Tityre, lentus in umbra
> Formosam resonare doces Amaryllida silvas.*

'O Papa, what is that?' I could not prevent myself from asking. He
translated the verses, he explained their meaning, but his exposition
gave me little interest. What to me was beautiful Amaryllis? She and
her love-sick Tityrus awakened no image whatever in my mind.

But a miracle had been revealed to me, the incalculable, the amazing beauty which could exist in the sound of verses. My prosodical
instinct* was awakened, quite suddenly that dim evening, as my
Father and I sat alone in the breakfast-room after tea, serenely
accepting the hour, for once, with no idea of exhortation or profit.
Verse, 'a breeze mid blossoms playing', as Coleridge says,* descended
from the roses as a moth might have done, and the magic of it took
hold of my heart for ever. I persuaded my Father, who was a little
astonished at my insistence, to repeat the lines over and over again.
At last my brain caught them, and as I walked in Benny's garden, or
as I hung over the tidal pools at the edge of the sea, all my inner
being used to ring out with the sound of

> Formosam resonare doces Amaryllida silvas.*

CHAPTER VIII

In the previous chapter I have dwelt on some of the lighter conditions of our life at this time; I must now turn to it in a less frivolous aspect. As my tenth year advanced, the development of my character gave my Father, I will not say, anxiety, but matter for serious reflection. My intelligence was now perceived to be taking a sudden start; visitors drew my Father's attention to the fact that I was 'coming out so much'. I grew rapidly in stature, having been a little shrimp of a thing up to that time, and I no longer appeared much younger than my years. Looking back, I do not think that there was any sudden mental development, but that the change was mainly a social one. I had been reserved, timid and taciturn; I had disliked the company of strangers. But with my tenth year, I certainly unfolded, so far as to become sociable and talkative, and perhaps I struck those around me as grown 'clever', because I said the things which I had previously only thought. There was a change, no doubt, yet I believe that it was mainly physical, rather than mental. My excessive fragility—or apparent fragility, for I must have been always wiry—decreased; I slept better, and therefore grew less nervous; I ate better, and therefore put on flesh. If I preserved a delicate look—people still used to say in my presence, 'That dear child is not long for this world!'—it was in consequence of a sort of habit into which my body had grown; it was a transparency which did not speak of what was in store for me, but of what I had already passed through.

The increased activity of my intellectual system now showed itself in what I believe to be a very healthy form, direct imitation. The rage for what is called 'originality' is pushed to such a length in these days that even children are not considered promising, unless they attempt things preposterous and unparalleled. From his earliest hour, the ambitious person is told that to make a road where none has walked before, to do easily what it is impossible for others to do at all, to create new forms of thought and expression, are the only recipes for genius; and in trying to escape on all sides from every resemblance to his predecessors, he adopts at once an air of eccentricity and pretentiousness. This continues to be the accepted view of originality; but, in spite of this conventional opinion, I hold that the healthy sign of an activity of mind in early youth is not to be striving after unheard-of miracles, but to imitate closely and carefully what is being said and done in the vicinity. The child of a great sculptor will hang about the studio, and will try to hammer a head out of a waste piece of marble with a nail; it does not follow that he too will be a sculptor. The child of a politician will sit in committee with a row of empty chairs, and will harangue an imaginary senate from behind the curtains. I, the son of a man who looked through a microscope and painted what he saw there, would fain observe for myself, and paint my observations. It did not follow, alas! that I was built to be a miniature-painter or a savant, but the activity of a childish intelligence was shown by my desire to copy the results of such energy as I saw nearest at hand.

In the secular direction, this now took the form of my preparing little monographs on sea-side creatures, which were arranged, tabulated and divided as exactly as possible on the pattern of those which my Father was composing for his 'Actinologia Britannica'. I wrote these out upon sheets of paper of the same size as his printed page, and I adorned them with water-colour plates, meant to emulate his precise and exquisite illustrations. One or two of these ludicrous postiches are still preserved, and in glancing at them now I wonder, not at any skill that they possess, but at the perseverance and the patience, the evidence of close and persistent labour. I was not set to these tasks by my Father, who, in fact, did not much approve of them. He was touched, too, with the 'originality' heresy, and exhorted me not to copy him, but to go out into the garden or the shore and describe something new, in a new way. That was quite impossible; I possessed no initiative. But I can now well understand why my Father, very indulgently and good-temperedly, deprecated these exercises of mine. They took up, and, as he might well think, wasted, an enormous quantity of time; and they were, moreover, parodies, rather than imitations, of his writings, for I invented new species, with sapphire spots and crimson tentacles and amber bands, which were close enough to his real species to be disconcerting. He came from conscientiously shepherding the flocks of ocean, and I do not wonder that my ring-straked, speckled and spotted varieties put him out of countenance. If I had not been so innocent and solemn, he might have fancied I was mocking him.

These extraordinary excursions into science, falsely so called, occupied a large part of my time. There was a little spare room at the back of our house, dedicated to lumber and to empty portmanteaux. There was a table in it already, and I added a stool; this cheerless apartment now became my study. I spent so many hours here, in solitude and without making a sound, that my Father's curiosity, if not his suspicion, was occasionally roused, and he would make a sudden raid on me. I was always discovered, doubled up over the table, with my pen and ink, or else my box of colours and tumbler of turbid water by my hand, working away like a Chinese student shut up in his matriculating box.

It might have been done for a wager, if anything so sinful had ever been dreamed of in our pious household. The apparatus was slow and laboured. In order to keep my uncouth handwriting in bounds, I was obliged to rule not lines only, but borders to my pages. The subject did not lend itself to any flow of language, and I was obliged incessantly to borrow sentences, word for word, from my Father's published books. Discouraged by every one around me, daunted by the laborious effort needful to carry out the scheme, it seems odd to me now that I persisted in so strange and wearisome an employment, but it became an absorbing passion, and was indulged in to the neglect of other lessons and other pleasures.

My Father, as the spring advanced, used to come up to the Box-room, as my retreat was called, and hunt me out into the sunshine. But I soon crept back to my mania. It gave him much trouble, and Miss Marks, who thought it sheer idleness, was vociferous in objection. She would gladly have torn up all my writings and paintings, and have set me to a useful task. My Father, with his strong natural individualism, could not take this view. He was interested in this strange freak of mine, and he could not wholly condemn it. But he must have thought it a little crazy, and it is evident to me now that it led to the revolution in domestic polity by which he began to encourage my acquaintance with other young people as much as he had previously discouraged it. He saw that I could not be allowed to spend my whole time in a little stuffy room making solemn and ridiculous imitations of Papers read before the Linnæan Society.* He was grieved, moreover, at the badness of my pictures, for I had no native skill; and he tried to teach me his own system of miniature-painting as applied to natural history. I was forced, in deep depression of spirits, to turn from my grotesque monographs, and paint

under my Father's eye, and from a finished drawing of his, a
gorgeous tropic bird in flight. Aided by my habit of imitation, I did
at length produce something which might have shown promise, if it
had not been wrung from me, touch by touch, pigment by pigment,
under the orders of a task-master.

All this had its absurd side, but I seem to perceive that it had also
its value. It is, surely, a mistake to look too near at hand for the
benefits of education. What is actually taught in early childhood is
often that part of training which makes least impression on the
character, and is of the least permanent importance. My labours
failed to make me a zoologist, and the multitude of my designs and
my descriptions have left me helplessly ignorant of the anatomy of a
sea-anemone. Yet I cannot look upon the mental discipline as useless.
It taught me to concentrate my attention, to define the nature of
distinctions, to see accurately, and to name what I saw. Moreover, it
gave me the habit of going on with any piece of work I had in hand,
not flagging because the interest or picturesqueness of the theme had
declined, but pushing forth towards a definite goal, well-foreseen
and limited beforehand. For almost any intellectual employment in
later life, it seems to me that this discipline was valuable. I am,
however, not the less conscious how ludicrous was the mode in
which, in my tenth year, I obtained it.

My spiritual condition occupied my Father's thoughts very insist-
ently at this time. Closing, as he did, most of the doors of worldly
pleasure and energy upon his conscience, he had continued to pursue his scientific investigations without any sense of sin. Most fortunate it was, that the collecting of marine animals in the tidal pools,
and the description of them in pages which were addressed to the
wide scientific public, at no time occurred to him as in any way
inconsistent with his holy calling. His conscience was so delicate, and
often so morbid in its delicacy, that if that had occurred to him, he
would certainly have abandoned his investigations, and have been
left without an employment. But happily he justified his investigation by regarding it as a glorification of God's created works. In the
introduction to his 'Actinologia Britannica', written at the time
which I have now reached in this narrative, he sent forth his labours
with a phrase which I should think unparalleled in connection with a
learned and technical biological treatise. He stated concerning that
book, that he published it 'as one more tribute humbly offered to the

glory of the Triune God, who is wonderful in counsel, and excellent in working'. Scientific investigation sincerely carried out in that spirit became a kind of week-day interpretation of the current creed of Sundays.

The development of my faculties, of which I have spoken, extended to the religious sphere no less than to the secular. Here also, as I look back, I see that I was extremely imitative. I expanded in the warmth of my Father's fervour, and, on the whole, in a manner that was satisfactory to him. He observed the richer hold that I was now taking on life; he saw my faculties branching in many directions, and he became very anxious to secure my maintenance in grace. In earlier years, certain sides of my character had offered a sort of passive resistance to his ideas. I had let what I did not care to welcome pass over my mind in the curious density that children adopt in order to avoid receiving impressions—blankly, dumbly, achieving by stupidity what they cannot achieve by argument. I think that I had frequently done this; that he had been brought up against a dead wall; although on other sides of my nature I had been responsive and docile. But now, in my tenth year, the imitative faculty got the upper hand, and nothing seemed so attractive as to be what I was expected to be. If there was a doubt now, it lay in the other direction; it seemed hardly normal that so young a child should appear so receptive and so apt.

My Father believed himself justified, at this juncture, in making a tremendous effort. He wished to secure me finally, exhaustively, before the age of puberty could dawn, before my soul was fettered with the love of carnal things. He thought that if I could now be identified with the 'saints', and could stand on exactly their footing, a habit of conformity would be secured. I should meet the paganising tendencies of advancing years with security if I could be forearmed with all the weapons of a sanctified life. He wished me, in short, to be received into the community of the Brethren on the terms of an adult. There were difficulties in the way of carrying out this scheme, and they were urged upon him, more or less courageously, by the elders of the church. But he overbore them. What the difficulties were, and what were the arguments which he used to sweep those difficulties away, I must now explain, for in this lay the centre of our future relations as father and son.

In dealing with the peasants around him, among whom he was engaged in an active propaganda, my Father always insisted on the necessity of conversion. There must be a new birth and being, a fresh creation in God. This crisis he was accustomed to regard as manifesting itself in a sudden and definite upheaval. There might have been prolonged practical piety, deep and true contrition for sin, but these, although the natural and suitable prologue to conversion, were not conversion itself. People hung on at the confines of regeneration, often for a very long time; my Father dealt earnestly with them, the elders ministered to them, with explanation, exhortation and prayer. Such persons were in a gracious state, but they were not in a state of grace. If they should suddenly die, they would pass away in an unconverted condition, and all that could be said in their favour was a vague expression of hope that they would benefit from God's uncovenanted mercies.

But on some day, at some hour and minute, if life was spared to them, the way of salvation would be revealed to these persons in such an aspect that they would be enabled instantaneously to accept it. They would take it consciously, as one takes a gift from the hand that offers it. This act of taking was the process of conversion, and the person who so accepted was a child of God now, although a single minute ago he had been a child of wrath. The very root of human nature had to be changed, and, in the majority of cases, this change was sudden, patent, palpable.

I have just said, 'in the majority of cases', because my Father admitted the possibility of exceptions. The formula was, 'If any man hath not the Spirit of Christ, he is none of his.' As a rule, no one could possess the Spirit of Christ, without a conscious and full abandonment of the soul, and this, however carefully led up to, and prepared for with tears and renunciations, was not, could not, be made, except at a set moment of time. Faith, in an esoteric and almost symbolic sense, was necessary, and could not be a result of argument, but was a state of heart. In these opinions my Father departed no wise from the strict evangelical doctrine of the Protestant churches, but he held it in a mode and with a severity peculiar to himself. Now, it is plain that this state of heart, this voluntary deed of acceptance, presupposed a full and rational consciousness of the relations of things. It might be clearly achieved by a person of humble cultivation, but only by one who was fully capable of independent thought, in other words by a more or less adult person. The man or woman claiming the privileges of conversion must be able to understand and to grasp what his religious education was aiming at.

It is extraordinary what trouble it often gave my Father to know whether he was justified in admitting to the communion people of very limited powers of expression. A harmless, humble labouring man would come with a request to be allowed to 'break bread'. It was only by the use of strong leading questions that he could be induced to mention Christ as the ground of his trust at all. I recollect an elderly agricultural labourer being closeted for a long time with my Father, who came out at last, in a sort of dazed condition, and replied to our inquiries,— with a shrug of his shoulders as he said it,— 'I was obliged to put the Name and Blood and Work of Jesus into his very mouth. It is true that he assented cordially at last, but I confess I was grievously daunted by the poor intelligence!'

But there was, or there might be, another class of persons, whom early training, separation from the world, and the care of godly parents had so early familiarised with the acceptable calling of Christ that their conversion had occurred, unperceived and therefore unrecorded, at an extraordinarily early age. It would be in vain to look for a repetition of the phenomenon in those cases. The heavenly fire must not be expected to descend a second time; the lips are touched with the burning coal once, and once only. If, accordingly, these precociously selected spirits are to be excluded because no new birth is observed in them at a mature age, they must continue outside in the cold, since the phenomenon cannot be repeated. When, therefore, there is not possible any further doubt of their being in possession of salvation, longer delay is useless, and worse than useless. The fact of conversion, though not recorded nor even recollected, must be accepted on the evidence of confession of faith, and as soon as the intelligence is evidently developed, the person not merely may, but should be accepted into communion, although still immature in body, although in years still even a child. This my Father believed to be my case, and in this rare class did he fondly persuade himself to station me.

As I have said, the congregation,—although docile and timid, and little able, as units, to hold their own against their minister,— behind his back were faintly hostile to this plan. None of their own children had ever been so much as suggested for membership, and each of themselves, in ripe years, had been subjected to severe cross-examination. I think it was rather a bitter pill for some of them to swallow that a pert little boy of ten should be admitted, as a grown-up person, to all the hard-won privileges of their order. Mary Grace Burmington came back from her visits to the cottagers, reporting disaffection here and there, grumblings in the rank and file. But quite as many, especially of the women, enthusiastically supported my Father's wish, gloried aloud in the manifestations of my early piety, and professed to see in it something of miraculous promise. The expression 'another Infant Samuel'* was widely used. I became quite a subject of contention. A war of the sexes threatened to break out over me; I was a disturbing element at cottage break-fasts. I was mentioned at public prayer-meetings, not indeed by name, but, in the extraordinary allusive way customary in our devotions, as 'one amongst us of tender years' or as 'a sapling in the Lord's vineyard'.

To all this my Father put a stop in his own high-handed fashion. After the morning meeting, one Sunday in the autumn of 1859, he desired the attention of the saints to a personal matter which was, perhaps, not unfamiliar to them by rumour. That was, he explained, the question of the admission of his beloved little son to the communion of saints in the breaking of bread. He allowed—and I sat there in evidence, palely smiling at the audience, my feet scarcely touching the ground—that I was not what is styled adult; I was not, he frankly admitted, a grown-up person. But I was adult in a knowledge of the Lord; I possessed an insight into the plan of salvation which many a hoary head might envy for its fulness, its clearness, its conformity with Scripture doctrine. This was a palpable hit at more than one stumbler and fumbler after the truth, and several hoary heads were bowed.

My Father then went on to explain very fully the position which I have already attempted to define. He admitted the absence in my case of a sudden, apparent act of conversion resulting upon conviction of sin. But he stated the grounds of his belief that I had, in still earlier infancy, been converted, and he declared that if so, I ought no longer to be excluded from the privileges of communion. He said, moreover, that he was willing on this occasion to waive his own privilege as a minister, and that he would rather call on Brother Fawkes and Brother Bere, the leading elders, to examine the candidate in his stead. This was a master-stroke, for Brothers Fawkes and

Bere had been suspected of leading the disaffection, and this threw all the burden of responsibility on them. The meeting broke up in great amiability, and my Father and I went home together in the very highest of spirits. I, indeed, in my pride, touched the verge of indiscretion by saying: 'When I have been admitted to fellowship, Papa, shall I be allowed to call you "belovèd Brother"?' My Father was too well pleased with the morning's work to be critical. He laughed, and answered: 'That, my Love, though strictly correct, would hardly, I fear, be thought judicious!'

It was suggested that my tenth birthday, which followed this public announcement by a few days, would be a capital occasion for me to go through the ordeal. Accordingly, after dark (for our new lamp was lighted for the first time in honour of the event), I withdrew alone into our drawing-room, which had just, at length, been furnished, and which looked, I thought, very smart. Hither came to me, first Brother Fawkes, by himself; then Brother Bere, by himself; and then both together, so that you may say, if you are pedantically inclined, that I underwent three successive interviews. My Father, out of sight somewhere, was, of course, playing the part of stage manager.

I felt not at all shy, but so highly strung that my whole nature seemed to throb with excitement. My first examiner, on the other hand, was extremely confused. Fawkes, who was a builder in a small business of his own, was short and fat; his complexion, which wore a deeper and more uniform rose-colour than usual, I observed to be starred with dew-drops of nervous emotion, which he wiped away at intervals with a large bandana handkerchief. He was so long in coming to the point, that I was obliged to lead him to it myself, and I sat up on the sofa in the full lamplight, and testified my faith in the atonement with a fluency that surprised myself. Before I had done, Fawkes, a middle-aged man with the reputation of being a very stiff employer of labour, was weeping like a child.

Bere, the carpenter, a long, thin and dry man, with a curiously immobile eye, did not fall so easily a prey to my fascinations. He put me through my paces very sharply, for he had something of the temper of an attorney mingled with his religiousness. However, I was equal to him, and he, too, though he held his own head higher, was not less impressed than Fawkes had been, by the surroundings of the occasion. Neither of them had ever been in our drawing-room since it was furnished, and I thought that each of them noticed how smart the wall-paper was. Indeed, I believe I drew their attention to it. After the two solitary examinations were over, the elders came in again, as I have said, and they prayed for a long time. We all three knelt at the sofa, I between them. But by this time, to my great exaltation of spirits there had succeeded an equally dismal depression. It was my turn now to weep, and I dimly remember my Father coming into the room, and my being carried up to bed, in a state of collapse and fatigue, by the silent and kindly Miss Marks.

On the following Sunday morning, I was the principal subject which occupied an unusually crowded meeting. My Father, looking whiter and yet darker than usual, called upon Brother Fawkes and Brother Bere to state to the assembled saints what their experiences had been in connection with their visits to 'one' who desired to be admitted to the breaking of bread. It was tremendously exciting to me to hear myself spoken of with this impersonal publicity, and I had no fear of the result.

Events showed that I had no need of fear. Fawkes and Bere were sometimes accused of a rivalry, which indeed broke out a few years later, and gave my Father much anxiety and pain. But on this occasion their unanimity was wonderful. Each strove to exceed the other in the tributes which they paid to my piety. My answers had been so full and clear, my humility (save the mark!) had been so sweet, my acquaintance with Scripture so amazing, my testimony to all the leading principles of salvation so distinct and exhaustive, that they could only say that they had felt confounded, and yet deeply cheered and led far along their own heavenly path, by hearing such accents fall from the lips of a babe and a suckling.* I did not like being described as a suckling, but every lot has its crumpled rose-leaf, and in all other respects the report of the elders was a triumph. My Father then clenched the whole matter by rising and announcing that I had expressed an independent desire to confess the Lord by the act of public baptism, immediately after which I should be admitted to communion 'as an adult'.* Emotion ran so high at this, that a large portion of the congregation insisted on walking with us back to our garden-gate, to the stupefaction of the rest of the villagers.

My public baptism was the central event of my whole childhood. Everything, since the earliest dawn of consciousness, seemed to have been leading up to it. Everything, afterwards, seemed to be leading down and away from it. The practice of immersing communicants on the sea-beach at Oddicombe had now been completely abandoned, but we possessed as yet no tank for a baptismal purpose in our own Room. The Room in the adjoining town, however, was really quite a large chapel, and it was amply provided with the needful conveniences. It was our practice, therefore, at this time, to claim the hospitality of our neighbours. Baptisms were made an occasion for friendly relations between the two congregations, and led to pleasant social intercourse. I believe that the ministers and elders of the two meetings arranged to combine their forces at these times, and to baptize communicants from both congregations.

The minister of the town meeting was Mr S., a very handsome old gentleman, of venerable and powerful appearance. He had snowy hair and a long white beard, but from under shaggy eyebrows there blazed out great black eyes which warned the beholder that the snow was an ornament and not a sign of decrepitude. The eve of my baptism at length drew near; it was fixed for October 12, almost exactly three weeks after my tenth birthday. I was dressed in old clothes, and a suit of smarter things was packed up in a carpet-bag. After night-fall, this carpet-bag, accompanied by my Father, myself, Miss Marks and Mary Grace, was put in a four-wheeled cab, and driven, a long way in the dark, to the chapel of our friends. There we were received, in a blaze of lights, with a pressure of hands, with a murmur of voices, with ejaculations and even with tears, and were conducted, amid unspeakable emotion, to places of honour in the front row of the congregation.

The scene was one which would have been impressive, not merely to such hermits as we were, but even to worldly persons accustomed to life and to its curious and variegated experiences. To me it was dazzling beyond words, inexpressibly exciting, an initiation to every kind of publicity and glory. There were many candidates, but the rest of them,—mere grown-up men and women,—gave thanks aloud that it was their privilege to follow where I led. I was the acknowledged hero of the hour. Those were days when newspaper enterprise was scarcely in its infancy, and the event owed nothing to journalistic effort. In spite of that, the news of this remarkable ceremony, the immersion of a little boy of ten years old 'as an adult', had spread far and wide through the county in the course of three weeks.

The chapel of our hosts was, as I have said, very large; it was commonly too large for their needs, but on this night it was crowded to the ceiling, and the crowd had come—as every soft murmurer assured me—to see *me*.

There were people there who had travelled from Exeter, from Dartmouth, from Totnes, to witness so extraordinary a ceremony. There was one old woman of eighty-five who had come, my neighbours whispered to me, all the way from Moreton-Hampstead, on purpose to see me baptized. I looked at her crumpled countenance with amazement, for there was no curiosity, no interest visible in it. She sat there perfectly listless, looking at nothing, but chewing between her toothless gums what appeared to be a jujube.*

In the centre of the chapel-floor a number of planks had been taken up, and revealed a pool which might have been supposed to be a small swimming-bath. We gazed down into this dark square of mysterious waters, from the tepid surface of which faint swirls of vapour rose. The whole congregation was arranged, tier above tier, about the four straight sides of this pool; every person was able to see what happened in it without any unseemly struggling or standing on forms. Mr S. now rose,* an impressive hieratic figure,* commanding attention and imploring perfect silence. He held a small book in his hand, and he was preparing to give out the number of a hymn, when an astounding incident took place.

There was a great splash, and a tall young woman was perceived to be in the baptismal pool, her arms waving above her head, and her figure held upright in the water by the inflation of the air underneath her crinoline, which was blown out like a bladder, as in some extravagant old fashion-plate. Whether her feet touched the bottom of the font I cannot say, but I suppose they did so. An indescribable turmoil of shieks and cries followed on this extraordinary apparition. A great many people excitedly called upon other people to be calm, and an instance was given of the remark of James Smith that

> He who, in quest of quiet, 'Silence!' hoots
> Is apt to make the hubbub he imputes.*

The young woman, in a more or less fainting condition, was presently removed from the water, and taken into the sort of tent which was prepared for candidates. It was found that she herself had wished to be a candidate and had earnestly desired to be baptized, but that this had been forbidden by her parents. On the supposition that she fell in by accident, a pious coincidence was detected in this affair; the Lord had pre-ordained that she should be baptized in spite of all opposition. But my Father, in his shrewd way, doubted. He pointed out to us, next morning, that, in the first place, she had not, in any sense, been baptized, as her head had not been immersed; and that, in the second place, she must have deliberately jumped in, since, had she stumbled and fallen forward, her hands and face would have struck the water, whereas they remained quite dry. She belonged, however, to the neighbour congregation, and we had no responsibility to pursue the inquiry any further.

Decorum being again secured, Mr S., with unimpaired dignity, proposed to the congregation a hymn, which was long enough to occupy them during the preparations for the actual baptism. He then retired to the vestry, and I (for I was to be the first to testify) was led by Miss Marks and Mary Grace into the species of tent of which I have just spoken. Its pale sides seemed to shake with the jubilant singing of the saints outside, while part of my clothing was removed and I was prepared for immersion. A sudden cessation of the hymn warned us that the Minister was now ready, and we emerged into the glare of lights and faces to find Mr S. already standing in the water up to his knees. Feeling as small as one of our microscopical specimens, almost infinitesimally tiny as I descended into his Titanic arms,* I was handed down the steps to him. He was dressed in a kind of long surplice, underneath which—as I could not, even in that moment, help observing—the air gathered in long bubbles which he strove to flatten out. The end of his noble beard he had tucked away; his shirt-sleeves were turned up at the wrist.

The entire congregation was now silent, so silent that the uncertain splashing of my feet as I descended seemed to deafen me. Mr S., a little embarrassed by my short stature, succeeded at length in securing me with one palm on my chest and the other between my shoulders. He said, slowly, in a loud, sonorous voice that seemed to enter my brain and empty it, 'I baptize thee, my Brother, in the name of the Father and of the Son and of the Holy Ghost!' Having intoned this formula, he then gently flung me backwards until I was wholly under the water, and then—as he brought me up again, and tenderly steadied my feet on the steps of the font, and delivered me, dripping and spluttering, into the anxious hands of the women, who hurried me to the tent—the whole assembly broke forth in a thunder of song, a pæan of praise to God for this manifestation of his marvellous goodness and mercy. So great was the enthusiasm, that it could hardly be restrained so as to allow the other candidates, the humdrum adults who followed in my wet and glorious footsteps, to undergo a ritual about which, in their case, no one in the congregation pretended to be able to take even the most languid interest.

My Father's happiness during the next few weeks it is now pathetic to me to look back upon. His sternness melted into a universal complaisance. He laughed and smiled, he paid to my opinions the tribute of the gravest consideration, he indulged—utterly unlike his wont,—in shy and furtive caresses. I could express no wish that he did not attempt to fulfil, and the only warning which he cared to give me was one, very gently expressed, against spiritual pride.

This was certainly required, for I was puffed out with a sense of my own holiness. I was religiously confidential with my Father, condescending with Miss Marks (who I think had given up trying to make it all out), haughty with the servants, and insufferably patronising with those young companions of my own age with whom I was now beginning to associate.

I would fain close this remarkable episode on a key of solemnity, but alas! if I am to be loyal to the truth, I must record that some of the other little boys presently complained to Mary Grace that I put out my tongue at them in mockery, during the service in the Room, to remind them that I now broke bread as one of the Saints and that they did not.

CHAPTER IX

THE result of my being admitted into the communion of the 'Saints' was that, as soon as the nine days' wonder of the thing passed by, my position became, if anything, more harassing and pressed than ever. It is true that freedom was permitted to me in certain directions; I was allowed to act a little more on my own responsibility, and was not so incessantly informed what 'the Lord's will' might be in this matter and in that, because it was now conceived that, in such dilemmas, I could command private intelligence of my own. But there was no relaxation of our rigid manner of life, and I think I now began, by comparing it with the habits of others, to perceive how very strict it was.

The main difference in my lot as a communicant from that of a mere dweller in the tents of righteousness was that I was expected to respond with instant fervour to every appeal of conscience. When I did not do this, my position was almost worse than it had been before, because of the livelier nature of the responsibility which weighed upon me. My little faults of conduct, too, assumed shapes of terrible importance, since they proceeded from one so signally enlightened. My Father was never tired of reminding me that, now that I was a professing Christian, I must remember, in everything I did, that I was an example to others. He used to draw dreadful pictures of supposititious little boys who were secretly watching me from afar, and whose whole career, in time and in eternity, might be disastrously affected if I did not keep my lamp burning.

The year which followed upon my baptism did not open very happily at the Room. Considerable changes had now taken place in the community. My Father's impressive services, a certain prestige in his preaching, the mere fact that so vigorous a person was at the head of affairs, had induced a large increase in the attendance. By this time, if my memory does not fail me as to dates, we had left the dismal loft over the stables, and had built ourselves a perfectly plain, but commodious and well-arranged chapel in the centre of the village. This greatly added to the prosperity of the meeting. Everything had combined to make our services popular, and had attracted to us a new element of younger people. Numbers of youthful masons and carpenters, shop-girls and domestic servants, found the Room a

pleasant trysting-place, and were more or less superficially induced
to accept salvation as it was offered to them in my Father's searching
addresses. My Father was very shrewd in dealing with mere curiosity
or idle motive, and sharply packed off any youths who simply came
to make eyes at the girls, or any 'maids' whose only object was to
display their new bonnet-strings. But he was powerless against a
temporary sincerity, the simulacrum of a true change of heart. I have
often heard him say,—of some young fellow who had attended our
services with fervour for a little while, and then had turned cold and
left us,—'and I thought that the Holy Ghost had wrought in him!'
Such disappointments grievously depress an evangelist.

Religious bodies are liable to strange and unaccountable fluctu-
ations. At the beginning of the third year since our arrival, the
congregation seemed to be in a very prosperous state, as regards
attendance, conversions and other outward signs of activity. Yet it
was quite soon after this that my Father began to be harassed by all
sorts of troubles, and the spring of 1860 was a critical moment in the
history of the community. Although he loved to take a very high tone
about the Saints, and involved them sometimes in a cloud of laud-
atory metaphysics, the truth was that they were nothing more than
peasants of a somewhat primitive type, not well instructed in the
rules of conduct and liable to exactly the same weaknesses as invade
the rural character in every country and latitude. That they were
exhorted to behave as 'children of light', and that the majority of
them sincerely desired to do credit to their high calling, could not
prevent their being beset by the sins which had affected their fore-
bears for generations past.

The addition of so many young persons of each sex to the communion led to an entirely new class of embarrassment. Now there
arose endless difficulties about 'engagements', about youthful brethren who 'went out walking' with even more youthful sisters. Glancing
over my Father's notes, I observe the ceaseless repetition of cases in
which So-and-So is 'courting' Such-an-one, followed by the melancholy record that he has 'deserted' her. In my Father's stern language, 'desertion' would very often mean no more than that the
amatory pair had blamelessly changed their minds; but in some cases
it meant more and worse than this. It was a very great distress to him
that sometimes the young men and women who showed the most
lively interest in Scripture, and who had apparently accepted the way

of salvation with the fullest intelligence, were precisely those who seemed to struggle with least success against a temptation to unchastity. He put this down to the concentrated malignity of Satan, who directed his most poisoned darts against the fairest of the flock.

In addition to these troubles, there came recriminations, mutual charges of drunkenness in private, all sorts of petty jealousy and scandal. There were frequent definite acts of 'backsliding' on the part of members, who had in consequence to be 'put away'.* No one of these cases might be in itself extremely serious, but when many of them came together they seemed to indicate that the church was in an unhealthy condition. The particulars of many of these scandals were concealed from me, but I was an adroit little pitcher, and had cultivated the art of seeming to be interested in something else, a book or a flower, while my elders were talking confidentially. As a rule, while I would fain have acquired more details, I was fairly well-informed about the errors of the Saints, although I was often quaintly ignorant of the real nature of those errors.

Not infrequently, persons who had fallen into sin repented of it under my Father's penetrating ministrations. They were apt in their penitence to use strange symbolic expressions. I remember Mrs Pewings,* our washerwoman, who had been accused of intemperance and had been suspended from communion, reappearing with a face that shone with soap and sanctification, and saying to me, 'Oh! blessed Child, you're wonderin' to zee old Pewings here again, but He have rolled away my mountain!' For once, I was absolutely at a loss, but she meant that the Lord had removed the load of her sins, and restored her to a state of grace.

It was in consequence of these backslidings, which had become alarmingly frequent, that early in 1860 my Father determined on proclaiming a solemn fast. He delivered one Sunday what seemed to me an awe-inspiring address, calling upon us all closely to examine our consciences, and reminding us of the appalling fate of the church of Laodicea.* He said that it was not enough to have made a satisfactory confession of faith, nor even to have sealed that confession in baptism, if we did not live up to our protestations. Salvation, he told us, must indeed precede holiness of life, yet both are essential. It was a dark and rainy winter morning when he made this terrible address, which frightened the congregation extremely. When the marrow was congealed within our bones, and when the bowed heads before him, and the faintly audible sobs of the women in the background, told him that his lesson had gone home, he pronounced the keeping of a day in the following week as a fast of contrition. 'Those of you who have to pursue your daily occupations will pursue them, but sustained only by the bread of affliction and by the water of affliction.'

His influence over these gentle peasant people was certainly remarkable, for no effort was made to resist his exhortation. It was his customary plan to stay a little while, after the morning meeting was over, and in a very affable fashion to shake hands with the saints. But on this occasion he stalked forth without a word, holding my hand tight until we had swept out into the street.

How the rest of the congregation kept this fast I do not know. But it was a dreadful day for us. I was awakened in the pitchy night to go off with my Father to the Room, where a scanty gathering held a penitential prayer-meeting. We came home, as dawn was breaking, and in process of time sat down to breakfast, which consisted—at that dismal hour—of slices of dry bread and a tumbler of cold water each. During the morning, I was not allowed to paint, or write, or withdraw to my study in the box-room. We sat, in a state of depression not to be described, in the breakfast-room, reading books of a devotional character, with occasional wailing of some very doleful hymn. Our midday dinner came at last; the meal was strictly confined, as before, to dry slices of the loaf and a tumbler of water.

The afternoon would have been spent as the morning was, and so my Father spent it. But Miss Marks, seeing my white cheeks and the dark rings round my eyes, besought leave to take me out for a walk. This was permitted, with a pledge that I should be given no species of refreshment. Although I told Miss Marks, in the course of the walk, that I was feeling 'so leer' (our Devonshire phrase for hungry), she dared not break her word. Our last meal was of the former character, and the day ended by our trapsing through the wet to another prayer-meeting, whence I returned in a state bordering on collapse, and was put to bed without further nourishment. There was no great hardship in all this, I daresay, but it was certainly rigorous. My Father took pains to see that what he had said about the bread and water of affliction was carried out in the bosom of his own family, and by no one more unflinchingly than by himself.

My attitude to other people's souls when I was out of my Father's sight was now a constant anxiety to me. In our tattling world of small things he had extraordinary opportunities of learning how I behaved when I was away from home; I did not realise this, and I used to think his acquaintance with my deeds and words savoured almost of wizardry. He was accustomed to urge upon me the necessity of 'speaking for Jesus in season and out of season', and he so worked upon my feelings that I would start forth like St Teresa, wild for the Moors and martyrdom.* But any actual impact with persons marvellously cooled my zeal, and I should hardly ever have 'spoken' at all if it had not been for that unfortunate phrase 'out of season'. It really seemed that one must talk of nothing else, since if an occasion was not in season it was out of season; there was no alternative, no close time for souls.*

My Father was very generous. He used to magnify any little effort that I made, with stammering tongue, to sanctify a visit; and people, I now see, were accustomed to give me a friendly lead in this direction, so that they might please him by reporting that I had 'testified' in the Lord's service. The whole thing, however, was artificial, and was part of my Father's restless inability to let well alone. It was not in harshness or in ill-nature that he worried me so much; on the contrary, it was all part of his too-anxious love. He was in a hurry to see me become a shining light, every thing that he had himself desired to be, yet with none of his shortcomings.

It was about this time that he harrowed my whole soul into painful agitation by a phrase that he let fall, without, I believe, attaching any particular importance to it at the time. He was occupied, as he so often was, in polishing and burnishing my faith, and he was led to speak of the day when I should ascend the pulpit to preach my first sermon. 'Oh! if I may be there, out of sight, and hear the gospel message proclaimed from your lips, then I shall say, "My poor work is done. Oh! Lord Jesus, receive my spirit." '* I cannot express the dismay which this aspiration gave me, the horror with which I anticipated such a *nunc dimittis*.* I felt like a small and solitary bird, caught and hung out hopelessly and endlessly in a great glittering cage. The clearness of the personal image affected me as all the texts and prayers and predictions had failed to do. I saw myself imprisoned forever in the religious system which had caught me and would whirl my helpless spirit as in the concentric wheels of my nightly vision. I did not struggle against it, because I believed that it was inevitable, and that there was no other way of making peace with the terrible and ever-watchful 'God who is a jealous God'.* But I looked forward to my fate without zeal and without exhilaration, and the fear of the Lord altogether swallowed up and cancelled any notion of the love of Him.

I should do myself an injustice, however, if I described my attitude to faith at this time as wanting in candour. I did very earnestly desire to follow where my Father led. That passion for imitation, which I have already discussed, was strongly developed at this time, and it induced me to repeat the language of pious books in godly ejaculations which greatly edified my grown-up companions, and were, so far as I can judge, perfectly sincere. I wished extremely to be good and holy, and I had no doubt in my mind of the absolute infallibility of my Father as a guide in heavenly things. But I am perfectly sure that there never was a moment in which my heart truly responded, with native ardour, to the words which flowed so readily, in such a stream of unction, from my anointed lips. I cannot recall anything but an intellectual surrender; there was never joy in the act of resignation, never the mystic's rapture at feeling his phantom self, his own threadbare soul, suffused, thrilled through, robed again in glory by a fire which burns up everything personal and individual about him.

Through thick and thin I clung to a hard nut of individuality, deep down in my childish nature. To the pressure from without, I resigned everything else, my thoughts, my words, my anticipations, my assurances, but there was something which I never resigned, my innate and persistent self. Meek as I seemed, and gently respondent, I was always conscious of that innermost quality which I had learned to recognise in my earlier days in Islington, that existence of two in the depths who could speak to one another in inviolable secrecy.

'This a natural man may discourse of, and that very knowingly, and give a kind of natural credit to it, as to a history that may be true; but firmly to believe that there is divine truth in all these things, and to have a persuasion of it stronger than of the very thing we see with our eyes; such an assent as this is the peculiar work of the Spirit of God, and is certainly saving faith.' This passage is not to be found in the writings of any extravagant Plymouth Brother, but in one of the most solid classics of the Church, in Archbishop Leighton's 'Commentary on the First Epistle of Peter'.* I quote it because it defines, more exactly than words of my own could hope to do, the difference which already existed, and in secrecy began forthwith to be more and more acutely accentuated, between my Father and myself. He did indeed possess this saving faith, which could move mountains of evidence,* and suffer no diminution under the action of failure or disappointment. I, on the other hand—as I began to feel dimly then, and see luminously now—had only acquired the habit of giving what the Archbishop means by 'a kind of natural credit' to the doctrine so persistently impressed upon my conscience. From its very nature this could not but be molten in the dews and exhaled in the sunshine of life and thought and experience.

My Father, by an indulgent act for the caprice of which I cannot wholly account, presently let in a flood of imaginative light which was certainly hostile to my heavenly calling. My instinctive interest in geography has already been mentioned. This was the one branch of knowledge in which I needed no instruction, geographical infor- mation seeming to soak into the cells of my brain without an effort. At the age of eleven, I knew a great deal more of maps, and of the mutual relation of localities all over the globe, than most grown-up people do. It was almost a mechanical acquirement. I was now greatly taken with the geography of the West Indies, of every part of which I had made MS maps. There was something powerfully attractive to my fancy in the great chain of the Antilles,* lying on the sea like an open bracelet, with its big jewels and little jewels strung on an invisible thread. I liked to shut my eyes and see it all, in a mental panorama, stretched from Cape Sant' Antonio to the Serpent's Mouth.* Several of these lovely islands, these emeralds and amethysts set on the Caribbean Sea, my Father had known well in his youth, and I was importunate in questioning him about them. One day, as I multiplied inquiries, he rose in his impetuous way, and climbing to the top of a bookcase, brought down a thick volume and presented it to me. 'You'll find all about the Antilles there,' he said, and left me with 'Tom Cringle's Log'* in my possession.

The embargo laid upon every species of fiction by my Mother's powerful scruple had never been raised, although she had been dead four years. As I have said in an earlier chapter, this was a point on which I believe that my Father had never entirely agreed with her. He had, however, yielded to her prejudice, and no work of romance, no fictitious story, had ever come in my way. It is remarkable that among our books, which amounted to many hundreds, I had never discovered a single work of fiction until my Father himself revealed the existence of Michael Scott's wild masterpiece. So little did I understand what was allowable in the way of literary invention that I began the story without a doubt that it was true, and I think it was my Father himself who, in answer to an inquiry, explained to me that it was 'all made up'. He advised me to read the descriptions of the sea, and of the mountains of Jamaica, and 'skip' the pages which gave imaginary adventures and conversations. But I did not take his counsel; these latter were the flower of the book to me. I had never read, never dreamed of anything like them, and they filled my whole horizon with glory and with joy.

I suppose that when my Father was a younger man, and less pietistic, he had read 'Tom Cringle's Log' with pleasure, because it recalled familiar scenes to him. Much was explained by the fact that the frontispiece of this edition was a delicate line-engraving of Blewfields, the great lonely house in a garden of Jamaican all-spice* where for eighteen months he had worked as a naturalist. He could not look at this print without recalling exquisite memories and airs that blew from a terrestrial paradise. But Michael Scott's noisy amorous novel of adventure was an extraordinary book to put in the hands of a child who had never been allowed to glance at the mildest and most febrifugal* story-book.

It was like giving a glass of brandy neat to some one who had never been weaned from a milk diet. I have not read 'Tom Cringle's Log' from that day to this, and I think that I should be unwilling now to break the charm of memory, which may be largely illusion. But I remember a great deal of the plot and not a little of the language, and, while I am sure it is enchantingly spirited, I am quite as sure that the persons it describes were far from being unspotted by the world. The scenes at night in the streets of Spanish Town* surpassed not merely my experience, but, thank goodness, my imagination. The nautical personages used, in their conversations, what is called 'a class of language', and there ran, if I am not mistaken, a glow and gust of life through the romance from beginning to end which was nothing if it was not resolutely pagan.*

There were certain scenes and images in 'Tom Cringle's Log' which made not merely a lasting impression upon my mind, but tinged my outlook upon life. The long adventures, fightings and escapes, sudden storms without, and mutinies within, drawn forth as they were, surely with great skill, upon the fiery blue of the boundless tropical ocean, produced on my inner mind a sort of glimmering hope, very vaguely felt at first, slowly developing, long stationary and faint, but always tending towards a belief that I should escape at last from the narrowness of the life we led at home, from this bondage to the Law and the Prophets.

I must not define too clearly, nor endeavour too formally to insist on the blind movements of a childish mind. But of this I am quite sure, that the reading and re-reading of 'Tom Cringle's Log' did more than anything else, in this critical eleventh year of my life, to give fortitude to my individuality, which was in great danger—as I now see—of succumbing to the pressure my Father brought to bear upon it from all sides. My soul was shut up, like Fatima,* in a tower to which no external influences could come, and it might really have been starved to death, or have lost the power of recovery and rebound, if my captor, by some freak not yet perfectly accounted for, had not gratuitously opened a little window in it and added a powerful telescope. The daring chapters of Michael Scott's picaresque romance of the tropics were that telescope and that window.

In the spring of this year, I began to walk about the village and even proceed for considerable distances into the country by myself, and after reading 'Tom Cringle's Log' those expeditions were accompanied by a constant hope of meeting with some adventures. I did not court events, however, except in fancy, for I was very shy of real people, and would break off some gallant dream of prowess on the high seas to bolt into a field and hide behind the hedge, while a couple of labouring men went by. Sometimes, however, the wave of a great purpose would bear me on, as when once, but certainly at an earlier date than I have now reached, hearing the dangers of a persistent drought much dwelt upon, I carried my small red wateringpot, full of water, up to the top of the village, and then all the way down Petit-tor Lane,* and discharged its contents in a cornfield, hoping by this act to improve the prospects of the harvest. A more eventful excursion must be described, because of the moral impression it left indelibly upon me.

I have described the sequestered and beautiful hamlet of Barton, to which I was so often taken visiting by Mary Grace Burmington. At Barton there lived a couple who were objects of peculiar interest to me, because of the rather odd fact that having come, out of pure curiosity, to see me baptized, they had been then and there deeply convinced of their spiritual danger. These were John Brooks, an Irish quarryman, and his wife, Ann Brooks.* These people had not merely been hitherto unconverted, but they had openly treated the Brethren with anger and contempt. They came, indeed, to my baptism to mock, but they went away impressed.

Next morning, when Mrs Brooks was at the wash-tub, as she told us, Hell opened at her feet, and the Devil came out holding a long scroll on which the list of her sins was written. She was so much excited, that the emotion brought about a miscarriage and she was seriously ill. Meanwhile, her husband, who had been equally moved at the baptism, was also converted, and as soon as she was well enough, they were baptized together, and then 'broke bread' with us. The case of the Brookses was much talked about, and was attributed, in a distant sense, to me; that is to say, if I had not been an object of public curiosity, the Brookses might have remained in the bond of iniquity. I, therefore, took a very particular interest in them, and as I presently heard that they were extremely poor, I was filled with a fervent longing to minister to their necessities.

Somebody had lately given me a present of money, and I begged little sums here and there until I reached the very considerable figure of seven shillings and sixpence. With these coins safe in a little linen bag, I started one Sunday afternoon, without saying anything to any one, and I arrived at the Brookses' cottage in Barton. John Brooks was a heavy dirty man, with a pock-marked face and two left legs; his broad and red face carried small side-whiskers in the manner of that day, but was otherwise shaved. When I reached the cottage, husband and wife were at home, doing nothing at all in the approved Sunday style. I was received by them with some surprise, but I quickly explained my mission, and produced my linen bag. To my disgust, all John Brooks said was, 'I know'd the Lord would provide', and after emptying my little bag into the palm of an enormous hand, he swept the contents into his trousers pocket, and slapped his leg. He said not one single word of thanks or appreciation, and I was absolutely cut to the heart.

I think that in the course of a long life I have never experienced a bitterer disappointment. The woman, who was quicker, and more sensitive, doubtless saw my embarrassment, but the form of comfort which she chose was even more wounding to my pride. 'Never mind, little master,' she said, 'you shall come and see me feed the pigs.' But there is a limit to endurance, and with a sense of having been cruelly torn by the tooth of ingratitude, I fled from the threshold of the Brookses, never to return.

At tea that afternoon, I was very much downcast, and under cross-examination from Miss Marks, all my little story came out. My Father, who had been floating away in a meditation, as he very often did, caught a word that interested him and descended to conscious-ness. I had to tell my tale over again, this time very sadly, and with a fear that I should be reprimanded. But on the contrary, both my Father and Miss Marks were attentive and most sympathetic, and I was much comforted. 'We must remember they are the Lord's chil-dren,' said my Father. 'Even the Lord can't make a silk purse out of a sow's ear,' said Miss Marks, who was considerably ruffled. 'Alas! alas!' replied my Father, waving his hand with a deprecating gesture. 'The dear child!' said Miss Marks, bristling with indignation, and patting my hand across the tea-table. 'The Lord will reward your zealous loving care of his poor, even if they have neither the grace nor the knowledge to thank you,' said my Father, and rested his brown eyes meltingly upon me. 'Brutes!' said Miss Marks, thinking of John and Mary Brooks.* 'Oh no! no!' replied my Father, 'but hewers of wood and drawers of water! We must bear with the limited intelligence.' All this was an emollient to my wounds, and I became consoled. But the springs of benevolence were dried up within me, and to this day I have never entirely recovered from the shock of John Brooks's coarse leer and his 'I know'd the Lord would provide'. The infant plant of philanthropy was burned in my bosom as if by quick-lime.

In the course of the summer, a young schoolmaster called on my Father to announce to him that he had just opened a day-school for the sons of gentlemen in our vicinity, and he begged for the favour of a visit. My Father returned his call; he lived in one of the small white villas, buried in laurels, which gave a discreet animation to our neighbourhood. Mr M.* was frank and modest, deferential to my Father's opinions and yet capable of defending his own. His school and he produced an excellent impression, and in August I began to be one of his pupils. The school was very informal; it was held in the two principal dwelling-rooms on the ground-floor of the villa, and I do not remember that Mr M. had any help from an usher.

There were perhaps twenty boys in the school at most, and often fewer. I made the excursion between home and school four times a day; if I walked fast, the transit might take five minutes, and, as there were several objects of interest in the way, it might be spread over an hour. In fine weather the going to and from school was very delightful, and small as the scope of it was, it could be varied almost indefinitely. I would sometimes meet with a schoolfellow proceeding in the same direction, and my Father, observing us over the wall one morning, was amused to notice that I always progressed by dancing along the curbstone sideways, my face turned inwards and my arms beating against my legs, conversing loudly all the time. This was a case of pure heredity, for so he used to go to his school, forty years before, along the streets of Poole.*

One day when fortunately I was alone, I was accosted by an old gentleman, dressed as a dissenting minister. He was pleased with my replies, and he presently made it a habit to be taking his constitutional when I was likely to be on the high road. We became great friends, and he took me at last to his house, a very modest place, where to my great amazement, there hung in the dining-room, two large portraits, one of a man, the other of a woman, in extravagant fancy-dress. My old friend told me that the former was a picture of himself as he had appeared, 'long ago, in my unconverted days, on the stage'.

I was so ignorant as not to have the slightest conception of what was meant by the stage, and he explained to me that he had been an actor and a poet, before the Lord had opened his eyes to better things. I knew nothing about actors, but poets were already the objects of my veneration. My friend was the first poet I had ever seen. He was no less a person than James Sheridan Knowles,* the famous author of *Virginius* and *The Hunchback*, who had become a Baptist minister in his old age. When, at home, I mentioned this acquaintance, it awakened no interest. I believe that my Father had never heard, or never noticed, the name of one who had been by far the most eminent English playwright of that age.

It was from Sheridan Knowles' lips that I first heard fall the name of Shakespeare. He was surprised, I fancy, to find me so curiously advanced in some branches of knowledge, and so utterly ignorant of others. He could hardly credit that the names of Hamlet and Falstaff and Prospero* meant nothing to a little boy who knew so much theology and geography as I did. Mr Knowles suggested that I should ask my schoolmaster to read some of the plays of Shakespeare with the boys, and he proposed *The Merchant of Venice* as particularly well-suited for this purpose. I repeated what my aged friend (Mr Sheridan Knowles must have been nearly eighty at that time) had said, and Mr M. accepted the idea with promptitude. (All my memories of this my earliest schoolmaster present him to me as intelligent, amiable and quick, although I think not very soundly prepared for his profession.)

Accordingly, it was announced that the reading of Shakespeare would be one of our lessons, and on the following afternoon we began *The Merchant of Venice*. There was one large volume, and it was handed about the class; I was permitted to read the part of Bassanio,* and I set forth, with ecstatic pipe, how

> In Belmont is a lady richly left,
> And she is fair, and fairer than that word!*

Mr M. must have had some fondness for the stage himself; his pleasure in the Shakespeare scenes was obvious, and nothing else that he taught me made so much impression on me as what he said about a proper emphasis in reading aloud. I was in the seventh heaven of delight, but alas! we had only reached the second act of the play, when the readings mysteriously stopped. I never knew the cause, but I suspect that it was at my Father's desire. He prided himself on never having read a page of Shakespeare, and on never having entered a theatre but once. I think I must have spoken at home about the readings, and that he must have given the schoolmaster a hint to return to the ordinary school curriculum.

The fact that I was 'a believer', as it was our custom to call one who had been admitted to the arcana of our religion, and that therefore, in all commerce with 'unbelievers', it was my duty to be 'testifying for my Lord, in season and out of season',—this prevented my forming any intimate friendships at my first school. I shrank from the toilsome and embarrassing act of button-holing a school-fellow as he rushed out of class, and of pressing upon him the probably unintelligible question 'Have you found Jesus?' It was simpler to avoid him, to slip like a lizard through the laurels and emerge into solitude.

The boys had a way of plunging out into the road in front of the school-villa when afternoon school was over; it was a pleasant rural road lined with high hedges and shadowed by elm-trees. Here, especially towards the summer twilight, they used to linger and play vague games, swooping and whirling in the declining sunshine, and I used to join these bat-like sports. But my company, though not avoided, was not greatly sought for. I think that something of my curious history was known, and that I was, not unkindly, but instinctively, avoided, as an animal of a different species, not allied to the herd. The conventionality of little boys is constant; the colour of their traditions is uniform. At the same time, although I made no friends, I found no enemies. In class, except in my extraordinary aptitude for geography, which was looked upon as incomprehensible and almost uncanny, I was rather behind than in front of the others. I, therefore, awakened no jealousies, and, intent on my own dreams, I think my little shadowy presence escaped the notice of most of my schoolfellows.

By the side of the road I have mentioned, between the school and my home, there was a large horse-pond. The hedge folded round three sides of it, while ancient pollard elms bent over it, and chequered with their foliage in it the reflection of the sky. The roadside edge of this pond was my favourite station; it consisted of a hard clay which could be moulded into fairly tenacious forms. Here I created a maritime empire—islands, a sea-board with harbours, lighthouses, fortifications. My geographical imitativeness had its full swing. Sometimes, while I was creating, a cart would be driven roughly into the pond, and a horse would drink deep of my ocean, his hooves trampling my archipelagoes and shattering my ports with what was worse than a typhoon. But I immediately set to work, as soon as the cart was gone and the mud had settled, to tidy up my coast-line again and to scoop out anew my harbours.

My pleasure in this sport was endless, and what I was able to see, in my mind's eye, was not the edge of a morass of mud, but a splendid line of coast, and gulfs of the type of Tor Bay.* I do not recollect a sharper double humiliation than when old Sam Lamble, the blacksmith, who was one of the 'saints', being asked by my Father whether he had met me, replied 'Yes, I zeed 'un up-long, making mud pies in the ro-ad!' What a position for one who had been received into communion 'as an adult'! What a blot on the scutcheon of a would-be Columbus! 'Mud-pies', indeed!

Yet I had an appreciator. One afternoon, as I was busy on my geographical operations, a good-looking middle-aged lady, with a soft pink cheek and a sparkling hazel eye, paused and asked me if my name was not what it was. I had seen her before; a stranger to our parts, with a voice without a trace in it of the Devonshire drawl. I knew, dimly, that she came sometimes to the meeting, that she was lodging at Upton with some friends of ours who accepted paying guests in an old house that was simply a basket of roses.* She was Miss Brightwen,* and I now conversed with her for the first time.

Her interest in my harbours and islands was marked; she did not smile; she asked questions about my peninsulas which were intelligent and pertinent. I was even persuaded at last to leave my creations and to walk with her towards the village. I was pleased with her voice, her refinement, her dress, which was more delicate, and her manners, which were more easy, than what I was accustomed to. We had some very pleasant conversation, and when we parted I had the satisfaction of feeling that our intercourse had been both agreeable to me and instructive to her. I told her that I should be glad to tell her more on a future occasion; she thanked me very gravely, and then she laughed a little. I confess I did not see that there was anything to laugh at. We parted on warm terms of mutual esteem, but I little thought that this sympathetic Quakerish lady was to become my stepmother.

CHAPTER X

I SLEPT in a little bed in a corner of the room, and my Father in the ancestral four-poster nearer to the door. Very early one bright September morning at the close of my eleventh year, my Father called me over to him. I climbed up, and was snugly wrapped in the coverlid; and then we held a momentous conversation. It began abruptly by his asking me whether I should like to have a new mamma. I was never a sentimentalist, and I therefore answered, cannily, that that would depend on who she was. He parried this, and announced that, any way, a new mamma was coming; I was sure to like her. Still in a non-committal mood, I asked: 'Will she go with me to the back of the lime-kiln?' This question caused my Father a great bewilderment. I had to explain that the ambition of my life was to go up behind the lime-kiln on the top of the hill that hung over Barton, a spot which was forbidden ground, being locally held one of extreme danger. 'Oh! I daresay she will,' my Father then said, 'but you must guess who she is.' I guessed one or two of the less comely of the female 'saints', and, this embarrassing my Father,—since the second I mentioned was a married woman who kept a sweet-shop in the village,—he cut my inquiries short by saying, 'It is Miss Brightwen.'

So far so good, and I was well pleased. But unfortunately I remembered that it was my duty to testify 'in season and out of season'. I therefore asked, with much earnestness, 'But, Papa, is she one of the Lord's children?' He replied, with gravity, that she was. 'Has she taken up her cross in baptism?' I went on, for this was my own strong point as a believer. My Father looked a little shame-faced, and replied: 'Well, she has not as yet seen the necessity of that, but we must pray that the Lord may make her way clear before her. You see, she has been brought up, hitherto, in the so-called Church of England.'

Our positions were now curiously changed. It seemed as if it were I who was the jealous monitor, and my Father the deprecating penitent. I sat up in the coverlid, and I shook a finger at him. 'Papa,' I said, 'don't tell me that she's a pedobaptist?'* I had lately acquired that valuable word, and I seized this remarkable opportunity of using it. It affected my Father painfully, but he repeated his assurance that if we united our prayers, and set the Scripture plan plainly before

Miss Brightwen, there could be no doubt that she would see her way to accepting the doctrine of adult baptism. And he said we must judge not, lest we ourselves be judged. I had just enough tact to let that pass, but I was quite aware that our whole system was one of judging, and that we had no intention whatever of being judged ourselves. Yet even at the age of eleven one sees that on certain occasions to press home the truth is not convenient.

Just before Christmas, on a piercing night of frost, my Father brought to us his bride. The smartening up of the house, the new furniture, the removal of my own possessions to a private bed-room, the wedding-gifts of the 'saints', all these things paled in interest before the fact that Miss Marks had made a 'scene', in the course of the afternoon. I was dancing about the drawing-room, and was saying: 'Oh! I am so glad my new Mamma is coming', when Miss Marks called out, in an unnatural voice, 'Oh! you cruel child.' I stopped in amazement and stared at her, whereupon she threw prudence to the winds, and moaned: 'I once thought I should be your dear mamma.' I was simply stupefied, and I expressed my horror in terms that were clear and strong. Thereupon Miss Marks had a wild fit of hysterics, while I looked on, wholly unsympathetic and still deeply affronted. She was right; I was cruel, alas! but then, what a silly woman she had been! The consequence was that she withdrew in a moist and quivering condition to her boudoir, where she had locked herself in when I, all smiles and caresses, was welcoming the bride and bridegroom on the doorstep as politely as if I had been a valued old family retainer.

My stepmother immediately became a great ally of mine. She was never a tower of strength to me, but at least she was always a lodge in my garden of cucumbers.* She was a very well-meaning pious lady, but she was not a fanatic, and her mind did not naturally revel in spiritual aspirations. Almost her only social fault was that she was sometimes a little fretful; this was the way in which her bruised individuality asserted itself. But she was affectionate, serene, and above all refined. Her refinement was extraordinarily pleasant to my nerves, on which much else in our surroundings jarred.

How life may have jarred, poor insulated lady, on her during her first experience of our life at the Room, I know not, but I think she was a philosopher. She had, with surprising rashness, and in opposition to the wishes of every member of her own family, taken her cake, and now she recognised that she must eat it, to the last crumb.

Over her wishes and prejudices my Father exercised a constant, cheerful and quiet pressure. He was never unkind or abrupt, but he went on adding avoirdupois* until her will gave way under the sheer weight. Even to public immersion, which, as was natural in a shy and sensitive lady of advancing years, she regarded with a horror which was long insurmountable,—even to baptism she yielded, and my Father had the joy to announce to the Saints one Sunday morning at the breaking of bread that 'my beloved wife has been able at length to see the Lord's Will in the matter of baptism, and will testify to the faith which is in her on Thursday evening next'. No wonder my stepmother was sometimes fretful.

On the physical side, I owe her an endless debt of gratitude. Her relations, who objected strongly to her marriage, had told her, among other pleasant prophecies, that 'the first thing you will have to do will be to bury that poor child'. Under the old-world sway of Miss Marks, I had slept beneath a load of blankets, had never gone out save weighted with great coat and comforter, and had been protected from fresh air as if from a pestilence. With real courage my stepmother reversed all this. My bed-room window stood wide open all night long, wraps were done away with, or exchanged for flannel garments next the skin, and I was urged to be out and about as much as possible.

All the quidnuncs* among the 'saints' shook their heads; Mary Grace Burmington, a little embittered by the downfall of her Marks, made a solemn remonstrance to my Father, who, however, allowed my stepmother to carry out her excellent plan. My health responded rapidly to this change of *régime*,* but increase of health did not bring increase of spirituality. My Father, fully occupied with moulding the will and inflaming the piety of my stepmother, left me now, to a degree not precedented, in undisturbed possession of my own devices. I did not lose my faith, but many other things took a prominent place in my mind.

It will, I suppose, be admitted that there is no greater proof of complete religious sincerity than fervour in private prayer. If an individual, alone by the side of his bed, prolongs his intercessions, lingers wrestling with his divine Companion, and will not leave off until he has what he believes to be evidence of a reply to his entreaties—then, no matter what the character of his public protest-ations, or what the frailty of his actions, it is absolutely certain that he believes in what he professes.

My Father prayed in private in what I may almost call a spirit of violence. He entreated for spiritual guidance with nothing less than importunity. It might be said that he stormed the citadels of God's grace, refusing to be baffled, urging his intercessions without mercy upon a Deity who sometimes struck me as inattentive to his prayers or wearied by them. My Father's acts of supplication, as I used to witness them at night, when I was supposed to be asleep, were accompanied by stretchings out of the hands, by crackings of the joints of the fingers, by deep breathings, by murmurous sounds which seemed just breaking out of silence, like Virgil's bees out of the hive, *magnis clamoribus.** My Father fortified his religious life by prayer as an athlete does his physical life by lung-gymnastics and vigorous rubbings.

It was a trouble to my conscience that I could not emulate this fervour. The poverty of my prayers had now long been a source of distress to me, but I could not discover how to enrich them. My Father used to warn us very solemnly against 'lip-service', by which he meant singing hymns of experience and joining in ministrations in which our hearts took no vital or personal part. This was an outward act, the tendency of which I could well appreciate, but there was a 'lip-service' even more deadly than that, against which it never occurred to him to warn me. It assailed me when I had come alone by my bedside, and had blown out the candle, and had sunken on my knees in my night-gown. Then it was that my deadness made itself felt, in the mechanical address I put up, the emptiness of my language, the absence of all real unction.

I never could contrive to ask God for spiritual gifts in the same voice and spirit in which I could ask a human being for objects which I knew he could give me and which I earnestly desired to possess. That sense of the reality of intercession was for ever denied me, and it was, I now see, the stigma of my want of faith. But at the time, of course, I suspected nothing of the kind, and I tried to keep up my zeal by a desperate mental flogging, as if my soul had been a peg-top.*

In nothing did I gain from the advent of my stepmother more than in the encouragement she gave to my friendships with a group of boys of my own age, of whom I had now lately formed the acquaintance. These friendships she not merely tolerated, but fostered; it was even due to her kind arrangements that they took a certain set form, that our excursions started from this house or from that on regular days. I hardly know by what stages I ceased to be a lonely little creature of mock-monographs and mud-pies, and became a member of a sort of club of eight or ten active boys. The long summer holidays of 1861 were set in an enchanting brightness.

Looking back, I cannot see a cloud on the terrestrial horizon—I see nothing but a blaze of sunshine; descents of slippery grass to moons of snow-white shingle, cold to the bare flesh; red promontories running out into a sea that was like sapphire; and our happy clan climbing, bathing, boating, lounging, chattering, all the hot day through. Once more I have to record the fact, which I think is not without interest, that precisely as my life ceases to be solitary, it ceases to be distinct. I have no difficulty in recalling, with the minuteness of a photograph, scenes in which my Father and I were the sole actors within the four walls of a room, but of the glorious life among wild boys on the margin of the sea I have nothing but vague and broken impressions, delicious and illusive.

It was a remarkable proof of my Father's temporary lapse into indulgence that he made no effort to thwart my intimacy with these my new companions. He was in an unusually humane mood himself. His marriage was one proof of it; another was the composition at this time of the most picturesque, easy and graceful of all his writings, 'The Romance of Natural History',* even now a sort of classic. Everything combined to make him believe that the blessing of the Lord was upon him, and to clothe the darkness of the world with at least a mist of rose-colour. I do not recollect that ever at this time he bethought him, when I started in the morning for a long day with my friends on the edge of the sea, to remind me that I must speak to them, in season and out of season, of the Blood of Jesus. And I, young coward that I was, let sleeping dogmas lie.

My companions were not all of them the sons of saints in our communion; their parents belonged to that professional class which we were only now beginning to attract to our services. They were brought up in religious, but not in fanatical, families, and I was the only 'converted' one among them. Mrs Paget, of whom I shall have presently to speak, characteristically said that it grieved her to see 'one lamb among so many kids'.* But 'kid' is a word of varied significance, and the symbol did not seem to us effectively applied. As a matter of fact, we made what I still feel was an excellent tacit compromise. My young companions never jeered at me for being 'in communion with the saints', and I, on my part, never urged the Atonement upon them. I began, in fact, more and more to keep my own religion for use on Sundays.

It will, I hope, have been observed that among the very curious grown-up people into whose company I was thrown, although many were frail and some were foolish, none, so far as I can discern, were hypocritical. I am not one of those who believe that hypocrisy is a vice that grows on every bush. Of course, in religious more than in any other matters, there is a perpetual contradiction between our thoughts and our deeds which is inevitable to our social order, and is bound to lead to 'cette tromperie mutuelle' of which Pascal speaks.* But I have often wondered, while admiring the splendid portrait of Tartufe,* whether such a monster ever, or at least often, has walked the stage of life; whether Molière* observed, or only invented him.

To adopt a scheme of religious pretension, with no belief whatever in its being true, merely for sensuous advantage, openly acknowledging to one's inner self the brazen system of deceit,—such a course may, and doubtless has been, trodden, yet surely much less frequently than cynics love to suggest. But at the juncture which I have now reached in my narrative, I had the advantage of knowing a person who was branded before the whole world, and punished by the law of his country, as a felonious hypocrite. My Father himself could only sigh and admit the charge. And yet—I doubt.

About half-way between our village and the town there lay a comfortable villa inhabited by a retired solicitor, or perhaps attorney, whom I shall name Mr Dormant. We often called at his half-way house, and, although he was a member of the town-meeting, he not unfrequently came up to us for 'the breaking of bread'. Mr Dormant was a solid, pink man, of a cosy habit. He had beautiful white hair, a very soft voice, and a welcoming, wheedling manner; he was extremely fluent and zealous in using the pious phraseology of the sect. My Father had never been very much attracted to him, but the man professed, and I think felt, an overwhelming admiration for my Father. Mr Dormant was not very well off, and in the previous year he had persuaded an aged gentleman of wealth to come and board with him. When, in the course of the winter, this gentleman died, much surprise was felt at the report that he had left almost his entire fortune, which was not inconsiderable, to Mr Dormant.

Much surprise—for the old gentleman had a son to whom he had always been warmly attached, who was far away, I think in South America, practising a perfectly respectable profession of which his father entirely approved. My own Father always preserved a delicacy and a sense of honour about money which could not have been more sensitive if he had been an ungodly man, and I am very much pleased to remember that when the legacy was first spoken of, he regretted that Mr Dormant should have allowed the old gentleman to make this will. If he knew the intention, my Father said, it would have shown a more proper sense of his responsibility if he had dissuaded the testator from so unbecoming a disposition. That was long before any legal question arose; and now Mr Dormant came into his fortune, and began to make handsome gifts to missionary societies, and to his own meeting in the town. If I do not mistake, he gave, unsolicited, a sum to our building fund, which my Father afterwards returned. But in process of time we heard that the son had come back from the Antipodes, and was making investigations. Before we knew where we were, the news burst upon us, like a bomb-shell, that Mr Dormant had been arrested on a criminal charge and was now in gaol at Exeter.

Sympathy was at first much extended amongst us to the prisoner. But it was lessened when we understood that the old gentleman had been 'converted' while under Dormant's roof, and had given the fact that his son was 'an unbeliever' as a reason for disinheriting him. All doubt was set aside when it was divulged, under pressure, by the nurse who attended on the old gentleman, herself one of the 'saints', that Dormant had traced the signature to the will by drawing the fingers of the testator over the document when he was already and finally comatose.

My Father, setting aside by a strong effort of will the repugnance which he felt, visited the prisoner in gaol before this final evidence had been extracted. When he returned he said that Dormant appeared to be enjoying a perfect confidence of heart, and had expressed a sense of his joy and peace in the Lord; my Father regretted that he had not been able to persuade him to admit any error, even of judgment. But the prisoner's attitude in the dock, when the facts were proved, and not by him denied, was still more extraordinary. He could be induced to exhibit no species of remorse, and, to the obvious anger of the judge himself, stated that he had only done his duty as a Christian, in preventing this wealth from coming into the hands of an ungodly man, who would have spent it in the service of the flesh and of the devil. Sternly reprimanded by the judge, he made the final statement that at that very moment he was conscious of his Lord's presence, in the dock at his side, whispering to him 'Well done, thou good and faithful servant!' In this frame of conscience, and with a glowing countenance, he was hurried away to penal servitude.

This was a very painful incident, and it is easy to see how compromising, how cruel, it was in its effect upon our communion; what occasion it gave to our enemies to blaspheme. No one, in either meeting, could or would raise a voice to defend Mr Dormant. We had to bow our heads when we met our enemies in the gate. The blow fell more heavily on the meeting of which he had been a prominent and communicating member, but it fell on us too, and my Father felt it severely. For many years he would never mention the man's name, and he refused all discussion of the incident.

Yet I was never sure and I am not sure now, that the wretched being was a hypocrite. There are as many vulgar fanatics as there are distinguished ones, and I am not convinced that Dormant, coarse and narrow as he was, may not have sincerely believed that it was better for the money to be used in religious propaganda than in the pleasures of the world, of which he doubtless formed a very vague idea. On this affair I meditated much, and it awakened in my mind, for the first time, a doubt whether our exclusive system of ethics was an entirely salutary one, if it could lead the conscience of a believer to tolerate such acts as these, acts which my Father himself had denounced as dishonourable and disgraceful.

My stepmother brought with her a little library of such books as we had not previously seen, but which yet were known to all the world except us. Prominent among these was a set of the poems of Walter Scott,* and in his unwonted geniality and provisional spirit of compromise, my Father must do no less than read these works aloud to my stepmother in the quiet spring evenings. This was a sort of aftermath of courtship, a tribute of song to his bride, very sentimental and pretty. She would sit, sedately, at her work-box, while he, facing her, poured forth the verses at her like a blackbird. I was not considered in this arrangement, which was wholly matrimonial, but I was present, and the exercise made more impression upon me than it did upon either of the principal agents.

My Father read the verse admirably, with a full,—some people (but not I) might say with too full—a perception of the metre as well as of the rhythm, rolling out the rhymes, and glorying in the proper names. He began, and it was a happy choice, with 'The Lady of the Lake'.* It gave me singular pleasure to hear his large voice do justice to 'Duncrannon' and 'Cambus-Kenneth', and wake the echoes with 'Roderigh Vich Alphine dhu, ho! ieroe!' I almost gasped with excitement, while a shudder floated down my backbone, when we came to:

> A sharp and shrieking echo gave,
> Coir-Uriskin, thy goblin cave!
> And the grey pass where birches wave,
>   On Beala-nam-bo,*

a passage which seemed to me to achieve the ideal of sublime romance. My thoughts were occupied all day long with the adventures of Fitzjames and the denizens of Ellen's Isle. It became an obsession, and when I was asked whether I remembered the name of the cottage where the minister of the Bible Christians lodged, I answered, dreamily, 'Yes,—Beala-nam-bo'.

Seeing me so much fascinated, thrown indeed into a temporary frenzy, by the epic poetry of Sir Walter Scott, my stepmother asked my Father whether I might not start reading the Waverley Novels. But he refused to permit this, on the ground that those tales gave false and disturbing pictures of life, and would lead away my attention from heavenly things. I do not fully apprehend what distinction he drew between the poems, which he permitted, and the novels, which he refused. But I suppose he regarded a work in verse as more artificial, and therefore less likely to make a realistic impression, than one in prose. There is something quaint in the conscientious scruple which allows 'The Lord of the Isles' and excludes 'Rob Roy'.*

But stranger still, and amounting almost to a whim, was his sudden decision that, although I might not touch the novels of Scott, I was free to read those of Dickens. I recollect that my stepmother showed some surprise at this, and that my Father explained to her that Dickens 'exposes the passion of love in a ridiculous light'. She did not seem to follow this recommendation, which indeed tends to the ultra-subtle, but she procured for me a copy of 'Pickwick',* by which I was instantly and gloriously enslaved. My shouts of laughing at the richer passages were almost scandalous, and led to my being reproved for disturbing my Father while engaged, in an upper room, in the study of God's Word. I must have expended months on the perusal of 'Pickwick', for I used to rush through a chapter, and then read it over again very slowly, word for word, and then shut my eyes to realise the figures and the action.

I suppose no child will ever again enjoy that rapture of unresisting humorous appreciation of 'Pickwick'. I felt myself to be in the company of a gentleman so extremely funny that I began to laugh before he began to speak; no sooner did he remark 'the sky was dark and gloomy, the air was damp and raw', than I was in fits of laughter. My retirement in our sequestered corner of life made me, perhaps, even in this matter, somewhat old-fashioned, and possibly I was the latest of the generation who accepted Mr Pickwick with an unquestioning and hysterical abandonment. Certainly few young people now seem sensitive, as I was, and as thousands before me had been, to the quality of his fascination.

It was curious that living in a household where a certain delicate art of painting was diligently cultivated, I had yet never seen a real picture, and was scarcely familiar with the design of one in engraving. My stepmother, however, brought a flavour of the fine arts with her; a kind of æsthetic odour, like that of lavender, clung to her as she moved. She had known authentic artists in her youth; she had watched Old Crome painting, and had taken a course of drawing-lessons from no less a person than Cotman.* She painted small water-colour landscapes herself, with a delicate economy of means and a graceful Norwich convention; her sketch-books were filled with abbeys gently washed in, river-banks in sepia by which the elect might be dimly reminded of *Liber Studiorum*,* and woodland scenes over which the ghost of Creswick* had faintly breathed. It was not exciting art, but it was, so far as it went, in its lady-like reserve, the real thing. Our sea-anemones, our tropic birds, our bits of spongy rock frilled and sprayed with corallines, had been very conscientious and skilful, but, essentially, so far as art was concerned, the wrong thing.

Thus I began to acquire, without understanding the value of it, some conception of the elegant phases of early English water-colour painting, and there was one singular piece of a marble well brimming with water, and a greyish-blue sky over it, and dark-green poplars, shaped like wet brooms, menacing the middle distance, which Cotman himself had touched; and this seemed beautiful and curious to me in its dim, flat frame, when it was hoisted to a place on our drawing-room wall.

But still I had never seen a subject-picture, although my step-mother used to talk of the joys of the Royal Academy,* and it was therefore with a considerable sense of excitement that I went, with my Father, to examine Mr Holman Hunt's *Finding of Christ in the Temple** which at this time was announced to be on public show at our neighbouring town. We paid our shillings and ascended with others to an upper room, bare of every disturbing object, in which a strong top-light raked the large and uncompromising picture. We looked at it for some time in silence, and then my Father pointed out to me various details, such as the phylacteries and the mitres,* and the robes which distinguished the high priest.

Some of the other visitors, as I recollect, expressed astonishment and dislike of what they called the 'Preraphaelite'* treatment, but we were not affected by that. Indeed, if anything, the exact, minute and hard execution of Mr Hunt was in sympathy with the methods we ourselves were in the habit of using when we painted butterflies and sea-weeds, placing perfectly pure pigments side by side, without any nonsense about *chiaroscuro*.* This large, bright, comprehensive picture made a very deep impression upon me, not exactly as a work of art, but as a brilliant natural specimen. I was pleased to have seen it, as I was pleased to have seen the comet, and the whale which was brought to our front door on a truck. It was a prominent addition to my experience.

The slender expansions of my interest which were now budding hither and thither do not seem to have alarmed my Father at all. His views were short; if I appeared to be contented and obedient, if I responded pleasantly when he appealed to me, he was not concerned to discover the source of my cheerfulness. He put it down to my happy sense of joy in Christ, a reflection of the sunshine of grace beaming upon me through no intervening clouds of sin or doubt. The 'saints' were, as a rule, very easy to comprehend; their emotions lay upon the surface. If they were gay, it was because they had no burden on their consciences, while, if they were depressed, the symptom might be depended upon as showing that their consciences were troubling them, and if they were indifferent and cold, it was certain that they were losing their faith and becoming hostile to godliness. It was almost a mechanical matter with these simple souls. But, although I was so much younger, I was more complex and more crafty than the peasant 'saints'. My Father, not a very subtle psychologist, applied to me the same formulas which served him well at the meeting, but in my case the results were less uniformly successful.

The excitement of school-life and the enlargement of my circle of interests, combined to make Sunday, by contrast, a very tedious occasion. The absence of every species of recreation on the Lord's Day grew to be a burden which might scarcely be borne. I have said that my freedom during the week had now become considerable; if I was at home punctually at meal-times, the rest of my leisure was not challenged. But this liberty, which in the summer holidays came to surpass that of 'fishes that tipple in the deep', was put into more and more painful contrast with the unbroken servitude of Sunday.

My Father objected very strongly to the expression Sabbath-day, as it is commonly used by Presbyterians and others. He said, quite justly, that it was an inaccurate modern innovation, that Sabbath was Saturday, the seventh day of the week, not the first, a Jewish festival and not a Christian commemoration. Yet his exaggerated view with regard to the observance of the First Day, namely, that it must be exclusively occupied with public and private exercises of divine worship, was based much more upon a Jewish than upon a Christian law. In fact, I do not remember that my Father ever produced a definite argument from the New Testament in support of his excessive passivity on the Lord's Day. He followed the early Puritan practice, except that he did not extend his observance, as I believe the old Puritans did, from sunset on Saturday to sunset on Sunday.

The observance of the Lord's Day has already become universally so lax that I think there may be some value in preserving an accurate record of how our Sundays were spent five and forty years ago. We came down to breakfast at the usual time. My Father prayed briefly before we began the meal; after it, the bell was rung, and, before the breakfast was cleared away, we had a lengthy service of exposition and prayer with the servants. If the weather was fine, we then walked about the garden, doing nothing, for about half an hour. We then sat, each in a separate room, with our Bibles open and some commentary on the text beside us, and prepared our minds for the morning service. A little before 11 A.M. we sallied forth, carrying our Bibles and hymn-books, and went through the morning-service of two hours at the Room; this was the central event of Sunday.

We then came back to dinner,—curiously enough to a hot dinner, always, with a joint, vegetables and puddings, so that the cook at least must have been busily at work,—and after it my Father and my stepmother took a nap, each in a different room, while I slipped out into the garden for a little while, but never venturing further afield. In the middle of the afternoon, my stepmother and I proceeded up the village to Sunday School, where I was early promoted to the tuition of a few very little boys. We returned in time for tea, immediately after which we all marched forth, again armed, as in the morning, with Bibles and hymn-books, and we went through the evening-service, at which my Father preached. The hour was now already past my week-day bedtime, but we had another service to attend, the Believers' Prayer Meeting, which commonly occupied forty minutes more. Then we used to creep home, I often so tired that the weariness was like physical pain, and I was permitted, without further 'worship', to slip upstairs to bed.

What made these Sundays, the observance of which was absolutely uniform, so peculiarly trying was that I was not permitted the indulgence of any secular respite. I might not open a scientific book, nor make a drawing, nor examine a specimen. I was not allowed to go into the road, except to proceed with my parents to the Room, nor to discuss worldly subjects at meals, nor to enter the little chamber where I kept my treasures. I was hotly and tightly dressed in black, all day long, as though ready at any moment to attend a funeral with decorum. Sometimes, towards evening, I used to feel the monotony and weariness of my position to be almost unendurable, but at this time I was meek, and I bowed to what I supposed to be the order of the universe.

CHAPTER XI

As my mental horizon widened, my Father followed the direction of my spiritual eyes with some bewilderment, and knew not at what I gazed. Nor could I have put into words, nor can I even now define, the visions which held my vague and timid attention. As a child develops, those who regard it with tenderness or impatience are seldom even approximately correct in their analysis of its intellectual movements, largely because, if there is anything to record, it defies adult definition. One curious freak of mentality I must now mention, because it took a considerable part in the enfranchisement of my mind, or rather in the formation of my thinking habits. But neither my Father nor my stepmother knew what to make of it, and to tell the truth I hardly know what to make of it myself.

Among the books which my new mother had brought with her were certain editions of the poets, an odd assortment. Campbell was there, and Burns, and Keats, and the 'Tales' of Byron.* Each of these might have been expected to appeal to me; but my emotion was too young, and I did not listen to them yet. Their imperative voices called me later. By the side of these romantic classics stood a small, thick volume, bound in black morocco, and comprising four reprinted works of the eighteenth century, gloomy, funereal poems of an order as wholly out of date as are the cross-bones and ruffled cherubim on the gravestones in a country churchyard. The four—and in this order, as I never shall forget—were 'The Last Day' of Dr Young, Blair's 'Grave', 'Death' by Bishop Beilby Porteus, and 'The Deity' of Samuel Boyse.* These lugubrious effusions, all in blank verse or in the heroic couplet, represented, in its most redundant form, the artistic theology of the middle of the eighteenth century. They were steeped in such vengeful and hortatory sentiments as passed for elegant piety in the reign of George II.*

How I came to open this solemn volume is explained by the oppressive exclusiveness of our Sundays. On the afternoon of the Lord's Day, as I have already explained, I might neither walk, nor talk, nor explore our scientific library, nor indulge in furious feats of water-colour painting. The Plymouth-Brother theology which alone was open to me produced, at length, and particularly on hot afternoons, a faint physical nausea, a kind of secret headache. But, hitting one day upon the doleful book of verses, and observing its religious character, I asked 'May I read that?' and after a brief, astonished glance at the contents, I received 'O certainly—if you can!'

The lawn sloped directly from a verandah at our drawing-room window, and it contained two immense elm-trees, which had originally formed part of the hedge of a meadow. In our trim and polished garden they then remained—they were soon afterwards cut down—rude and obtuse, with something primeval about them, something autochthonous;* they were like two peasant ancestors surviving in a family that had advanced to gentility. They rose each out of a steep turfed hillock, and the root of one of them was long my favourite summer reading-desk; for I could lie stretched on the lawn, with my head and shoulders supported by the elm-tree hillock, and the book in a fissure of the rough turf. Thither then I escaped with my grave-yard poets, and who shall explain the rapture with which I followed their austere morality?

Whether I really read consecutively in my black-bound volume I can no longer be sure, but it became a companion whose society I valued, and at worst it was a thousand times more congenial to me than Jukes' 'On the Apocalypse' or than a perfectly excruciating work ambiguously styled 'The Javelin of Phineas',* which lay smouldering in a dull red cover on the drawing-room table. I dipped my bucket here and there into my poets, and I brought up strange things. I brought up out of the depths of 'The Last Day'* the following ejaculation of a soul roused by the trump of resurrection:—

> Father of mercies! Why from silent earth
> Didst thou awake, and curse me into birth?
> Tear me from quiet, ravish me from night,
> And make a thankless present of thy light?
> Push into being a reverse of thee,
> And animate a clod with misery?*

I read these lines with a shiver of excitement, and in a sense I suppose little intended by the sanctimonious rector of Welwyn.* I also read in the same piece the surprising description of how

> Now charnels rattle, scattered limbs, and all
> The various bones, obsequious to the call,
> Self-mov'd, advance—the neck perhaps to meet
> The distant head, the distant legs the feet,*

but rejected it as not wholly supported by the testimony of Scripture. I think that the rhetoric and vigorous advance of Young's verse were pleasant to me. Beilby Porteus I discarded from the first as impenetrable. In 'The Deity',—I knew nothing then of the life of its extravagant and preposterous author,—I took a kind of persistent, penitential pleasure, but it was Blair's 'Grave' that really delighted me, and I frightened myself with its melodious doleful images in earnest.

About this time there was a great flow of tea-table hospitality in the village, and my friends and their friends used to be asked out, by respective parents and by more than one amiable spinster, to faint little entertainments where those sang who were ambitious to sing, and where all played post and forfeits after a rich tea. My Father was constantly exercised in mind as to whether I should or should not accept these glittering invitations. There hovered before him a painful sense of danger in resigning the soul to pleasures which savoured of 'the World'. These, though apparently innocent in themselves, might give an appetite for yet more subversive dissipations.

I remember, on one occasion,—when the Browns, a family of Baptists who kept a large haberdashery shop in the neighbouring town, asked for the pleasure of my company 'to tea and games', and carried complacency so far as to offer to send that local vehicle, 'the midge', to fetch me and bring me back,—my Father's conscience was so painfully perplexed, that he desired me to come up with him to the now-deserted 'boudoir' of the departed Marks, that we might 'lay the matter before the Lord'. We did so, kneeling side by side, with our backs to the window and our foreheads pressed upon the horsehair cover of the small, coffin-like sofa. My Father prayed aloud, with great fervour, that it might be revealed to me, by the voice of God, whether it was or was not the Lord's will that I should attend the Browns' party. My Father's attitude seemed to me to be hardly fair, since he did not scruple to remind the Deity of various objections to a life of pleasure and of the snakes that lie hidden in the grass of evening parties. It would have been more scrupulous, I thought, to give no sort of hint of the kind of answer he desired and expected.

It will be justly said that my life was made up of very trifling things, since I have to confess that this incident of the Browns' invitation was one of its landmarks. As I knelt, feeling very small, by

the immense bulk of my Father, there gushed through my veins like
a wine the determination to rebel. Never before, in all these years of
my vocation, had I felt my resistance take precisely this definite
form. We rose presently from the sofa, my forehead and the backs of
my hands still chafed by the texture of the horsehair, and we faced
one another in the dreary light. My Father, perfectly confident in the
success of what had really been a sort of incantation, asked me in a
loud wheedling voice, 'Well, and what is the answer which our Lord
vouchsafes?' I said nothing, and so my Father, more sharply, continued, 'We have asked Him to direct you to a true knowledge of His
will. We have desired Him to let you know whether it is, or is not, in
accordance with His wishes that you should accept this invitation
from the Browns.' He positively beamed down at me; he had no
doubt of the reply. He was already, I believe, planning some little
treat to make up to me for the material deprivation. But my answer
came, in the high-piping accents of despair: 'The Lord says I may go
to the Browns.' My Father gazed at me in speechless horror. He was
caught in his own trap, and though he was certain that the Lord had
said nothing of the kind, there was no road open for him but just
sheer retreat. Yet surely it was an error in tactics to slam the door.

It was at this party at the Browns—to which I duly went, although
in sore disgrace—that my charnel poets played me a mean trick. It
was proposed that 'our young friends' should give their elders the
treat of repeating any pretty pieces that they knew by heart. Accordingly a little girl recited 'Casabianca', and another little girl 'We are
Seven',* and various children were induced to repeat hymns, 'some
rather long', as Calverley* says, but all very mild and innocuously
evangelical. I was then asked by Mrs Brown's maiden sister, a gush-
ing lady in corkscrew curls, who led the revels, whether I also would
not indulge them 'by repeating some sweet stanzas'. No one more
ready than I. Without a moment's hesitation, I stood forth, and in a
loud voice I began one of my favourite passages from Blair's
'Grave':—

> If death were nothing, and nought after death,—
> If when men died at once they ceased to be,—
> Returning to the barren Womb of Nothing
> Whence first they sprung, then might the debauchee . . .*

'Thank you, dear, that will do nicely!' interrupted the lady with the curls. 'But that's only the beginning of it,' I cried. 'Yes, dear, but that will quite do! We won't ask you to repeat any more of it', and I withdrew to the borders of the company in bewilderment. Nor did the Browns or their visitors ever learn what it was the debauchee might have said or done in more favourable circumstances.

The growing eagerness which I displayed for the society of selected schoolfellows and for such gentle dissipations as were within my reach exercised my Father greatly. His fancy rushed forward with the pace of a steam-engine, and saw me the life and soul of a gambling club, or flaunting it at the Mabille.* He had no confidence in the action of moderating powers, and he was fond of repeating that the downward path is easy. If one fretted to be bathing with one's companions on the shingle, and preferred this exercise to the study of God's Word, it was a symbol of a terrible decline, the angle of which would grow steeper and steeper, till one plunged into perdition. He was, himself, timid and reclusive, and he shrank from all avoidable companionship with others, except on the footing of a master and teacher. My stepmother and I, who neither taught nor ruled, yearned for a looser chain and lighter relationships. With regard to myself, my Father about this time hit on a plan from which he hoped much, but from which little resulted. He looked to George to supply what my temperament seemed to require of congenial juvenile companionship.

If I have not mentioned 'George' until now, it is not that he was a new acquaintance. When we first came down into the country, our sympathy had been called forth by an accident to a little boy, who was knocked over by a horse, and whose thigh was broken. Somebody (I suppose Mary Grace, since my Father could rarely bring himself to pay these public visits) went to see the child in the infirmary, and accidentally discovered that he was exactly the same age that I was. This, and the fact that he was a meditative and sober little boy, attracted us all still further to George, who became converted under one of my Father's sermons. He attended my public baptism, and was so much moved by this ceremony that he passionately desired to be baptized also, and was in fact so immersed, a few months later, slightly to my chagrin, since I thereupon ceased to be the only infant prodigy in communion. When we were both in our thirteenth year, George became an outdoor servant to us, and did odd jobs under the gardener. My Father, finding him, as he said, 'docile, obedient and engaging', petted George a good deal, and taught him a little botany. He called George, by a curious contortion of thought, my 'spiritual foster-brother', and anticipated for him, I think, a career, like mine, in the Ministry.

Our garden suffered from an incursion of slugs, which laid the verbenas in the dust, and shore off the carnations as if with pairs of scissors. To cope with this plague we invested in a drake and a duck, who were christened Philemon and Baucis.* Every night large cabbage-leaves, containing the lees of beer, were spread about the flower-beds as traps, and at dawn these had become green parlours crammed with intoxicated slugs. One of George's earliest morning duties was to free Philemon and Baucis from their coop, and, armed with a small wand, to guide their foot-steps to the feast in one cabbage-leaf after another. My Father used to watch this perform-ance from an upper window, and, in moments of high facetiousness, he was wont to parody the poet Gray:*

How jocund doth George drive his team afield!

This is all, or almost all, that I remember about George's occupa-tions, but he was singularly blameless.

My Father's plan now was that I should form a close intimacy with George, as a boy of my own age, of my own faith, of my own future. My stepmother, still in bondage to the social conventions, was pas-sionately troubled at this, and urged the barrier of class-differences. My Father replied that such an intimacy would keep me 'lowly', and that from so good a boy as George I could learn nothing undesirable. 'He will encourage him not to wipe his boots when he comes into the house,' said my stepmother, and my Father sighed to think how narrow is the horizon of Woman's view of heavenly things.

In this caprice, if I may call it so, I think that my Father had before him the fine republican example of 'Sandford and Merton',* some parts of which book he admired extremely. Accordingly George and I were sent out to take walks together, and as we started, my Father, with an air of great benevolence, would suggest some passage of Scripture, 'some aspect of God's bountiful scheme in creation, on which you may profitably meditate together'. George and I never pursued the discussion of the text with which my Father started us for more than a minute or two; then we fell into silence, or investigated current scenes and rustic topics.

As is natural among the children of the poor, George was precocious where I was infantile, and undeveloped where I was elaborate. Our minds could hardly find a point at which to touch. He gave me, however, under cross-examination, interesting hints about rural matters, and I liked him, although I felt his company to be insipid. Sometimes he carried my books by my side to the larger and more distant school which I now attended, but I was always in a fever of dread lest my school-fellows should see him, and should accuse me of having to be 'brought' to school. To explain to them that the companionship of this wholesome and rather blunt young peasant was part of my spiritual discipline would have been all beyond my powers.

It was soon after this that my stepmother made her one vain effort to break through the stillness of our lives. My Father's energy seemed to decline, to become more fitful, to take unseasonable directions. My mother instinctively felt that his peculiarities were growing upon him; he would scarcely stir from his microscope, except to go to the chapel, and he was visible to fewer and fewer visitors. She had taken a pleasure in his literary eminence, and she was aware that this, too, would slip from him; that, so persistently kept out of sight, he must soon be out of mind. I know not how she gathered courage for her tremendous effort, but she took me, I recollect, into her counsels. We were to unite to oblige my Father to start to his feet and face the world. Alas! we might as well have attempted to rouse the summit of Yes Tor* into volcanic action. To my mother's arguments, my Father—with that baffling smile of his—replied: 'I esteem the reproach of Christ greater riches than the treasures of Egypt!' and that this answer was indirect made it none the less conclusive. My mother wished him to give lectures, to go to London, to read papers before the Royal Society, to enter into controversy with foreign *savants*, to conduct classes of out-door zoology at fashionable watering-places. I held my breath with admiration as she poured forth her scheme, so daring, so brilliant, so sure to cover our great man with glory. He listened to her with an ambiguous smile, and shook his head at us, and resumed the reading of his Bible.

At the date at which I write these pages, the arts of illustration are so universally diffused that it is difficult to realise the darkness in which a remote English village was plunged half a century ago. No opportunity was offered to us dwellers in remote places of realising the outward appearances of unfamiliar persons, scenes or things. Although ours was perhaps the most cultivated household in the parish, I had never seen so much as a representation of a work of sculpture till I was thirteen. My mother then received from her earlier home certain volumes, among which was a gaudy gift-book of some kind, containing a few steel engravings of statues.

These attracted me violently, and here for the first time I gazed on Apollo with his proud gesture, Venus in her undulations, the kirtled shape of Diana, and Jupiter* voluminously bearded. Very little information, and that to me not intelligible, was given in the text, but these were said to be figures of the old Greek gods. I asked my Father to tell me about these 'old Greek gods'. His answer was direct and disconcerting. He said—how I recollect the place and time, early in the morning, as I stood beside the window in our garish breakfast-room—he said that the so-called gods of the Greeks were the shadows cast by the vices of the heathen, and reflected their infamous lives; 'it was for such things as these that God poured down brimstone and fire on the Cities of the Plain,* and there is nothing in the legends of these gods, or rather devils, that it is not better for a Christian not to know.' His face blazed white with Puritan fury as he said this—I see him now in my mind's eye, in his violent emotion. You might have thought that he had himself escaped with horror from some Hellenic hippodrome.*

My Father's prestige was by this time considerably lessened in my mind, and though I loved and admired him, I had now long ceased to hold him infallible. I did not accept his condemnation of the Greeks, although I bowed to it. In private I returned to examine my steel engravings of the statues, and I reflected that they were too beautiful to be so wicked as my Father thought they were. The dangerous and pagan notion that beauty palliates evil budded in my mind, without any external suggestion,* and by this reflection alone I was still further sundered from the faith in which I had been trained. I gathered very diligently all I could pick up about the Greek gods and their statues; it was not much, it was indeed ludicrously little and false, but it was a germ. And at this æsthetic juncture I was drawn into what was really rather an extraordinary circle of incidents.

Among the 'Saints' in our village there lived a shoemaker and his wife, who had one daughter, Susan Flood. She was a flighty, excited young creature, and lately, during the passage of some itinerary revivalists, she had been 'converted' in the noisiest way, with sobs, gasps and gurglings. When this crisis passed, she came with her parents to our meetings, and was received quietly enough to the breaking of bread. But about the time I speak of, Susan Flood went up to London to pay a visit to an unconverted uncle and aunt. It was first whispered amongst us, and then openly stated, that these relatives had taken her to the Crystal Palace,* where, in passing through the Sculpture Gallery, Susan's sense of decency had been so grievously affronted, that she had smashed the naked figures with the handle of her parasol, before her horrified companions could stop her. She had, in fact, run amok among the statuary, and had, to the intense chagrin of her uncle and aunt, very worthy persons, been arrested and brought before a magistrate, who dismissed her with a warning to her relations that she had better be sent home to Devonshire and 'looked after'. Susan Flood's return to us, however, was a triumph; she had no sense of having acted injudiciously or unbecomingly; she was ready to recount to every one, in vague and veiled language, how she had been able to testify for the Lord 'in the very temple of Belial',* for so she poetically described the Crystal Palace. She was, of course, in a state of unbridled hysteria,* but such physical explanations were not encouraged amongst us, and the case of Susan Flood awakened a great deal of sympathy.

There was held a meeting of the elders in our drawing-room to discuss it, and I contrived to be present, though out of observation. My Father, while he recognised the purity of Susan Flood's zeal, questioned its wisdom. He noted that the statuary was not her property, but that of the Crystal Palace. Of the other communicants, none, I think, had the very slightest notion what the objects were that Susan had smashed, or tried to smash, and frankly maintained that they thought her conduct magnificent. As for me, I had gathered by persistent inquiry enough information to know that what her sacrilegious parasol had attacked were bodies of my mysterious friends, the Greek gods, and if all the rest of the village applauded iconoclastic Susan, I at least would be ardent on the other side.*

But I was conscious that there was nobody in the world to whom I could go for sympathy. If I had ever read 'Hellas'* I should have murmured

> Apollo, Pan and Love,
> And even Olympian Jove,
> Grew weak, when killing Susan glared on them.

On the day in question, I was unable to endure the drawing-room meeting to its close, but, clutching my volume of the Funereal Poets, I made a dash for the garden. In the midst of a mass of laurels, a clearing had been made, where ferns were grown and a garden-seat was placed. There was no regular path to this asylum; one dived under the snake-like boughs of the laurel and came up again in absolute seclusion.

Into this haunt I now fled to meditate about the savage godliness of that vandal, Susan Flood. So extremely ignorant was I that I supposed her to have destroyed the originals of the statues, marble and unique. I knew nothing about plaster casts, and I thought the damage (it is possible that there had really been no damage whatever) was of an irreparable character. I sank into the seat, with the great wall of laurels whispering around me, and I burst into tears. There was something, surely, quaint and pathetic in the figure of a little Plymouth Brother sitting in that advanced year of grace, weeping bitterly for indignities done to Hermes and to Aphrodite.* Then I opened my book for consolation, and read a great block of pompous verse out of 'The Deity', in the midst of which exercise, yielding to the softness of the hot and aromatic air, I fell fast asleep.

Among those who applauded the zeal of Susan Flood's parasol, the Pagets were prominent. These were a retired Baptist minister and his wife, from Exmouth, who had lately settled amongst us, and joined in the breaking of bread. Mr Paget was a fat old man, whose round pale face was clean-shaven, and who carried a full crop of loose white hair above it; his large lips were always moving, whether he spoke or not. He resembled, as I now perceive, the portraits of S. T. Coleridge* in age, but with all the intellect left out of them. He lived in a sort of trance of solemn religious despondency. He had thrown up his cure of souls, because he became convinced that he had committed the Sin against the Holy Ghost.* His wife was younger than he, very small, very tight, very active, with black eyes like pin-pricks at the base of an extremely high and narrow forehead, bordered with glossy ringlets. He was very cross to her, and it was murmured that 'dear Mrs Paget had often had to pass through the waters of affliction'. They were very poor, but rigidly genteel, and she was careful, so far as she could, to conceal from the world the caprices of her poor lunatic husband.

In our circle, it was never for a moment admitted that Mr Paget was a lunatic. It was said that he had gravely sinned, and was under the Lord's displeasure; prayers were abundantly offered up that he might be led back into the pathway of light, and that the Smiling Face might be drawn forth for him from behind the Frowning Providence. When the man had an epileptic seizure in the High Street, he was not taken to a hospital, but we repeated to one another, with shaken heads, that Satan, that crookèd Serpent, had been unloosed for a season. Mr Paget was fond of talking in private and in public, of his dreadful spiritual condition, and he would drop his voice while he spoke of having committed the Unpardonable Sin, with a sort of shuddering exultation, such as people sometimes feel. in the possession of a very unusual disease.

It might be thought that the position held in any community by persons so afflicted and eccentric as the Pagets would be very precarious. But it was not so with us; on the contrary, they took a prominent place at once. Mr Paget, in spite of his spiritual bankruptcy, was only too anxious to help my Father in his ministrations, and used to beg to be allowed to pray and exhort. In the latter case he took the tone of a wounded veteran, who, though fallen on the bloody field himself, could still encourage younger warriors to march forward to victory. Everybody longed to know what the exact nature had been of that sin against the Holy Ghost which had deprived Mr Paget of every glimmer of hope for time or for eternity. It was whispered that even my Father himself was not precisely acquainted with the character of it.

This mysterious disability clothed Mr Paget for us with a kind of romance. We watched him as the women watched Dante in Verona, whispering:

> Behold him, how Hell's reek
> Has crisped his hair and singed his cheek!*

His person lacked, it is true, something of the dignity of Dante's, for it was his caprice to walk up and down the High Street at noonday with one of those cascades of coloured paper which were known as 'ornaments for your fire-place' slung over the back and another over the front of his body. These he manufactured for sale, and he adopted the quaint practice of wearing the exuberant objects as a means for their advertisement.

Mrs Paget had been accustomed to rule in the little ministry from which Mr Paget's celebrated Sin had banished them, and she was inclined to clutch at the sceptre now. She was the only person I ever met with who was not afraid of the displeasure of my Father. She would fix her viper-coloured eyes on his, and say with a kind of gimlet* firmness, 'I hardly think that is the true interpretation, Brother G.', or, 'But let us turn to Colossians,* and see what the Holy Ghost says there upon this matter.' She fascinated my Father, who was not accustomed to this kind of interruption, and as she was not to be softened by any flattery (such as:—'Marvellous indeed, Sister, is your acquaintance with the means of grace!') she became almost a terror to him.

She abused her powers by taking great liberties, which culminated in her drawing his attention to the fact that my poor stepmother displayed 'an overweening love of dress'. The accusation was perfectly false; my stepmother was, if rather richly, always plainly dressed, in the sober Quaker mode; almost her only ornament was a large carnelian brooch, set in flowered flat gold. To this the envenomed Paget drew my Father's attention as 'likely to lead "the little ones of the flock" into temptation'. My poor Father felt it his duty, thus directly admonished, to speak to my mother. 'Do you not think, my Love, that you should, as one who sets an example to others, discard the wearing of that gaudy brooch?' 'One must fasten one's collar with something, I suppose?' 'Well, but how does Sister Paget fasten her collar?' 'Sister Paget', replied my Mother, stung at last into rejoinder, 'fastens her collar with a pin,—and that is a thing which I would rather die than do!'

Nor did I escape the attentions of this zealous reformer. Mrs Paget was good enough to take a great interest in me, and she was not satisfied with the way in which I was being brought up. Her presence seemed to pervade the village, and I could neither come in nor go out without seeing her hard bonnet and her pursed-up lips. She would hasten to report to my Father that she saw me laughing and talking 'with a lot of unconverted boys', these being the companions with whom I had full permission to bathe and boat. She urged my Father to complete my holy vocation by some definite step, by which he

would dedicate me completely to the Lord's service. Further school-
ing she thought needless, and merely likely to foster intellectual
pride. Mr Paget, she remarked, had troubled very little in his youth
about worldly knowledge, and yet how blessed he had been in the
conversion of souls until he had incurred the displeasure of the Holy
Ghost!

I do not know exactly what she wanted my Father to do with me;
perhaps she did not know herself; she was meddlesome, ignorant and
fanatical, and she liked to fancy that she was exercising influence.
But the wonderful, the inexplicable thing is that my Father,—who,
with all his limitations, was so distinguished and high-minded,—
should listen to her for a moment, and still more wonderful is it that
he really allowed her, grim vixen that she was, to disturb his plans
and retard his purposes. I think the explanation lay in the perfectly
logical position she took up. My Father found himself brought face
to face at last, not with a disciple, but with a trained expert in his
own peculiar scheme of religion. At every point she was armed with
arguments the source of which he knew and the validity of which he
recognised. He trembled before Mrs Paget as a man in a dream may
tremble before a parody of his own central self, and he could not
blame her without laying himself open somewhere to censure.

But my stepmother's instincts were more primitive and her
actions less wire-drawn than my Father's. She disliked Mrs Paget as
much as one earnest believer can bring herself to dislike a sister in
the Lord. My stepmother had quietly devoted herself to what she
thought the best way of bringing me up, and she did not propose
now to be thwarted by the wife of a lunatic Baptist. At this time I was
a mixture of childishness and priggishness, of curious knowledge
and dense ignorance. Certain portions of my intellect were growing
with unwholesome activity, while others were stunted, or had never
stirred at all. I was like a plant on which a pot has been placed, with
the effect that the centre is crushed and arrested, while shoots are
straggling up to the light on all sides. My Father himself was aware
of this, and in a spasmodic way he wished to regulate my thoughts.
But all he did was to try to straighten the shoots, without removing
the pot which kept them resolutely down.

It was my mother who decided that I was now old enough to go to
boarding-school, and my Father, having discovered that an elderly
couple of Plymouth Brethren kept an 'academy for young gentlemen'

in a neighbouring sea-port town,*—in the prospectus of which the knowledge and love of the Lord were mentioned as occupying the attention of the head-master and his assistants far more closely than any mere considerations of worldly tuition,—was persuaded to entrust me to its care. He stipulated, however, that I should always come home from Saturday night to Monday morning, not, as he said, that I might receive any carnal indulgence, but that there might be no cessation of my communion as a believer with the Saints in our village on Sundays. To this school, therefore, I presently departed, gawky and homesick, and the rift between my soul and that of my Father widened a little more.

CHAPTER XII

LITTLE boys from quiet, pious households, commonly found, in those days, a chasm yawning at the feet of their inexperience when they arrived at Boarding-school. But the fact that I still slept at home on Saturday and Sunday nights preserved me, I fancy, from many surprises. There was a crisis, but it was broad and slow for me. On the other hand, for my Father I am inclined to think that it was definite and sharp. Permission for me to desert the parental hearth, even for five days in certain weeks, was tantamount, in his mind, to admitting that the great scheme, so long caressed, so passionately fostered, must in its primitive bigness be now dropped.

The Great Scheme (I cannot resist giving it the mortuary honour of capital letters) had been, as my readers know, that I should be exclusively and consecutively dedicated, through the whole of my life, to the manifest and uninterrupted and uncompromised 'service of the Lord'. That had been the aspiration of my Mother, and at her death she had bequeathed that desire to my Father, like a dream of the Promised Land.* In their ecstasy, my parents had taken me, as Elkanah and Hannah had long ago taken Samuel, from their moun-tain-home of Rama-thaim-Zophim down to sacrifice to the Lord of Hosts in Shiloh. They had girt me about with a linen ephod, and had hoped to leave me there; 'as long as he liveth,' they had said, 'he shall be lent unto the Lord.'*

Doubtless in the course of these fourteen years it had occasionally flashed upon my Father, as he overheard some speech of mine, or detected some idiosyncrasy, that I was not one of those whose tem-perament points them out as ultimately fitted for an austere life of religion. What he hoped, however, was that when the little rough-nesses of childhood were rubbed away, there would pass a deep mellowness over my soul. He had a touching way of condoning my faults of conduct, directly after reproving them, and he would softly deprecate my frailty, saying, in a tone of harrowing tenderness, 'Are you not the child of many prayers?' He continued to think that prayer, such passionate importunate prayer as his, must prevail. Faith could move mountains;* should it not be able to mould the little ductile heart of a child, since he was sure that his own faith was

154 *Father and Son*

unfaltering? He had yearned and waited for a son who should be totally without human audacities, who should be humble, pure, not troubled by worldly agitations, a son whose life should be cleansed and straightened from above, *in custodiendo sermones Dei;** in whom everything should be sacrificed except the one thing needful to salvation.

How such a marvel of lowly piety was to earn a living had never, I think, occurred to him. My Father was singularly indifferent about money. Perhaps his notion was that, totally devoid of ambitions as I was to be, I should quietly become adult, and continue his ministrations among the poor of the Christian flock. He had some dim dream, I think, of there being just enough for us all without my having to take up any business or trade. I believe it was immediately after my first term at boarding-school, that I was a silent but indignant witness of a conversation between my Father and Mr Thomas Brightwen, my stepmother's brother, who was a banker in one of the Eastern Counties.

This question 'what is he to be?' in a worldly sense, was being discussed, and I am sure that it was for the first time, at all events in my presence. Mr Brightwen, I fancy, had been worked upon by my stepmother, whose affection for me was always on the increase, to suggest, or faintly to stir the air in the neighbourhood of suggesting, a query about my future. He was childless and so was she, and I think a kind impulse led them to 'feel the way', as it is called. I believe he said that the banking business, wisely and honourably conducted, sometimes led, as we know that it is apt to lead, to affluence. To my horror, my Father, with rising emphasis, replied that 'if there were offered to his belovèd child what is called "an opening" that would lead to an income of £10,000 a year, and that would divert his thoughts and interest from the Lord's work, he would reject it on his child's behalf'. Mr Brightwen, a precise and polished gentleman, who evidently never made an exaggerated statement in his life, was, I think, faintly scandalised; he soon left us, and I do not recollect his paying us a second visit.

For my silent part, I felt very much like Gehazi,* and I would fain have followed after the banker if I had dared to do so, into the night. I would have excused to him the ardour of my Elisha, and I would have reminded him of the sons of the prophets—'Give me, I pray thee,' I would have said, 'a talent of silver and two changes of garments.' It seemed to me very hard that my Father should dispose of my possibilities of wealth in so summary a fashion, but the fact that I did resent it, and regretted what I supposed to be my 'chance', shows how far apart we had already swung. My Father, I am convinced, thought that he gave words to my inward instincts when he repudiated the very mild and inconclusive benevolence of his brother-in-law. But he certainly did not do so. I was conscious of a sharp and instinctive disappointment at having had, as I fancied, wealth so near my grasp, and at seeing it all cast violently into the sea of my Father's scruples.

Not one of my village friends attended the boarding-school to which I was now attached, and I arrived there without an acquaintance. I should soon, however, have found a corner of my own if my Father had not unluckily stipulated that I was not to sleep in the dormitory with boys of my own age, but in the room occupied by the two elder sons of a prominent Plymouth Brother whom he knew. From a social point of view, this was an unfortunate arrangement, since these youths were some years older and many years riper than I; the eldest, in fact, was soon to leave; they had enjoyed their independence, and they now greatly resented being saddled with the presence of an unknown urchin. The supposition had been that they would protect and foster my religious practices; would encourage me, indeed, as my Father put it, to approach the Throne of Grace with them at morning and evening prayer. They made no pretence, however, to be considered godly; they looked upon me as an intruder; and after a while the younger, and ruder, of them openly let me know that they believed I had been put into their room to 'spy upon' them: it had been a plot, they knew, between their father and mine: and he darkly warned me that I should suffer if 'anything got out'. I had, however, no wish to trouble them, nor any faint interest in their affairs. I soon discovered that they were absorbed in a silly kind of amorous correspondence with the girls of a neighbouring academy, but 'what were all such toys to me?'

These young fellows, who ought long before to have left the school, did nothing overtly unkind to me, but they condemned me to silence. They ceased to address me except with an occasional command. By reason of my youth, I was in bed and asleep before my companions arrived upstairs, and in the morning I was always routed up and packed about my business while they still were drowsing. But the fact that I had been cut off from my coevals by night, cut me off from them also by day—so that I was nothing to them, neither a boarder nor a day-scholar, neither flesh, fish nor fowl. The loneliness of my life was extreme, and that I always went home on Saturday afternoon and returned on Monday morning still further checked my companionships at school. For a long time, round the outskirts of that busy throng of opening lives, I 'wandered lonely as a cloud',* and sometimes I was more unhappy than I had ever been before. No one, however, bullied me, and though I was dimly and indefinably witness to acts of uncleanness and cruelty, I was the victim of no such acts and the recipient of no dangerous confidences. I suppose that my queer reputation for sanctity, half dreadful, half ridiculous, surrounded me with a non-conducting atmosphere.

We are the victims of hallowed proverbs, and one of the most classic of these tells us that 'the child is father of the man'.* But in my case I cannot think that this was true. In mature years I have always been gregarious, a lover of my kind, dependent upon the company of friends for the very pulse of moral life. To be marooned, to be shut up in a solitary cell, to inhabit a lighthouse, or to camp alone in a forest, these have always seemed to me afflictions too heavy to be borne, even in imagination. A state in which conversation exists not, is for me an air too empty of oxygen for my lungs to breathe it.

Yet when I look back upon my days at boarding school, I see myself unattracted by any of the human beings around me. My grown-up years are made luminous to me in memory by the ardent faces of my friends, but I can scarce recall so much as the names of more than two or three of my schoolfellows. There is not one of them whose mind or whose character made any lasting impression upon me. In later life, I have been impatient of solitude, and afraid of it; at school, I asked for no more than to slip out of the hurly-burly and be alone with my reflections and my fancies. That magnetism of humanity which has been the agony of mature years, of this I had not a trace when I was a boy. Of those fragile loves to which most men look back with tenderness and passion, emotions to be explained only as Montaigne explained them, '*parceque c'était lui, parceque c'était moi*',* I knew nothing. I, to whom friendship has since been like sunlight and like sleep, left school unbrightened and unrefreshed by commerce with a single friend.

If I had been clever, I should doubtless have attracted the jealousy of my fellows, but I was spared this by the mediocrity of my success in the classes. One little fact I may mention, because it exemplifies the advance in observation which has been made in forty years. I was extremely nearsighted and in consequence was placed at a gross disadvantage, by being unable to see the slate or the black-board on which our tasks were explained. It seems almost incredible, when one reflects upon it, but during the whole of my school life, this fact was never commented upon or taken into account by a single person, until the Polish lady who taught us the elements of German and French drew some one's attention to it in my sixteenth year. I was not quick, but I passed for being denser than I was because of the myopic haze that enveloped me. But this is not an autobiography,* and with the cold and shrouded details of my uninteresting school life I will not fatigue the reader.

I was not content, however, to be the cipher that I found myself, and when I had been at school for about a year, I 'broke out', greatly, I think, to my own surprise, in a popular act. We had a young usher whom we disliked. I suppose, poor half-starved phthisic lad,* that he was the most miserable of us all. He was, I think, unfitted for the task which had been forced upon him; he was fretful, unsympathetic, agitated. The school-house, an old rambling place, possessed a long cellar-like room that opened from our general corridor and was lighted by deep windows, carefully barred, which looked into an inner garden. This vault was devoted to us and to our play-boxes: by a tacit law, no master entered it. One evening, just at dusk, a great number of us were here when the bell for night-school rang, and many of us dawdled at the summons. Mr B., tactless in his anger, bustled in among us, scolding in a shrill voice, and proceeded to drive us forth. I was the latest to emerge, and as he turned away to see if any other truant might not be hiding, I determined upon action. With a quick movement, I drew the door behind me and bolted it, just in time to hear the imprisoned usher scream with vexation. We boys all trooped upstairs, and it is characteristic of my isolation that I had not one 'chum'* to whom I could confide my feat.

That Mr B. had been shut in became, however, almost instantly known, and the night-class, usually so unruly, was awed by the event into exemplary decorum. There, with no master near us, in a silence rarely broken by a giggle or a cat-call, we sat diligently working, or pretending to work. Through my brain, as I hung over my book, a thousand new thoughts began to surge. I was the liberator, the tyrannicide,* I had freed all my fellows from the odious oppressor. Surely, when they learned that it was I, they would cluster round me; surely, now, I should be somebody in the school-life, no longer a mere trotting shadow or invisible presence. The interval seemed long; at length Mr B. was released by a servant, and he came up into the school-room to find us in that ominous condition of suspense.

At first he said nothing. He sank upon a chair in a half-fainting attitude, while he pressed his hand to his side; his distress and silence redoubled the boys' surprise, and filled me with something like remorse. For the first time, I reflected that he was human, that perhaps he suffered. He rose presently and took a slate, upon which he wrote two questions: 'Did you do it?' 'Do you know who did?' and these he propounded to each boy in rotation. The prompt, redoubled 'No' in every case seemed to pile up his despair.

One of the last to whom he held, in silence, the trembling slate was the perpetrator. As I saw the moment approach, an unspeakable timidity swept over me. I reflected that no one had seen me, that no one could accuse me. Nothing could be easier or safer than to deny, nothing more perplexing to the enemy, nothing less perilous for the culprit. A flood of plausible reasons invaded my brain; I seemed to see this to be a case in which to tell the truth would be not merely foolish, it would be wrong. Yet when the usher stood before me, holding the slate out in his white and shaking hand, I seized the pencil, and, ignoring the first question, I wrote 'Yes' firmly against the second. I suppose that the ambiguity of this action puzzled Mr B. He pressed me to answer: 'Did *you* do it?' but to that I was obstinately dumb; and away I was hurried to an empty bed-room, where for the whole of that night and the next day I was held a prisoner, visited at intervals by the head-master and other in-quisitorial persons, until I was gradually persuaded to make a full confession and apology.

This absurd little incident had one effect, it revealed me to my schoolfellows as an existence. From that time forth I lay no longer under the stigma of invisibility; I had produced my material shape and had thrown my shadow for a moment into a legend. But, in other respects, things went on much as before: curiously uninfluenced by my surroundings, I in my turn failed to exercise influence, and my practical isolation was no less than it had been before. It was thus that it came about that my social memories of my boarding-school life are monotonous and vague. It was a period during which, as it appears to me now on looking back, the stream of my spiritual nature spread out into a shallow pool which was almost stagnant. I was labouring to gain those elements of conventional knowledge, which had, in many cases, up to that time been singularly lacking. But my brain was starved, and my intellectual perceptions were veiled. Elder persons who in later years would speak to me frankly of my school-days assured me that, while I had often struck them as a smart and quaint and even interesting child, all promise seemed to fade out of me as a school-boy, and that those who were most inclined to be indulgent gave up the hope that I should prove a man in any way remarkable. This was particularly the case with the most indulgent of my protectors, my refined and gentle stepmother.

As this record can, however, have no value that is not based on its rigorous adhesion to the truth, I am bound to say that the dreariness and sterility of my school-life were more apparent than real. I was pursuing certain lines of moral and mental development all the time, and since my schoolmasters and my schoolfellows combined in thinking me so dull, I will display a tardy touch of 'proper spirit' and ask whether it may not partly have been because they were themselves so commonplace. I think that if some drops of sympathy, that magic dew of Paradise, had fallen upon my desert, it might have blossomed like the rose, or, at all events, like that chimerical flower, the Rose of Jericho.* As it was, the conventionality around me, the intellectual drought, gave me no opportunity of outward growth. They did not destroy, but they cooped up, and rendered slow and inefficient, that internal life which continued, as I have said, to live on unseen. This took the form of dreams and speculations, in the course of which I went through many tortuous processes of the mind, the actual aims of which were futile, although the movements themselves were useful. If I may more minutely define my meaning, I would say that in my school-days, without possessing thoughts, I yet prepared my mind for thinking, and learned how to think.

The great subject of my curiosity at this time was words, as instruments of expression. I was incessant in adding to my vocabulary, and in finding accurate and individual terms for things. Here, too, the exercise preceded the employment, since I was busy providing myself with words before I had any ideas to express with them. When I read Shakespeare* and came upon the passage in which

Prospero tells Caliban that he had no thoughts till his master taught
him words, I remember starting with amazement at the poet's intu-
ition, for such a Caliban had I been:

> I pitied thee,
> Took pains to make thee speak, taught thee each hour
> One thing or other, when thou didst not, savage,
> Know thine own meaning, but wouldst gabble, like
> A thing most brutish; I endow'd thy purposes
> With words that made them know.

For my Prosperos I sought vaguely in such books as I had access to,
and I was conscious that as the inevitable word seized hold of me,
with it out of the darkness into strong light came the image and the
idea.

My Father possessed a copy of Bailey's 'Etymological Dictionary',
a book published early in the eighteenth century.* Over this I would
pore for hours, playing with the words in a fashion which I can no
longer reconstruct, and delighting in the savour of the rich, old-
fashioned country phrases. My Father finding me thus employed,
fell to wondering at the nature of my pursuit, and I could offer him,
indeed, no very intelligible explanation of it. He urged me to give up
such idleness, and to make practical use of language. For this purpose he conceived an exercise which he obliged me to adopt,
although it was hateful to me. He sent me forth, it might be, up the
lane to Warbury Hill* and round home by the copses; or else down
one chine* to the sea and along the shingle to the next cutting in the
cliff, and so back by way of the village; and he desired me to put
down, in language as full as I could, all that I had seen in each
excursion. As I have said, this practice was detestable and irksome to
me, but, as I look back, I am inclined to believe it to have been the
most salutary, the most practical piece of training which my Father
ever gave me. It forced me to observe sharply and clearly, to form
visual impressions, to retain them in the brain, and to clothe them in
punctilious and accurate language.

It was in my fifteenth year that I became again, this time intelli-
gently, acquainted with Shakespeare. I got hold of a single play, *The
Tempest*, in a school edition, prepared, I suppose, for one of the
university examinations which were then being instituted in the
provinces. This I read through and through, not disdaining the help

of the notes, and revelling in the glossary. I studied *The Tempest* as I had hitherto studied no classic work, and it filled my whole being with music and romance. This book was my own hoarded posses-sion; the rest of Shakespeare's works were beyond my hopes. But gradually I contrived to borrow a volume here and a volume there. I completed *The Merchant of Venice*, read *Cymbeline, Julius Cæsar* and *Much Ado*; most of the others, I think, remained closed to me for a long time. But these were enough to steep my horizon with all the colours of sunrise. It was due, no doubt, to my bringing up, that the plays never appealed to me as bounded by the exigencies of a stage or played by actors. The images they raised in my mind were of real people moving in the open air, and uttering, in the natural play of life, sentiments that were clothed in the most lovely, and yet, as it seemed to me, the most obvious and the most inevitable language.

It was while I was thus under the full spell of the Shakespearean necromancy* that a significant event occurred. My Father took me up to London for the first time since my infancy. Our visit was one of a few days only, and its purpose was that we might take part in some enormous Evangelical conference. We stayed in a dark hotel off the Strand,* where I found the noise by day and night very afflicting. When we were not at the conference, I spent long hours, among crumbs and blue-bottle flies, in the coffee-room of this hotel, my Father being busy at the British Museum and the Royal Society. The conference was held in an immense hall, somewhere in the north of London.* I remember my short-sighted sense of the terrible vastness of the crowd, with rings on rings of dim white faces fading in the fog. My Father, as a privileged visitor, was obliged with seats on the platform, and we were in the heart of the first really large assemblage of persons that I had ever seen.

The interminable ritual of prayers, hymns and addresses left no impression on my memory, but my attention was suddenly stung into life by a remark. An elderly man, fat and greasy, with a voice like a bassoon, and an imperturbable assurance, was denouncing the spread of infidelity, and the lukewarmness of professing Christians, who refrained from battling the wickedness at their doors. They were like the Laodiceans, whom the Angel of the Apocalypse spewed out of his mouth. For instance, who, the orator asked, is now rising to check the outburst of idolatry in our midst? 'At this very moment,' he went on, 'there is proceeding, unreproved, a blasphemous celebration of the birth of Shakespeare,* a lost soul now suffering for his sins in hell!' My sensation was that of one who has suddenly been struck on the head; stars and sparks beat round me. If some person I loved had been grossly insulted in my presence, I could not have felt more powerless in anguish. No one in that vast audience raised a word of protest, and my spirits fell to their nadir. This, be it remarked, was the earliest intimation that had reached me of the tercentenary of the Birth at Stratford,* and I had not the least idea what could have provoked the outburst of outraged godliness.

But Shakespeare was certainly in the air. When we returned to the hotel that noon, my Father of his own accord reverted to the subject. I held my breath, prepared to endure fresh torment. What he said, however, surprised and relieved me. 'Brother So-and-so', he remarked, 'was not, in my judgment, justified in saying what he did. The uncovenanted mercies of God are not revealed to us. Before so rashly speaking of Shakespeare as "a lost soul in hell", he should have remembered how little we know of the poet's history. The light of salvation was widely disseminated in the land during the reign of Queen Elizabeth, and we cannot know that Shakespeare did not accept the atonement of Christ in simple faith before he came to die.' The concession will to-day seem meagre to gay and worldly spirits, but words cannot express how comfortable it was to me. I gazed at my Father with loving eyes across the cheese and celery, and if the waiter had not been present I believe I might have hugged him in my arms.

This anecdote may serve to illustrate the attitude of my conscience, at this time, with regard to theology. I was not consciously in any revolt against the strict faith in which I had been brought up, but I could not fail to be aware of the fact that literature tempted me to stray up innumerable paths which meandered in directions at right angles to that direct strait way which leadeth to salvation. I fancied, if I may pursue the image, that I was still safe up these pleasant lanes if I did not stray far enough to lose sight of the main road. If, for instance, it had been quite certain that Shakespeare had been irrecoverably damnable and damned, it would scarcely have been possible for me to have justified myself in going on reading *Cymbeline*. One who broke bread with the Saints every Sunday morning, who 'took a class' at Sunday school, who made, as my Father loved to remind me, a public weekly confession of his willingness to bear the

Cross of Christ, such an one could hardly, however bewildering and torturing the thought, continue to admire a lost soul. But that happy possibility of an ultimate repentance, how it eased me! I could always console myself with the belief that when Shakespeare wrote any passage of intoxicating beauty, it was just then that he was beginning to breathe the rapture that faith in Christ brings to the anointed soul. And it was with a like casuistry that I condoned my other intellectual and personal pleasures.

My Father continued to be under the impression that my boarding-school, which he never again visited after originally leaving me there, was conducted upon the same principles as his own household. I was frequently tempted to enlighten him, but I never found the courage to do so. As a matter of fact the piety of the establishment, which collected to it the sons of a large number of evangelically minded parents throughout that part of the country, resided mainly in the prospectus. It proceeded no further than the practice of reading the Bible aloud, each boy in successive order one verse, in the early morning before breakfast. There was no selection and no exposition; where the last boy sat, there the day's reading ended, even if it were in the middle of a sentence, and there it began next morning.

Such reading of 'the chapter' was followed by a long dry prayer. I do not know that this morning service would appear more perfunctory than usual to other boys, but it astounded and disgusted me, accustomed as I was to the ministrations at home, where my Father read 'the word of God' in a loud passionate voice, with dramatic emphasis, pausing for commentary and paraphrase, and treating every phrase as if it were part of a personal message or of thrilling family history. At school, 'morning prayer' was a dreary, unintelligible exercise, and with this piece of mumbo-jumbo,* religion for the day began and ended. The discretion of little boys is extraordinary. I am quite certain no one of us ever revealed this fact to our godly parents at home.

If any one was to do this, it was of course I who should first of all have 'testified'.* But I had grown cautious about making confidences. One never knew how awkwardly they might develop or to what disturbing excesses of zeal they might precipitously lead. I was on my guard against my Father, who was, all the time, only too openly yearning that I should approach him for help, for comfort, for ghostly counsel. Still 'delicate', though steadily gaining in solidity of constitution, I was liable to severe chills and to fugitive neuralgic pangs. My Father was, almost maddeningly, desirous that these afflictions should be sanctified to me, and it was in my bed, often when I was much bowed in spirit by indisposition, that he used to triumph over me most pitilessly. He retained the singular superstition, amazing in a man of scientific knowledge and long human experience, that all pains and ailments were directly sent by the Lord in chastisement for some definite fault, and not in relation to any physical cause. The result was sometimes quite startling, and in particular I recollect that my stepmother and I exchanged impressions of astonishment at my Father's action when Mrs Goodyer, who was one of the 'Saints' and the wife of a young journeyman cobbler, broke her leg. My Father, puzzled for an instant as to the meaning of this accident, since Mrs Goodyer was the gentlest and most inoffensive of our church members, decided that it must be because she had made an idol of her husband, and he reduced the poor thing to tears by standing at her bed-side and imploring the Holy Spirit to bring this sin home to her conscience.

When, therefore, I was ill at home with one of my trifling disorders, the problem of my spiritual state always pressed violently upon my Father, and this caused me no little mental uneasiness. He would appear at my bed-side, with solemn solicitude, and sinking on his knees would earnestly pray aloud that the purpose of the Lord in sending me this affliction might graciously be made plain to me; and then, rising, and standing by my pillow, he would put me through a searching spiritual inquiry as to the fault which was thus divinely indicated to me as observed and reprobated on high.

It was not on points of moral behaviour that he thus cross-examined me; I think he disdained such ignoble game as that. But uncertainties of doctrine, relinquishment of faith in the purity of this dogma or of that, lukewarm zeal in 'taking up the cross of Christ', growth of intellectual pride,—such were the insidious offences in consequence of which, as he supposed, the cold in the head or the toothache had been sent as heavenly messengers to recall my straggling conscience to its plain path of duty.

What made me very uncomfortable on these occasions was my consciousness that confinement to bed was hardly an affliction at all. It kept me from the boredom of school, in a fire-lit bed-room at home, with my pretty, smiling stepmother lavishing luxurious attendance upon me, and it gave me long, unbroken days for reading. I was awkwardly aware that I simply had not the effrontery to 'approach the Throne of Grace' with a request to know for what sin I was condemned to such a very pleasant disposition of my hours.

The current of my life ran, during my school-days, most merrily and fully in the holidays, when I resumed my out-door exercises with those friends in the village of whom I have spoken earlier. I think they were more refined and better bred than any of my school-fellows, at all events it was among these homely companions alone that I continued to form congenial and sympathetic relations. In one of these boys,—one of whom I have heard or seen nothing now for nearly a generation,—I found tastes singularly parallel to my own, and we scoured the horizon in search of books in prose and verse, but particularly in verse.

As I grew stronger in muscle, I was capable of adding considerably to my income by an exercise of my legs. I was allowed money for the railway ticket between the town where the school lay and the station nearest to my home. But, if I chose to walk six or seven miles along the coast, thus more than halving the distance by rail from school house to home, I might spend as pocket-money the railway fare I thus saved. Such considerable sums I fostered in order to buy with them editions of the poets. These were not in those days, as they are now, at the beck and call of every purse, and the attainment of each little masterpiece was a separate triumph. In particular I shall never forget the excitement of reaching at last the exorbitant price the bookseller asked for the only, although imperfect, edition of the poems of S. T. Coleridge. At last I could meet his demand, and my friend and I went down to consummate the solemn purchase. Coming away with our treasure, we read aloud from the orange-coloured volume, in turns, as we strolled along, until at last we sat down on the bulging root of an elm-tree in a secluded lane. Here we stayed, in a sort of poetical *nirvana*,* reading, reading, forgetting the passage of time, until the hour of our neglected mid-day meal was a long while past, and we had to hurry home to bread and cheese and a scolding.

There was occasionally some trouble about my reading, but now not much nor often. I was rather adroit, and careful not to bring prominently into sight anything of a literary kind which could become a stone of stumbling. But, when I was nearly sixteen, I made a purchase which brought me into sad trouble, and was the cause of a permanent wound to my self-respect. I had long coveted in the book-shop window a volume in which the poetical works of Ben Jonson and Christopher Marlowe* were said to be combined. This I bought at length, and I carried it with me to devour as I trod the desolate road that brought me along the edge of the cliff on Saturday afternoons. Ben Jonson I could make nothing of, but when I turned to 'Hero and Leander',* I was lifted to a heaven of passion and music. It was a marvellous revelation of romantic beauty to me, and as I paced along that lonely and exquisite high-way, with its immense command of the sea, and its peeps every now and then, through slanting thickets, far down to the snow-white shingle, I lifted up my voice, singing the verses, as I strolled along:

> Buskins of shells, all silver'd, usèd she,
> And branch'd with blushing coral to the knee,
> Where sparrows perched, of hollow pearl and gold,
> Such as the world would wonder to behold,—*

so it went on, and I thought I had never read anything so lovely,—

> Amorous Leander, beautiful and young,
> Whose tragedy divine Musaeus sung,—*

it all seemed to my fancy intoxicating beyond anything I had ever even dreamed of, since I had not yet become acquainted with any of the modern romanticists.*

When I reached home, tired out with enthusiasm and exercise, I must needs, so soon as I had eaten, search out my stepmother that she might be a partner in my joys. It is remarkable to me now, and a disconcerting proof of my still almost infantile innocence, that, having induced her to settle to her knitting, I began, without hesitation, to read Marlowe's voluptuous poem aloud to that blameless Christian gentlewoman. We got on very well in the opening, but at the episode of Cupid's pining, my stepmother's needles began nervously to clash, and when we launched on the description of Leander's person,* she interrupted me by saying, rather sharply, 'Give me that book, please, I should like to read the rest to myself.' I resigned the reading in amazement, and was stupefied to see her take the volume, shut it with a snap and hide it under her needlework. Nor could I extract from her another word on the subject.

The matter passed from my mind, and I was therefore extremely alarmed when, soon after my going to bed that night, my Father came into my room with a pale face and burning eyes, the prey of violent perturbation. He set down the candle and stood by the bed, and it was some time before he could resolve on a form of speech. Then he denounced me, in unmeasured terms, for bringing into the house, for possessing at all or reading, so abominable a book. He explained that my stepmother had shown it to him, and that he had looked through it, and had burned it.

The sentence in his tirade which principally affected me was this. He said, 'You will soon be leaving us, and going up to lodgings in London, and if your landlady should come into your room, and find such a book lying about, she would immediately set you down as a profligate.' I did not understand this at all, and it seems to me now that the fact that I had so very simply and childishly volunteered to read the verses to my stepmother should have proved to my Father that I connected it with no ideas of an immoral nature.

I was greatly wounded and offended, but my indignation was smothered up in the alarm and excitement which followed the news that I was to go up to live in lodgings and, as it was evident, alone, in London. Of this no hint or whisper had previously reached me. On reflection, I can but admit that my Father, who was little accustomed to seventeenth-century literature, must have come across some start-ling exposures in Ben Jonson, and probably never reached 'Hero and Leander' at all. The artistic effect of such poetry on an innocently pagan mind* did not come within the circle of his experience. He judged the outspoken Elizabethan poets, no doubt, very much in the spirit of the problematical landlady.

Of the world outside, of the dim wild whirlpool of London, I was much afraid, but I was now ready to be willing to leave the narrow Devonshire circle, to see the last of the red mud, of the dreary village street, of the plethoric elders,* to hear the last of the drawling voices of the 'Saints'. Yet I had a great difficulty in persuading myself that I could ever be happy away from home, and again I compared my lot with that of one of the speckled soldier-crabs that roamed about in my Father's aquarium, dragging after them great whorl-shells. They, if by chance they were turned out of their whelk-habitations, trailed about a pale soft body in search of another house, visibly broken-hearted and the victims of every ignominious accident.

My spirits were divided pathetically between the wish to stay on, a guarded child, and to proceed into the world, a budding man, and, in my utter ignorance, I sought in vain to conjure up what my immediate future would be. My Father threw no light upon the subject, for he had not formed any definite idea of what I could possibly do to earn an honest living. As a matter of fact I was to stay another year at school and home.

This last year of my boyish life passed rapidly and pleasantly. My sluggish brain waked up at last and I was able to study with application. In the public examinations I did pretty well, and may even have been thought something of a credit to the school. Yet I formed no close associations, and I even contrived to avoid, as I had afterwards occasion to regret, such lessons as were distasteful to me, and therefore particularly valuable. But I read with unchecked voracity, and in several curious directions. Shakespeare now passed into my possession entire, in the shape of a reprint more hideous and more offensive to the eyesight than would in these days appear conceivable. I made acquaintance with Keats,* who entirely captivated me; with Shelley, whose 'Queen Mab'* at first repelled me from the threshold of his edifice; and with Wordsworth,* for the exercise of whose magic I was still far too young. My Father presented me with the entire bulk of Southey's stony verse,* which I found it impossible to penetrate, but my stepmother lent me 'The Golden Treasury',* in which almost everything seemed exquisite.

Upon this extension of my intellectual powers, however, there did not follow any spirit of doubt or hostility to the faith. On the contrary, at first there came a considerable quickening of fervour. My prayers became less frigid and mechanical; I no longer avoided as far as possible the contemplation of religious ideas; I began to search the Scriptures for myself with interest and sympathy, if scarcely with ardour. I began to perceive, without animosity, the strange narrowness of my Father's system, which seemed to take into consideration only a selected circle of persons, a group of disciples peculiarly illuminated, and to have no message whatever for the wider Christian community.

On this subject I had some instructive conversations with my Father, whom I found not reluctant to have his convictions pushed to their logical extremity. He did not wish to judge, he protested; but he could not admit that a single Unitarian (or 'Socinian', as he preferred to say)* could possibly be redeemed; and he had no hope of eternal salvation for the inhabitants of Catholic countries. I recollect his speaking of Austria. He questioned whether a single Austrian subject, except, as he said, here and there a pious and extremely ignorant individual, who had not comprehended the errors of the Papacy, but had humbly studied his Bible, could hope to find eternal life. He thought that the ordinary Chinaman or savage native of Fiji had a better chance of salvation than any cardinal in the Vatican. And even in the priesthood of the Church of England he believed that while many were called, few indeed would be found to have been chosen.

I could not sympathise, even in my then state of ignorance, with so rigid a conception of the Divine mercy. Little inclined as I was to be sceptical, I still thought it impossible, that a secret of such stupendous importance should have been entrusted to a little group of Plymouth Brethren, and have been hidden from millions of disinterested and pious theologians. That the leaders of European Christianity were sincere, my Father did not attempt to question. But they were all of them wrong, *incorrect*; and no matter how holy their lives, how self-sacrificing their actions, they would have to suffer for their inexactitude through æons of undefined torment. He would speak with a solemn complacency of the aged nun, who, after a long life of renunciation and devotion, died at last, 'only to discover her mistake'.

He who was so tender-hearted that he could not bear to witness the pain or distress of any person, however disagreeable or undeserving, was quite acquiescent in believing that God would punish human beings, in millions, for ever, for a purely intellectual error of comprehension. My Father's inconsistencies of perception seem to me to have been the result of a curious irregularity of equipment. Taking for granted, as he did, the absolute integrity of the Scriptures, and applying to them his trained scientific spirit, he contrived to stifle with a deplorable success alike the function of the imagination, the sense of moral justice, and his own deep and instinctive tenderness of heart.

There presently came over me a strong desire to know what doctrine indeed it was that the other Churches taught. I expressed a wish to be made aware of the practices of Rome, or at least of Canterbury, and I longed to attend the Anglican and the Roman services. But to do so was impossible. My Father did not, indeed, forbid me to enter the fine parish church of our village, or the stately Puginesque cathedral* which Rome had just erected at its side, but I knew that I could not be seen at either service without his immediately knowing it, or without his being deeply wounded. Although I was sixteen years of age, and although I was treated with indulgence and affection, I was still but a bird fluttering in the net-work of my Father's will, and incapable of the smallest independent action. I resigned all thought of attending any other services than those at our 'Room', but I did no longer regard this exclusion as a final one. I bowed, but it was in the house of Rimmon,* from which I now knew that I must inevitably escape. All the liberation, however, which I desired or dreamed of was only just so much as would bring me into communion with the outer world of Christianity, without divesting me of the pure and simple principles of faith.

Of so much emancipation, indeed, I now became ardently desirous, and in the contemplation of it I rose to a more considerable degree of religious fervour than I had ever reached before or was ever to experience later. Our thoughts were at this time abundantly exercised with the expectation of the immediate coming of the Lord, who, as my Father and those who thought with him believed, would suddenly appear, without the least warning, and would catch up to be with Him in everlasting glory all whom acceptance of the Atonement had sealed for immortality. These were, on the whole, not numerous, and our belief was that the world, after a few days' amazement at the total disappearance of these persons, would revert to its customary habits of life, merely sinking more rapidly into a moral corruption due to the removal of these souls of salt. This event an examination of prophecy had led my Father to regard as absolutely imminent, and sometimes, when we parted for the night, he would say with a sparkling rapture in his eyes, 'Who knows? We may meet next in the air, with all the cohorts of God's saints!'

This conviction I shared, without a doubt; and, indeed,—in perfect innocency, I hope, but perhaps with a touch of slyness too,—I proposed at the end of the summer holidays that I should stay at home. 'What is the use of my going to school? Let me be with you when we rise to meet the Lord in the air!' To this my Father sharply and firmly replied that it was our duty to carry on our usual avocations to the last, for we knew not the moment of His coming, and we should be together in an instant on that day, how far soever we might be parted upon earth. I was ashamed, but his argument was logical, and, as it proved, judicious. My Father lived for nearly a quarter of a century more, never losing the hope of 'not tasting death', and as the last moments of mortality approached, he was bitterly disappointed at what he held to be a scanty reward of his long faith and patience. But if my own life's work had been, as I proposed, shelved in expectation of the Lord's imminent advent, I should have cumbered the ground until this day.

To school, therefore, I returned with a brain full of strange discords, in a huddled mixture of 'Endymion' and the Book of Revelation, John Wesley's hymns and *Midsummer Night's Dream*.* Few boys of my age, I suppose, carried about with them such a confused throng of immature impressions and contradictory hopes. I was at one moment devoutly pious, at the next haunted by visions of material beauty and longing for sensuous impressions. In my hot and silly brain, Jesus and Pan held sway together,* as in a wayside chapel discordantly and impishly consecrated to Pagan and to Christian rites. But for the present, as in the great chorus which so marvellously portrays our double nature, 'the folding-star of Bethlehem'* was still dominant. I became more and more pietistic. Beginning now to versify, I wrote a tragedy in pale imitation of Shakespeare,* but on a Biblical and evangelistic subject; and odes that were imitations of those in 'Prometheus Unbound',* but dealt with the approaching advent of our Lord and the rapture of His saints. My unwholesome excitement, bubbling up in this violent way, reached at last a climax and foamed over.

It was a summer afternoon, and, being now left very free in my movements, I had escaped from going out with the rest of my schoolfellows in their formal walk in charge of an usher. I had been reading a good deal of poetry, but my heart had translated Apollo and Bacchus* into terms of exalted Christian faith. I was alone, and I lay on a sofa, drawn across a large open window at the top of the schoolhouse, in a room which was used as a study by the boys who were 'going up for examination'.* I gazed down on a labyrinth of gardens sloping to the sea, which twinkled faintly beyond the towers of the town. Each of these gardens held a villa in it, but all the near landscape below me was drowned in foliage. A wonderful warm light of approaching sunset modelled the shadows and set the broad summits of the trees in a rich glow. There was an absolute silence below and around me, a magic of suspense seemed to keep every topmost twig from waving.

Over my soul there swept an immense wave of emotion. Now, surely, now the great final change must be approaching. I gazed up into the faintly-coloured sky, and I broke irresistibly into speech. 'Come now, Lord Jesus,' I cried, 'come now and take me to be for ever with Thee in Thy Paradise. I am ready to come. My heart is purged from sin, there is nothing that keeps me rooted to this wicked world. Oh, come now, now, and take me before I have known the temptations of life, before I have to go to London and all the dreadful things that happen there!' And I raised myself on the sofa, and leaned upon the window-sill, and waited for the glorious apparition.

This was the highest moment of my religious life, the apex of my striving after holiness. I waited awhile, watching; and then I had a little shame at the theatrical attitude I had adopted, although I was alone. Still I gazed and still I hoped. Then a little breeze sprang up, and the branches danced. Sounds began to rise from the road beneath me. Presently the colour deepened, the evening came on. From far below there rose to me the chatter of the boys returning home. The tea-bell rang,—last word of prose to shatter my mystical poetry. 'The Lord has not come, the Lord will never come,' I muttered, and in my heart the artificial edifice of extravagant faith began to totter and crumble. From that moment forth my Father and I, though the fact was long successfully concealed from him and even from myself, walked in opposite hemispheres of the soul, with 'the thick o' the world between us'.*

EPILOGUE

THIS narrative, however, must not be allowed to close with the son in the foreground of the piece. If it has a value, that value consists in what light it may contrive to throw upon the unique and noble figure of the father. With the advance of years, the characteristics of this figure became more severely outlined, more rigorously confined within settled limits. In relation to the son—who presently departed, at a very immature age, for the new life in London*—the attitude of the father continued to be one of extreme solicitude, deepening by degrees into disappointment and disenchantment. He abated no jot or tittle of his demands upon human frailty. He kept the spiritual cord drawn tight; the Biblical bearing-rein was incessantly busy, jerking into position the head of the dejected neophyte.*

That young soul, removed from the father's personal inspection, began to blossom forth crudely and irregularly enough into new provinces of thought, through fresh layers of experience. To the painful mentor at home in the West, the centre of anxiety was still the meek and docile heart, dedicated to the Lord's service, which must, at all hazards and with all defiance of the rules of life, be kept unspotted from the world.

The torment of a postal inquisition began directly I was settled in my London lodgings. To my Father—with his ample leisure, his palpitating apprehension, his ready pen,—the flow of correspondence offered no trouble at all; it was a grave but gratifying occupation. To me the almost daily letter of exhortation, with its string of questions about conduct, its series of warnings, grew to be a burden which could hardly be borne, particularly because it involved a reply as punctual and if possible as full as itself. At the age of seventeen, the metaphysics of the soul are shadowy, and it is a dreadful thing to be forced to define the exact outline of what is so undulating and so shapeless. To my Father there seemed no reason why I should hesitate to give answers of full metallic ring to his hard and oft-repeated questions; but to me this correspondence was torture. When I feebly expostulated, when I begged to be left a little to myself, these appeals of mine automatically stimulated, and indeed blew up into fierce flames, the ardour of my Father's alarm.

The letter, the only too-confidently expected letter, would lie on the table as I descended to breakfast.* It would commonly be, of course, my only letter, unless tempered by a cosy and chatty note from my dear and comfortable stepmother, dealing with such perfectly tranquillising subjects as the harvest of roses in the garden or the state of health of various neighbours. But the other, the solitary letter, in its threatening whiteness, with its exquisitely penned address—there it would lie awaiting me, destroying the taste of the bacon, reducing the flavour of the tea to insipidity. I might fatuously dally with it, I might pretend not to observe it, but there it lay. Before the morning's exercise began, I knew that it had to be read, and what was worse, that it had to be answered. Useless the effort to conceal from myself what it contained. Like all its precursors, like all its followers, it would insist, with every variety of appeal, on a reiterated declaration that I still fully intended, as in the days of my earliest childhood, 'to be on the Lord's side' in everything.

In my replies, I would sometimes answer precisely as I was desired to answer; sometimes I would evade the queries, and write about other things; sometimes I would turn upon the tormentor, and urge that my tender youth might be let alone. It little mattered what form of weakness I put forth by way of baffling my Father's direct, firm, unflinching strength. To an appeal against the bondage of a correspondence of such unbroken solemnity I would receive—with what a paralysing promptitude!—such a reply as this:—

'Let me say that the "solemnity" you complain of has only been the expression of tender anxiousness of a father's heart, that his only child, just turned out upon the world, and very far out of his sight and hearing, should be walking in God's way. Recollect that it is not now as it was when you were at school, when we had personal communication with you at intervals of five days:—we now know absolutely nothing of you, save from your letters, and if they do not indicate your spiritual prosperity, the deepest solicitudes of our hearts have nothing to feed on. But I will try henceforth to trust you, and lay aside my fears; for you are worthy of my confidence; and your own God and your father's God will hold you with His right hand.'

Over such letters as these I am not ashamed to say that I sometimes wept; the old paper I have just been copying shows traces of tears shed upon it more than forty years ago, tears commingled of despair at my own feebleness, distraction at my want of will, pity for my Father's manifest and pathetic distress. He would 'try henceforth to trust' me, he said. Alas! the effort would be in vain; after a day or two, after a hollow attempt to write of other things, the importunate subject would recur; there would intrude again the inevitable questions about the Atonement and the Means of Grace, the old anxious fears lest I was 'yielding' my intimacy to agreeable companions who were not 'one with me in Christ', fresh passionate entreaties to be assured, in every letter, that I was walking in the clear light of God's presence.

It seems to me now profoundly strange, although I knew too little of the world to remark it at the time, that these incessant exhortations dealt, not with conduct, but with faith. Earlier in this narrative I have noted how disdainfully, with what an austere pride, my Father refused to entertain the subject of personal shortcomings in my behaviour. There were enough of them to blame, heaven knows, but he was too lofty-minded a gentleman to dwell upon them, and, though by nature deeply suspicious of the possibility of frequent moral lapses, even in the very elect, he refused to stoop to anything like espionage.

I owe him a deep debt of gratitude for his beautiful faith in me in this respect, and now that I was alone in London, at this tender time of life, 'exposed', as they say, to all sorts of dangers, as defenceless as a fledgling that has been turned out of its nest, yet my Father did not, in his uplifted Quixotism,* allow himself to fancy me guilty of any moral misbehaviour, but concentrated his fears entirely upon my faith.

'Let me know more of your inner light. Does the candle of the Lord shine on your soul?' This would be the ceaseless inquiry. Or, again, 'Do you get any spiritual companionship with young men? You passed over last Sunday without even a word, yet this day is the most interesting to me in your whole week. Do you find the ministry of the Word pleasant, and, above all, profitable? Does it bring your soul into exercise before God? The Coming of Christ draweth nigh. Watch, therefore and pray always, that you may be counted worthy to stand before the Son of Man.'

If I quote such passages as this from my Father's letters to me, it is not that I seek entertainment in a contrast between his earnestness and the casuistical inattention and provoked distractedness of a young man to whom the real world now offered its irritating and stimulating scenes of animal and intellectual life, but to call out sympathy, and perhaps wonder, at the spectacle of so blind a Roman firmness as my Father's spiritual attitude displayed.

His aspirations were individual and metaphysical. At the present hour, so complete is the revolution which has overturned the puritanism of which he was perhaps the latest surviving type, that all classes of religious persons combine in placing philanthropic activity, the objective attitude, in the foreground. It is extraordinary how far-reaching the change has been, so that nowadays a religion which does not combine with its subjective faith a strenuous labour for the good of others is hardly held to possess any religious principle worth holding.

This propaganda of beneficence, this constant attention to the moral and physical improvement of persons who have been neglected, is quite recent as a leading feature of religion, though indeed it seems to have formed some part of the Saviour's original design. It was unknown to the great divines of the seventeenth century, whether Catholic or Protestant, and it offered but a shadowy attraction to my Father, who was the last of their disciples.* When Bossuet desired his hearers to listen to the '*cri de misère à l'entour de nous, qui devrait nous fondre le cœur*',* he started a new thing in the world of theology. We may search the famous 'Rule and Exercises of Holy Living' from cover to cover, and not learn that Jeremy Taylor would have thought that any activity of the district-visitor or the Salvation lassie* came within the category of saintliness.

My Father, then, like an old divine, concentrated his thoughts upon the intellectual part of faith. In his obsession about me, he believed that if my brain could be kept unaffected by any of the tempting errors of the age, and my heart centred in the adoring love of God, all would be well with me in perpetuity. He was still convinced that by intensely directing my thoughts, he could compel them to flow in a certain channel, since he had not begun to learn the lesson, so mournful for saintly men of his complexion, that 'virtue would not be virtue, could it be given by one fellow creature to another'. He had recognised, with reluctance, that holiness was not hereditary, but he continued to hope that it might be compulsive. I was still 'the child of many prayers', and it was not to be conceded that these prayers could remain unanswered.

The great panacea was now, as always, the study of the Bible, and this my Father never ceased to urge upon me. He presented to me a copy of Dean Alford's edition of the Greek New Testament,* in four great volumes, and these he had had so magnificently bound in full morocco that the work shone on my poor shelf of sixpenny poets like a duchess among dairy-maids. He extracted from me a written promise that I would translate and meditate upon a portion of the Greek text every morning before I started for business. This promise I presently failed to keep, my good intentions being undermined by an invincible *ennui*;* I concealed the dereliction from him, and the sense that I was deceiving my Father ate into my conscience like a canker. But the dilemma was now before me that I must either deceive my Father in such things or paralyse my own character.

My growing distaste for the Holy Scriptures began to occupy my thoughts, and to surprise as much as it scandalised me. My desire was to continue to delight in those sacred pages, for which I still had an instinctive veneration. Yet I could not but observe the difference between the zeal with which I snatched at a volume of Carlyle or Ruskin*—since these magicians were now first revealing themselves to me—and the increasing languor with which I took up Alford for my daily 'passage'. Of course, although I did not know it, and believed my reluctance to be sinful, the real reason why I now found the Bible so difficult to read was my familiarity with its contents. These had the colourless triteness of a story retold a hundred times. I longed for something new, something that would gratify curiosity and excite surprise. Whether the facts and doctrines contained in the Bible were true or false was not the question that appealed to me; it was rather that they had been presented to me so often and had sunken into me so far that, as some one has said, they 'lay bedridden in the dormitory of the soul',* and made no impression of any kind upon me.

It often amazed me, and I am still unable to understand the fact, that my Father, through his long life—or till nearly the close of it—continued to take an eager pleasure in the text of the Bible. As I think I have already said, before he reached middle life, he had committed practically the whole of it to memory, and if started anywhere, even in a Minor Prophet,* he could go on without a break as long as ever he was inclined for that exercise. He, therefore, at no time can have been assailed by the satiety of which I have spoken, and that it came so soon to me I must take simply as an indication of difference of temperament. It was not possible, even through the dark glass of correspondence, to deceive his eagle eye in this matter, and his suspicions accordingly took another turn. He conceived me to have become, or to be becoming, a victim of 'the infidelity of the age'.

In this new difficulty, he appealed to forms of modern literature by the side of which the least attractive pages of Leviticus or Deuteronomy* struck me as even thrilling. In particular, he urged upon me a work, then just published, called 'The Continuity of Scripture' by William Page Wood, afterwards Lord Chancellor Hatherley.* I do not know why he supposed that the lucubrations of an exemplary lawyer, delivered in a style that was like the trickling of sawdust, would succeed in rousing emotions which the glorious rhetoric of the Orient* had failed to awaken; but Page Wood had been a Sunday School teacher for thirty years, and my Father was always unduly impressed by the acumen of pious barristers.

As time went on, and I grew older and more independent in mind, my Father's anxiety about what he called 'the pitfalls and snares which surround on every hand the thoughtless giddy youth of London' became extremely painful to himself. By harping in private upon these 'pitfalls'*—which brought to my imagination a funny rough woodcut in an old edition of Bunyan,* where a devil was seen capering over a sort of box let neatly into the ground—he worked himself up into a frame of mind which was not a little irritating to his hapless correspondent, who was now 'snared' indeed, limed by the pen like a bird by the feet, and could not by any means escape. To a peck or a flutter from the bird the implacable fowler would reply:

'You charge me with being suspicious, and I fear I cannot deny the charge. But I can appeal to your own sensitive and thoughtful mind for a considerable allowance. My deep and tender love for you; your youth and inexperience; the examples of other young men; your distance from parental counsel; our absolute and painful ignorance of all the details of your daily life, except what you yourself tell us:—try to throw yourself into the standing of a parent, and say if my suspiciousness is unreasonable. I rejoicingly acknowledge that from all I see you are pursuing a virtuous, steady, worthy course. One good thing my suspiciousness does:—ever and anon it brings out from you assurances, which greatly refresh and comfort me. And again, it carries me ever to God's Throne of Grace on your behalf. Holy Job* *suspected* that his sons might have sinned, and cursed God in their heart. Was not his suspicion much like mine, grounded on the same reasons, and productive of the same results? For it drove him to God in intercession. I have adduced the example of this Patriarch before, and he will endure being looked at again.'

In fact, Holy Job continued to be frequently looked at, and for this Patriarch I came to experience a hatred which was as venomous as it was undeserved. But what youth of eighteen would willingly be compared with the sons of Job? And indeed, for my part, I felt much more like that justly exasperated character, Elihu the Buzite, of the kindred of Ram.*

As time went on, the peculiar strain of inquisition was relaxed, and I endured fewer and fewer of the torments of religious correspondence. Nothing abides in one tense projection, and my Father, resolute as he was, had other preoccupations. His orchids, his microscope, his physiological researches, his interpretations of prophecy, filled up the hours of his active and strenuous life, and, out of his sight, I became not indeed out of his mind, but no longer ceaselessly in the painful foreground of it. Yet, although the reiteration of his anxiety might weary him a little as it had wearied me well nigh to groans of despair, there was not the slightest change in his real attitude towards the subject or towards me.

I have already had occasion to say that he had nothing of the mystic or the visionary about him. At certain times and on certain points, he greatly desired that signs and wonders, such as had astonished and encouraged the infancy of the Christian Church, might again be vouchsafed to it, but he did not pretend to see such miracles himself, nor give the slightest credence to others who asserted that they did. He often congratulated himself on the fact that although his mind dwelt so constantly on spiritual matters it was never betrayed into any suspension of the rational functions.

Cross-examination by letter slackened, but on occasion of my brief and usually summer visits to Devonshire I suffered acutely from my Father's dialectical appetites. He was surrounded by peasants, on whom the teeth of his arguments could find no purchase. To him, in that intellectual Abdera,* even an unwilling youth from London offered opportunities of pleasant contest. He would declare himself ready, nay eager, for argument. With his mental sleeves turned up, he would adopt a fighting attitude, and challenge me to a round on any portion of the Scheme of Grace. His alacrity

was dreadful to me, his well aimed blows fell on what was rather a
bladder or a pillow than a vivid antagonist.

He was, indeed most unfairly handicapped,—I was naked, he in a
suit of chain armour,—for he had adopted a method which I
thought, and must still think, exceedingly unfair. He assumed that
he had private knowledge of the Divine Will, and he would meet my
temporising arguments by asseverations,—'So sure as my God
liveth!' or by appeals to a higher authority,—'But what does *my* Lord
tell me in Paul's Letter to the Philippians?' It was the prerogative of
his faith to know, and of his character to overpower objection;
between these two millstones I was rapidly ground to powder.

These 'discussions', as they were rather ironically called, invariably ended for me in disaster. I was driven out of my *papier-mâché*
fastnesses,* my canvas walls rocked at the first peal from my Father's
clarion, and the foe pursued me across the plains of Jericho* until I
lay down ignominiously and covered my face. I seemed to be pushed
with horns of iron, such as those which Zedekiah the son of
Chenaanah prepared for the encouragement of Ahab.*

When I acknowledged defeat and cried for quarter, my Father
would become radiant, and I still seem to hear the sound of his full
voice, so thrilling, so warm, so painful to my over-strained nerves,
bursting forth in a sort of benediction at the end of each of these
one-sided contentions, with 'I bow my knees unto the Father of our
Lord Jesus Christ, that He would grant you, according to the riches
of his glory, to be strengthened with might by His Spirit in the inner
man; that Christ may dwell in your heart by faith; that you, being
rooted and grounded in love, may be able to comprehend with all
saints what is the breadth, and length, and depth, and height, and to
know, the love of Christ which passeth knowledge, that you might be
filled with the fullness of God.'

Thus solemn, and thus ceremonious was my Father apt to
become, without a moment's warning, on plain and domestic occasions; abruptly brimming over with emotion like a basin which an
unseen flow of water has filled and over-filled.

I earnestly desire that no trace of that absurd self-pity which is apt
to taint recollections of this nature should give falsity to mine. My
Father, let me say once more, had other interests than those of his
religion. In particular, at this time, he took to painting in water-
colours in the open air, and he resumed the assiduous study of

botany. He was no fanatical monomaniac. Nevertheless, there was, in everything he did and said, the central purpose present. He acknowledged it plainly; 'with me,' he confessed, 'every question assumes a Divine standpoint and is not adequately answered if the judgment-seat of Christ is not kept in sight.'

This was maintained whether the subject under discussion was poetry, or society, or the Prussian war with Austria,* or the stamen of a wild flower. Once, at least, he was himself conscious of the fatiguing effect on my temper of this insistency, for, raising his great brown eyes with a flash of laughter in them, he closed the Bible suddenly after a very lengthy disquisition, and quoted his Virgil to startling effect:—

Claudite jam rivos, pueri: sat prata biberunt.*

The insistency of his religious conversation was, probably, the less incomprehensible to me on account of the evangelical training to which I had been so systematically subjected. It was, however, none the less intolerably irksome, and would have been exasperating, I believe, even to a nature in which a powerful and genuine piety was inherent. To my own, in which a feeble and imitative faith was expiring, it was deeply vexatious. It led, alas! to a great deal of bowing in the house of Rimmon,* to much hypocritical ingenuity in drawing my Father's attention away, if possible, as the terrible subject was seen to be looming and approaching. In this my stepmother would aid and abet, sometimes producing incongruous themes, likely to attract my Father aside, with a skill worthy of a parlour conjurer, and much to my admiration. If, however, she was not unwilling to come, in this way, to the support of my feebleness, there was no open collusion between us. She always described my Father, when she was alone with me, admiringly, as one 'whose trumpet gave no uncertain sound'. There was not a tinge of infidelity upon her candid mind, but she was human, and I think that now and then she was extremely bored.

My Father was entirely devoid of the prudence which turns away its eyes and passes as rapidly as possible in the opposite direction. The peculiar kind of drama in which every sort of social discomfort is welcomed rather than that the characters should be happy when guilty of 'acting a lie', was not invented in those days, and there can hardly be imagined a figure more remote from my Father than Ibsen.*

Yet when I came, at a far later date, to read 'The Wild Duck',*
memories of the embarrassing household of my infancy helped me
to realise Gregers Werle, with his determination to pull the veil of
illusion away from every compromise that makes life bearable.

I was docile, I was plausible, I was anything but combative; if my
Father could have persuaded himself to let me alone, if he could
merely have been willing to leave my subterfuges and my explanations unanalysed, all would have been well. But he refused to see
any difference in temperament between a lad of twenty and a sage of
sixty. He had no vital sympathy for youth, which in itself had no
charm for him. He had no compassion for the weaknesses of
immaturity, and his one and only anxiety was to be at the end of his
spiritual journey, safe with me in the house where there are many
mansions.* The incidents of human life upon the road to glory were
less than nothing to him.

My Father was very fond of defining what was his own attitude at
this time, and he was never tired of urging the same ambition upon
me. He regarded himself as the faithful steward of a Master who
might return at any moment,* and who would require to find everything ready for his convenience. That master was God, with whom
my Father seriously believed himself to be in relations much more
confidential than those vouchsafed to ordinary pious persons. He
awaited, with anxious hope, 'the coming of the Lord', an event which
he still frequently believed to be imminent. He would calculate, by
reference to prophecies in the Old and New Testament, the exact
date of this event; the date would pass, without the expected Advent,
and he would be more than disappointed,—he would be incensed.
Then he would understand that he must have made some slight error
in calculation, and the pleasures of anticipation would recommence.

Me in all this he used as a kind of inferior coadjutor, much as a
responsible and upper servant might use a footboy. I, also, must be
watching; it was not important that I should be seriously engaged in
any affairs of my own. I must be ready for the Master's coming; and
my Father's incessant cross-examination was made in the spirit of a
responsible servant who fidgets lest some humble but essential piece
of household work has been neglected.

My holidays, however, and all my personal relations with my
Father were poisoned by this insistency. I was never at my ease in his
company; I never knew when I might not be subjected to a series of

searching questions which I should not be allowed to evade. Meanwhile, on every other stage of experience I was gaining the reliance upon self and the respect for the opinion of others which come naturally to a young man of sober habits who earns his own living and lives his own life. For this kind of independence my Father had no respect or consideration, when questions of religion were introduced, although he handsomely conceded it on other points. And now first there occurred to me the reflection, which in years to come I was to repeat over and over, with an ever sadder emphasis,—what a charming companion, what a delightful parent, what a courteous and engaging friend, my Father would have been, and would pre-eminently have been to me, if it had not been for this stringent piety which ruined it all.

Let me speak plainly. After my long experience, after my patience and forbearance, I have surely the right to protest against the untruth (would that I could apply to it any other word!) that evangelical religion, or any religion in a violent form, is a wholesome or valuable or desirable adjunct to human life. It divides heart from heart. It sets up a vain, chimerical ideal, in the barren pursuit of which all the tender, indulgent affections, all the genial play of life, all the exquisite pleasures and soft resignations of the body, all that enlarges and calms the soul, are exchanged for what is harsh and void and negative. It encourages a stern and ignorant spirit of condemnation; it throws altogether out of gear the healthy movement of the conscience; it invents virtues which are sterile and cruel; it invents sins which are no sins at all, but which darken the heaven of innocent joy with futile clouds of remorse. There is something horrible, if we will bring ourselves to face it, in the fanaticism that can do nothing with this pathetic and fugitive existence of ours but treat it as if it were the uncomfortable ante-chamber to a palace which no one has explored and of the plan of which we know absolutely nothing. My Father, it is true, believed that he was intimately acquainted with the form and furniture of this habitation, and he wished me to think of nothing else but of the advantages of an eternal residence in it.

Then came a moment when my self-sufficiency revolted against the police-inspection to which my 'views' were incessantly subjected. There was a morning, in the hot-house at home, among the gorgeous waxen orchids which reminded my Father of the tropics in his youth,* when my forbearance or my timidity gave way. The enervated air, soaked with the intoxicating perfumes of all those voluptuous flowers, may have been partly responsible for my outburst. My Father had once more put to me the customary interrogatory. Was I 'walking closely with God'? Was my sense of the efficacy of the Atonement clear and sound? Had the Holy Scriptures still their full authority with me? My replies on this occasion were violent and hysterical. I have no clear recollection what it was that I said,—I desire not to recall the whimpering sentences in which I begged to be let alone, in which I demanded the right to think for myself, in which I repudiated the idea that my Father was responsible to God for my secret thoughts and my most intimate convictions.

He made no answer; I broke from the odorous furnace of the conservatory, and buried my face in the cold grass upon the lawn. My visit to Devonshire, already near its close, was hurried to an end. I had scarcely arrived in London before the following letter, furiously despatched in the track of the fugitive, buried itself like an arrow in my heart:

'When your sainted Mother died, she not only tenderly committed you to God, but left you also as a solemn charge to me, to bring you up in the nurture and admonition of the Lord. That responsibility I have sought constantly to keep before me: I can truly aver that it *has* been ever before me—in my choice of a housekeeper, in my choice of a school, in my ordering of your holidays, in my choice of a second wife, in my choice of an occupation for you, in my choice of a residence for you; and in multitudes of lesser things—I have sought to act for you, not in the light of this present world, but with a view to Eternity.

'Before your childhood was past, there seemed God's manifest blessing on our care; for you seemed truly converted to Him; you confessed, in solemn baptism, that you had died and had been raised with Christ; and you were received with joy into the bosom of the Church of God, as one alive from the dead.

'All this filled my heart with thankfulness and joy, whenever I thought of you:—how could it do otherwise? And when I left you in London, on that dreary winter evening, my heart, full of sorrowing love, found its refuge and its resource in this thought,—that you were one of the lambs of Christ's flock; sealed with the Holy Spirit as His; renewed in heart to holiness, in the image of God.

'For a while, all appeared to go on fairly well: we yearned, indeed, to discover more of heart in your allusions to religious matters, but your expressions towards us were filial and affectionate; your conduct, so far as we could see, was moral and becoming; you mingled with the people of God, spoke of occasional delight and profit in His ordinances; and employed your talents in service to Him.

'But of late, and specially during the past year, there has become manifest a rapid progress towards evil. (I must beg you here to pause, and again to look to God for grace to weigh what I am about to say; or else wrath will rise.)

'When you came to us in the summer, the heavy blow fell full upon me; and I discovered how very far you had departed from God. It was not that you had yielded to the strong tide of youthful blood, and had fallen a victim to fleshly lusts; in that case, however sad, your enlightened conscience would have spoken loudly, and you would have found your way back to the blood which cleanseth us from all sin, to humble confession and self-abasement, to forgiveness and to re-communion with God. It was not this; it was worse. It was that horrid, insidious infidelity, which had already worked in your mind and heart with terrible energy. Far worse, I say, because this was sapping the very foundations of faith, on which all true godliness, all real religion, must rest.

'Nothing seemed left to which I could appeal. We had, I found, no common ground. The Holy Scriptures had no longer any authority: you had taught yourself to evade their inspiration. Any particular Oracle of God which pressed you, you could easily explain away; even the very character of God you weighed in your balance of fallen reason, and fashioned it accordingly. You were thus sailing down the rapid tide of time towards Eternity, without a single authoritative guide (having cast your chart overboard), except what you might fashion and forge on your own anvil,—except what you might *guess*, in fact.

'Do not think I am speaking in passion, and using unwarrantable strength of words. If the written Word is not absolutely authoritative, what do we know of God? What more than we can infer, that is, guess,—as the thoughtful heathens guessed,—Plato, Socrates, Cicero,*—from dim and mute surrounding phenomena? What do we know of Eternity? Of our relations to God? Especially of the relations of a *sinner* to God? What of reconciliation? What of the capital question—How can a God of perfect spotless rectitude deal with me, a corrupt sinner, who have trampled on those of His laws which were even written on my conscience? . . .

'This dreadful conduct of yours I had intended, after much prayer, to pass by in entire silence; but your apparently sincere inquiries after the cause of my sorrow have led me to go to the root of the matter, and I could not stop short of the development contained in this letter. It is with pain, not in anger, that I send it; hoping that you may be induced to review the whole course, of which this is only a stage, before God. If this grace were granted to you, oh! how joyfully should I bury all the past, and again have sweet and tender fellowship with my beloved Son, as of old.'

The reader who has done me the favour to follow this record of the clash of two temperaments will not fail to perceive the crowning importance of the letter from which I have just made a long quotation. It sums up, with the closest logic, the whole history of the situation, and I may leave it to form the epigraph of this little book.

All that I need further say is to point out that when such defiance is offered to the intelligence of a thoughtful and honest young man with the normal impulses of his twenty-one years, there are but two alternatives. Either he must cease to think for himself; or his individualism must be instantly confirmed, and the necessity of religious independence* must be emphasised.

No compromise, it is seen, was offered; no proposal of a truce would have been acceptable. It was a case of 'Everything or Nothing'; and thus desperately challenged, the young man's conscience threw off once for all the yoke of his 'dedication', and, as respectfully as he could, without parade or remonstrance, he took a human being's privilege to fashion his inner life for himself.

APPENDIX 1

from *A Memorial of the Last Day on Earth of Emily Gosse* by Her Husband, Philip Henry Gosse, FRS
(London: James Nisbett & Co., 1857)

ABOUT the end of April, 1856, my beloved Emily became conscious of a hard lump in her left breast, the first intimation of that dreadful disease, which was commissioned to dissolve her earthly house of this tabernacle in nine short months.

It is observable, that on her birthday preceding, she had afresh made a solemn dedication of herself to God, and had besought of Him, that the year then commenced might be one of peculiar blessing. This I knew soon afterwards, because of the way in which the Lord graciously began to answer her prayers; and since her departure, I find in her private diary, under that date, the following entry:—

'Lord, forgive the sins of the past, and help me to be faithful in future! *May this be a year of much blessing—a year of jubilee!* May I be kept lowly, trusting, loving! *May I have more blessing than in all former years combined!* May I be happier as a wife, mother, sister, writer, mistress, friend!'

How little do we know in what way the Lord will answer our petitions! I believe my beloved's prayer was fully answered, and that this *was* the best year of her life; but through much tribulation, through great agony of body, was her spirit made ripe for the glory. In a great measure laid aside from her favourite employment, the writing of Gospel Tracts, she was called to glorify Him whom she loved, by a patient endurance of his will, in bearing the most torturing pain. But 'He doeth all things well': and this she knew, and loved to testify [. . .]

But the year of blessing thus auspiciously begun was scarcely half passed away before there appeared, as I have already said, the messenger commissioned to take down her tabernacle, and consummate her joy by removing her hence to the presence of her Lord. Hitherto we had known nothing but ease and happiness in the seven years of our married life; and it was not unfrequently remarked by us to each other, that the common lot, the badge of discipleship, seemed to be unknown to us. My beloved very frequently observed to me, and that especially during the year or two that preceded her mortal disease, 'How very happy we are! surely this cannot last!' Alas! it was soon to end. It is not for the eternal bliss of God's

children, that their nest (Job xxix. 18) should be undisturbed; and therefore He pulls it to pieces, and says, 'Set your affections on things above!'
He cares for our eternal happiness, and makes our temporal joy give place
to the eternal. Even so, Father!

Slightly alarmed at the lump in her breast, my dearest Emily took
the first opportunity of showing it to her tried friend, Miss Stacey, of
Tottenham, who immediately accompanied her to Dr Laseron. She
returned to me in the afternoon, met me with her usual quiet smile,
and with unbroken calmness told me that he pronounced it cancer! The
next day we consulted a relative of my own, an eminent physician, by
whose recommendation we saw the first authority on cancer in London,
Mr Paget:* by both the case was declared to be indubitable cancer, and
instant excision was recommended.*

But my relative had heard of an American,* who professed to cure
cancer by a new process, without the need of an operation; and as he was
said to invite the notice of the faculty, Dr S——* kindly offered to attend
on one of his public days, and let us know the result. He accordingly went,
and from his report, we determined to consult the American physician,
residing at Pimlico.

On our visit, he professed to be in possession of a secret medicament,
by the external application of which to a cancer the diseased portion
gradually became dead, spontaneously separated from the healthy flesh,
and sloughed away, leaving a cavity, which soon healed, and the patient
was well. He showed us photographs of many patients in different stages
of cure, many large tumours preserved in spirit, which had been sloughed
away under his testament, and, what was still more to the point, we saw
one of his patients dressed [. . .]

After much prayer, then, we perfectly agreed that the American's mode
of treatment seemed to promise best. According to the sources of information open to us, it appeared to present comparative freedom from pain in
the process, and a far greater probability of ultimate cure. With the knowledge we afterwards attained, we should no doubt have decided far otherwise; but it was not the Lord's will that we *should* decide differently,
and therefore He saw fit to withhold from us that knowledge. He surely
guided us, however, with infinite wisdom, to fulfil his purpose, which was
infinitely good.

On the 12th of May, my dearest wife was placed under the care of
Dr F——. He conceived hopes that the tumour might be dispersed or
absorbed without extraction; and at all events recommended that this
alternative should be tried for some time. He distinctly assured us, over
and over, that even should this hope be disappointed, the tumour would
not be in a condition appreciably less favourable for the extractive treat-

ment, after the lapse of a few months, than at that time; and he entertained confidence that the case was one which he should be able to bring to a happy issue.

He commenced by applying two or three kinds of ointment to the breast, using them alternately on successive days; and this mode of treatment was continued until the end of August. It involved the necessity of my beloved wife's going from Islington to Pimlico three times a-week—a wearisome task, but which opened up to her, what she greatly loved and valued, opportunities of serving her Lord in testimony, both by distribution of Gospel Tracts, and by conversation with strangers.

It was one prominent feature of her character, that she was ever on the watch for occasions of speaking a word for Jesus. Scarcely ever did she get into a railway carriage or into an omnibus, but she presently offered tracts to those sitting within reach, and endeavoured to begin a conversation with some one on spiritual things; the free grace of God in Christ, and the sufficiency of the blood of Jesus to cleanse from all sin, being her ordinary topics. She thus acquired an ever-increasing acquaintance with the human heart, and with the various devices employed by Satan to keep sinners from Christ; and thus obtained, by the help of the Holy Spirit, power to bring the Word to bear on such and similar cases—an important gift in those who testify the Gospel of the grace of God. Not a few of her tracts were founded on actual conversations sustained under circumstances such as I have described [. . .]

[The Gosses travel to Tenby in South Wales.]

We returned home on the 2d of October, and immediately saw Dr F——, who advised the removal of the tumour. The lack of any apparent result from the five months' attempt to disperse it, had led us to look to such a course as the most hopeful. On the 10th, therefore, my beloved, accompanied by our little boy, her faithful companion and assiduous nurse throughout her trial, removed to a lodging in Pimlico, uncomfortable in many respects, but presenting the advantage of being next door to Dr F——'s own residence. The next morning, October 11th, the process of extraction commenced.

The whole surface of the left breast, an area of four inches in diameter was wetted with nitric acid, applied by means of a small bit of sponge tied to the end of a stick. The object of this application was to remove the skin. The smart was very trying, and continued for several hours augmenting; the effect being to blister and destroy the whole skin, exactly as if a severe burn had taken place.

On the succeeding day, the doctor proceeded to incise the tumour, in order that it might be penetrated by the peculiar medicament which he used for its separation. With the scalpel he drew, on the surface of the now exposed flesh, a series of parallel scratches, about half an inch apart, reaching from the top to the bottom. When these were made, a plaister of a purple mucilaginous substance was spread over the whole. The next day, on renewing this plaister, the scalpel was passed again along the scratches deepening them a little; and a fresh plaister was applied. By the daily repetition of this operation, the scratches were in a few days deepened into long parallel cuts or scores, into which narrow strips of linen rag, covered with the purple mucilage,* were pressed, instead of the common plaister. Every day these strips of rag were renewed, and the scores were made deeper and deeper.

The effect of this application was very distressing. In about an hour after its renewal every morning, the breast began to be the seat of an aching, piercing pain, under which my beloved sufferer was fain to wander up and down her narrow room, leaning now and then her head upon the mantel-piece or against the wall, unable from the agony to lie, sit, or stand. For several hours this continued, after which the intensity of the anguish commonly abated. Abatement of suffering was the most she could look for; suffering never *ceased* from the beginning of the operation, till her spirit was freed from the worn-out body [. . .]

When the incisions had reached the depth of about an inch and a quarter, the operator announced that he had now reached the bottom of the cancer. He now scored no more, but applied a 'girdle', or annular* plaister, around the line where the killed tumour adjoined the living flesh; a line which was marked with perfect definiteness. The object was now to promote a suppuration, whereby the tumour should be gradually detached from the flesh, and sloughed off, like a stone dropped out of a basin. It was nearly four weeks after the removal of the skin that the 'girdle' was first put on, and two weeks more before the tumour came away. A furrow, gradually deepening, formed between the living flesh and the hard and black tumour, and this was filled with pus. The sensation now became that of a heavy weight dragging at the breast and this feeling increased as the connexion between the parts daily diminished. At length, on Sunday, the 23rd of November, to our delight, the great insensible tumour fell out of its cavity, hanging only by a slender fleshy thread, which presently yielded, and the breast was relieved of its load—the dead body that it had so long carried about [. . .]

[The operation has left a piece of the tumour still lodged deep in the breast. The operation has to be repeated; Emily offers succour to the other patients at Dr Fell's.]

It frequently happens that the sevenfold furnace of affliction is to God's people the occasion and scene of their most exalted joys. It was not so with my beloved. She very often complained of the dulness of her spirit; she was unable to read more than a verse or two at a time; unable to concentrate her thoughts, so as to meditate upon any subject; frequently unable even to bear that one should read to her, if the subject required the least thought. She often said that she seemed incapable of any higher thoughts than the longing for deliverance from present pain; and even here, her mind rarely dwelt on the ultimate issue, but just looked forward to the next lull, the cessation of the present paroxysm [. . .]

[Dr Fell removes the remaining portion of the tumour.]

At length, on Monday the 22d [of December], he said, after examining the wound, 'Mrs Gosse, I'm very sorry for this. I shall have to take out another piece under the arm.' Her heart sank under this announcement, but she replied, 'And what then, Doctor?' 'Then I must treat this other part on the inner side of the breast.' 'But how do you account for this spreading of the disease beyond the part you have all along been dealing with?' 'Oh, 'tis in your blood.'

She said no more, but calmly took her leave; and in the afternoon, when I returned to her from my daily work, she told me of the result [. . .]

[Both Emily and PHG knew that this was her death sentence.]

Long before this, it had of course become evident to us both, that the severance of that happy union, which, without a single interruption of its peace and love, had been vouchsafed to us for the last eight years, was an event not very far from us. We looked it in the face; we well knew no blessing, no strength, was to be gained from concealing it from ourselves or from each other, and we talked of it freely. To me the prospect was dark indeed; but to her death had no terrors. Our dear child she was able to leave in the hands of that loving Lord, for whom she had trained him from earliest infancy, and to whose tender care she now, in the confidence of faith, committed him; but her loving heart deeply tasted the bitterness of the cup which she saw I should soon have to drink. It was but a day or two before her departure that she said to me, with a look of unutterable affection, and with peculiar emphasis, dwelling on each precious word, now embalmed in my inmost heart: 'I love *you*,—better than on my wedding-day—better than when I was taken ill—better than when I came home from Pimlico.'

At another time she said, 'My beloved Henry, gladly would I remain, if such were the Lord's will, and be your companion for the rest of your pilgrimage!'

Nor was this the language of mere natural affection, however tender or refined; it was evoked by that which in her was ever the master-principle, an earnest longing after the spiritual welfare of those whom she loved. She was not ignorant, she could not be, how often the Lord had used her unworldly faith, her unselfish love, her saintly devotion, her wise and godly counsel, to the promotion of my best interests, checking and counteracting the earthly tendencies of her heart, and its proneness to love this present world. The faith that could leave her child to the care of her covenant God, could with difficulty leave her husband to the same care [. . .]

Amidst all, from first to last, her quiet, patient, cheerful submission to the will of God never failed. Throughout her illness, even in the very worst agonies, I never heard an approach to a murmur. A week or two before her departure, the course of reading in family worship brought us to John xiii. I had made a few remarks on the grace of the Lord in purging his own from defilement, and on the various modes in which He effects it; and turning to her, I said, 'Jesus is washing *your* feet now, love!' This little observation was used to her great comfort and refreshment, as she repeatedly told me afterwards; and thenceforth it became one of her favourite words until the last,—'Jesus is washing my feet!' [. . .]

The anticipation of being soon in the presence of the Lord, who had redeemed her, was delightful to her. To a friend, who called a few days before her departure, she said, 'This will be the happiest year of my life; for I shall see Jesus!' [. . .]

No portrait of my beloved existed, except one which was taken in her early childhood, and another taken in youth, which is in the possession of a distant relative in America. We had often intended to have one, and in the preceding summer had even waited for several hours in the rooms of Maull and Polyblank, the eminent photographers; but the weather became unsuitable before her turn arrived. This was a subject of regret to her, for our little boy's sake; she would have liked him to possess some means of keeping in remembrance his mother's features; she knew they could never fade from my memory. Our dear friends, Mr Hislop and Miss Georgiana Long, knowing of this regret, with the most prompt kindness proffered their aid, the former to take a photograph, the latter a water-colour miniature. I thankfully accepted both offers; and on the sixth of February, only four days before her departure, the kind artists, with the camera and the palette, were introduced into the bedroom. The circumstances were almost as unfavourable as they well could be, yet the resemblances produced are to me beyond all price. A third photograph was taken on the following Monday, about twelve hours before death. It is characteristic and pleasing, though somewhat undefined, because of the motion arising from her laborious breathing: she appears as if sleeping, but this was owing to the bright sun's rays compelling her to keep her eyes closed during the exposure [. . .]

Her last day on earth was now come. It was one of brilliant sunshine—a lovely day for mid-winter; and as we moved her couch towards the window, for the taking of the third photograph, and saw the bright sunlight stream upon her countenance, we little thought she would see that sun no more. She was cheerful in conversation, as indeed she ever was; took an interest in the likeness, and wished to see the result; and in the afternoon conversed freely with her physician.

As she lay still, she said, 'I shall see his bright face, and shall shine in his brightness, and shall sing his praise in strains never uttered below.' I have no doubt she alluded to a deficiency which she had always regretted; from the want of ear and voice, she had never been able to sing.

Even up to the last her mind was set upon doing her Master's work; nearly a hundred 'British Messengers' the excellent publisher, Mr Drummond, of Stirling, had been in the habit of sending her every month for distribution; and on this very last day, one of the servants was seated at a table by her bedside, with heaps of Tracts and Messengers before her, folding and addressing each, under her dictation. It was her last act of earthly service.

In the course of the afternoon, as I was hanging over her, she said, 'O that I loved Him more!' I replied, 'You will soon.' She said, 'Yes, I hope so!' and then with an expression approaching to archness, she added, 'I don't love Satan!' 'Nor sin,' I suggested. 'No; and I don't want to enjoy the pleasures of sin for a season.'

As night drew on, a change became manifest. The physician had said that the whole blood in the system was poisoned by the cancer, and that the rapidity of its downward course was beyond that of any case he had ever witnessed. The breathing became shorter and more laborious, accompanied with much heaving of the chest. Soon after eight o'clock, she experienced a partial paralysis of the tongue, causing her speech to be thick, and with difficulty intelligible. In allusion to this, and in the dread that she might linger some time without the power of speech, she said, 'The Lord has hitherto raised me up above circumstances; He has made me to ride upon the high places of the earth, and now He has brought me down; and now He has made me to fear.'

'Fear what, my darling?' I asked.

'Paralysis.'

A little before ten, she murmured, 'I'm going home—I must go home!'

'Yes,' I replied, 'what a blessing that you have a home to go to!'

She immediately added, though almost inarticulately, 'And a hearty welcome!' There was here an allusion to one of her last three Tracts, 'A Home Welcome', as its title now stands, but which in her MS had been entitled, 'A Home and a Hearty Welcome'.

The two maids, who truly loved their mistress, refused to go to bed, and they with me continued to watch for the end. After a while my precious sufferer said, 'I shall walk with Him in white; won't you take your lamb, and walk with me?' The last sentence she repeated twice or thrice, as she saw that I did not readily catch her meaning. I believe, however, she alluded to our dear little boy. Her speech was now so thick, that a great deal of what she said was unintelligible; only a sentence now and then could be made out.

Presently she said, ' 'Tis a pleasant way—more pleasant than when I could not pray for what would make you unhappy.' I suppose she referred to the circumstance that, within the last day or two, I had been able solemnly to resign her into the hand of Him, who for a season had lent her to me, and who now reclaimed his loan.

She looked on us hanging over her, and said, two or three times, as if the thought of eternal union were delightful, 'One family!' and then added, 'One song!—One family: one song!'

At times she dropped into a momentary slumber, during which she still spoke, incoherently, or at least unintelligibly, but still of Him whose 'best wine for his beloved, that goeth down sweetly, causeth the lips of those that are asleep to speak' (Song vii. 9).* In one of these murmurings, on putting our ears close to her mouth, we could make out the words—'Open the gates! Open the gates, and let me in!' Ah! the 'blessed of the Lord' had not much longer to 'stand without!'

About a quarter to eleven, I spoke to her of the freeness of gospel grace, which she had proclaimed so fully in her Tracts; when she replied, 'I see it!'

'See what, love?' I asked.

'I see the freeness of gospel grace that I have set before others; but in extreme weakness'; immediately adding, lest the expression might be misunderstood, as meaning dimness of apprehension of the truth—'in extreme weakness *of body*'.

Soon after this she turned her dimming eyes on me, and said, 'Dear Papa, I'm all ready.'

'What has made you ready?' I asked.

'The blood.' Then she added, after a momentary pause, 'The blood of the Lamb.'

This precious testimony was the last sentence that issued from her lips. It had been her joy in life to proclaim the sufficiency of that book, and now she died on it.

A few minutes after this she fell into a heavy doze, breathing stertorously with laborious heaving and with opened mouth. I lay down in the room, the maids still hanging over her. In about three quarters of an hour I resumed my place by her side; she was as when I left her, and they told me she had not uttered a word, except once, that she said, 'Papa!' The breathing was now feebler, with less of the rattling of the phlegm. Presently she again breathed the familiar word, 'Papa!' which was the last word she uttered on earth.

Her eyes now became fixed, and she was evidently unconscious, in no way noticing anything we said or did, till, exactly at one o'clock, she breathed a long expiration, and ceased. I laid her dear head, which for an hour had been on my arm, on the pillow, closed her eyes, and, all kneeling round the bed, gave thanks to God, amidst sobs and tears, for her peaceful admission into her happy Home.

Her dust was deposited, on the Friday following, the 13th of February, 1857, in Abney Park Cemetery, in the presence of many of God's elect, who loved her, and who look forward with sweet hope to the approaching day of the manifestation of Jesus, when she shall be restored to our glad embrace, in resurrection power and glory.

APPENDIX 2

from *Omphalos: An Attempt To Untie the Geological Knot* by Philip Henry Gosse, FRS
(London: John Van Voorst, 1857)

'—τὸν τροχὸν τῆς γενέσεως' —JAMES iii. 6.*

THE course of nature is a circle. I do not mean the *plan* of nature; I am not speaking of a circular arrangement of species, genera, families, and classes, as maintained by MacLeay, Swainson, and others.* Their theories may be true, or they may be false; I decide nothing concerning them; I am not alluding to any *plan* of nature, but to its *course, cursus,*—the way in which it *runs on.* This is a circle.

Here is in my garden a scarlet runner. It is a slender twining stem some three feet long, beset with leaves, with a growing bud at one end, and with the other inserted in the earth. What was it a month ago? A tiny shoot protruding from between two thick fleshy leaves scarcely raised above the ground. A month before that? The thick fleshy leaves were two oval cotyledons,* closely appressed face to face, with the minute plumule* between them, the whole enclosed in an unbroken, tightly-fitting, spotted, leathery coat. It was a bean, a seed.

Was this the commencement of its existence? O no! Six months earlier still it was snugly lying, with several others like itself, in a green fleshy pod, to the interior of which it was organically attached. A month before that, this same pod with its contents was the centre of a scarlet butterfly-like flower, the bottom of its pistil,* within which, if you had split it open, you would have discerned the tiny beans, whose history we are tracing backwards, each imbedded in the soft green tissue, but no bigger than the eye of a cambric needle.

But where was this flower? It was one of many that glowed on my garden wall all through last summer; each cluster springing as a bud from a slender twining stem, which was the exact counterpart of that with which we commenced this little life-history.

And this earlier stem,—what of it? It too had been a shoot, a pair of cotyledons with a plumule, a seed, an integral part of a carpel, which was a part of an earlier flower, that expanded from an earlier bud, that grew out of an earlier stem, that had been a still earlier seed, that had been—and backward, *ad infinitum*, for aught that I can perceive.

The course, then, of a scarlet runner is a circle, without beginning or end:—that is, I mean, without a natural, a normal beginning or end. For at what point of its history can you put your finger, and say, 'Here is the commencement of this organism, before which there is a blank; here it began to exist?' There is no such point; no stage which does not look back to a previous stage, on which *this* stage is inevitably and absolutely dependent.

[. . .]

This, then, is the order of all organic nature. When once we are in any portion of the course, we find ourselves running in a circular groove, as endless as the course of a blind horse in a mill. It is evident that there is no one point in the history of any single creature, which is a legitimate beginning of existence. And this is not the law of some particular species, but of all: it pervades all classes of animals, all classes of plants, from the queenly palm down to the protococcus,* from the monad* up to man: the life of every organic being is whirling in a ceaseless circle, to which one knows not how to assign any commencement,—I will not say any certain or even probable, but any *possible*, commencement. The cow is as inevitable a sequence of the embryo, as the embryo is of the cow. Looking only at nature, or looking at it only with the lights of experience and reason, I see not how it is possible to avoid one of these two theories, the development of all organic existence out of gaseous elements, or the eternity of matter in its present forms.

Creation, however, solves the dilemma. I have, in my postulates, begged the fact of creation, and I shall not, therefore, attempt to prove it. Creation, the sovereign fiat of Almighty Power, gives us the commencing point, which we in vain seek in nature. But what is creation? It is *the sudden bursting into a circle*. Since there is no one stage in the course of existence, which more than any other affords a natural commencing point, whatever stage is selected by the arbitrary will of God, must be an unnatural, or rather a preter-natural, commencing point.

The life-history of every organism commenced at some point or other of its circular course. It was created, called into being, in some definite stage. Possibly, various creatures differed in this respect; perhaps some began existence in one stage of development, some in another; but every separate organism had a distinct point at which it began to live. Before that point there was nothing; this particular organism had till then no existence; its history presents an absolute blank; *it was not*.

But the whole organisation of the creature thus newly called into existence, looks back to the course of an endless circle in the past. Its whole structure displays a series of developments, which as distinctly witness to former conditions as do those which are presented in the cow, the butterfly, and the fern, of the present day. But what former conditions? The conditions thus witnessed unto, as being necessarily implied in the present organisation, were non-existent; the history was a perfect blank till the moment of creation. The past conditions or stages of existence in question, can indeed be as triumphantly inferred by legitimate deduction from the present, as can those of our cow or butterfly; they rest on the very same evidences; they are identically the same in every respect, except in this one, that they were *unreal*. They exist only in their results; they are effects which never had causes.

Perhaps it may help to clear my argument if I divide the past developments of organic life, which are necessarily, or at least legitimately, inferrible from present phenomena, into two categories, separated by the violent act of creation. Those unreal developments whose apparent results are seen in the organism at the moment of its creation, I will call *prochronic*, because time was not an element in them; while those which have subsisted since creation, and which have had actual existence, I will distinguish as *diachronic*, as occurring during time.

Now, again I repeat, there is no imaginable difference to sense between the prochronic and the diachronic development. Every argument by which the physiologist can prove to demonstration that yonder cow was once a fœtus in the uterus of its dam, will apply with exactly the same power to show that the newly created cow was an embryo, some years before its creation.

Look again at the diagram by which I have represented the life-history of this animal. The only mode in which it can begin is by a sudden sovereign act of power, an irruption into the circle. You may choose *where* the irruption shall occur; there must be a bursting-in at some point. Suppose it is at 'calf'; or suppose it is at 'embr. vesicle'. Put a wafer at the point you choose, say the latter. This then is the real, actual commencement of a circle, to be henceforth ceaseless. But the embryonic vesicle necessarily implies a germinal vesicle, and this necessitates an ovum, and the ovum necessitates an ovary, and the ovary necessitates an entire animal,—and thus we have got a quarter round the circle in back development; we are irresistibly carried along the prochronic stages,—the stages of existence which were before existence commenced,—as if they had been diachronic, actually occurring within our personal experience.

If I know, as a *historic fact*, that the circle was commenced where I have put my wafer, I may begin it there; but there is, and can be, nothing in the *phenomena* to indicate a commencement there, any more than anywhere else, or, indeed, anywhere at all. The commencement, as a fact, I must learn from testimony; I have no means whatever of inferring it from phenomena.

Permit me, therefore, to repeat, as having been proved, these two propositions:—

ALL ORGANIC NATURE MOVES IN A CIRCLE.

CREATION IS A VIOLENT IRRUPTION INTO THE CIRCLE OF NATURE.

[PHG now considers whether the same laws operate in the case of human beings.]

So far, then, we can with certainty trace back the history of this being, as an independent organism; but did his history then commence? O no; we can carry him much farther back than this. What means this curious depression in the centre of the abdomen, and the corrugated knob which occupies the cavity?[1]

This is the NAVEL. The corrugation is the cicatrice* left where once was attached the umbilical cord, and whence its remains, having died, sloughed away. This organ introduces us to the fœtal life of Man; for it was the link of connexion between the unborn infant and the parent; the channel, through whose arteries and veins the oxygenated and the effete blood passed to and from the parental system, when as yet the unused lungs had not received one breath of vital air.

And thus the life of the individual Man before us passes, by a necessary retrogression, back to the life of another individual, from whose substance his own substance was formed by gemmation;* one of the component cells of whose structure was the primordial cell, from which have been developed successively all the cells which now make up his mature and perfect organism.

How is it possible to avoid this conclusion? Has not the physiologist irrefragable grounds for it, founded on universal experience? Has not observation abundantly shown, that, wherever the bones, flesh, blood, teeth, nails, hair of man exist, the aggregate body has passed through stages exactly correspondent to those alluded to above, and has originated in the uterus of a mother, its fœtal life being, so to speak, a budding out of

---

[1] Sir Thomas Browne* indeed, denies Adam a navel; I presume, however, physiologists will rather take my view. Sir Thomas did not know that the prochronism which he thought absurd pervaded every part of organic structure. The following is his verdict:—

'Another Mistake there may be in the Picture of our first Parents, who after the manner of theyre Posteritie are bothe delineated with a Navill: and this is observable not only in ordinarie and stayned peeces, but in the Authenticke Draughts of Vrbin, Angelo, and others.* Which, notwythstandynge, cannot be allowed, except wee impute that vnto the first Cause, which we impose not on the second; or what wee deny vnto Nature, wee impute vnto Naturity it selfe; that is, that in the first and moste accomplyshed Peece, the Creator affected Superfluities, or ordayned Parts withoute all Vse or Offyce.' *Pseudodoxia Epidemica,* lib. v.; cap. v.

hers? Has the combined experience of mankind ever seen a solitary exception to this law? How, then, can we refuse the concession that, in the individual before us, in whom we find all the phenomena that we are accustomed to associate with adult Man, repeated in the most exact verisimilitude, without a single flaw—how, I say, can we hesitate to assert that such was his origin too?

And yet, in order to assert it, we must be prepared to adopt the old Pagan doctrine of the eternity of matter; *ex nihilo nihil fit.** But those with whom I argue are precluded from this, by my first Postulate.

[. . .]

In order to perfect the analogy between an organism and the world, so as to show that the law which prevails in the one obtains also in the other, it would be necessary to prove that the development of the physical history of the world is circular, like that already shown to characterise the course of organic nature. And this I cannot prove. But neither, as I think, can the contrary be proved.

The life of *the individual* consists of a series of processes which are cyclical. In the tree this is shown by the successive growths and deaths of series of leaves: in the animal by the development and exuviation of nails, hair, epidermis, &c.

The life of *the species* consists of a series of processes which are cyclical. This has been sufficiently illustrated in the preceding pages, in the successive developments and deaths of generations of individuals.

[. . .]

Here I close my labours. How far I have succeeded in accomplishing the task to which I bent myself, it is not for me to judge. Others will determine that; and I am quite sure it will be determined fairly, on the whole. To prevent misapprehension, however, it may be as well to enunciate what the task was, which I prescribed, especially because other (collateral, hypothetical) points have been mooted in these pages.

All, then, that I consider myself responsible for is summed up in these sentences:—

I. The conclusions hitherto received have been but inferences deduced from certain premises: the witness who reveals the premises does *not* testify to the inferences.

II. The process of deducing the inferences has been liable to a vast incoming of error, arising from the operation of a *Law*, proved to exist, but hitherto unrecognised.

III. The amount of the error thus produced we have no means of knowing; much less of eliminating it.

IV. The whole of the facts deposed to by this witness are irrelevant to the question; and the witness is, therefore, out of court.

V. The field is left clear and undisputed for the one Witness on the opposite side, whose testimony is as follows:—

'IN SIX DAYS JEHOVAH MADE HEAVEN AND EARTH, THE SEA, AND ALL THAT IN THEM IS.'

APPENDIX 3

from *The Life of Philip Henry Gosse FRS*
by his son Edmund Gosse
(London: Kegan Paul, Trench, Trübner & Co., 1890)

IT will perhaps be assumed from this sketch of my father's religious views, that he was gloomy and saturnine in manner. It is true that, at the very end of his life, wrapped up as he grew to be more and more in meta-physical lucubrations, his extreme self-absorption took a stern com-plexion. But it had not always been so in earlier years. He was subject to long fits of depression, the result in great measure of dyspepsia, but when these passed away he would be cheerful and even gay for weeks at a time. Never lonely, never bored, he was contented with small excite-ments and monotonous amusements, and asked no more than to be left alone among his orchids, his cats, and his butterflies, happy from morning till night. On the first day of his seventy-eighth year, he wrote to me in these terms:—

'My health is fair and my vigour considerable. I am free from pains and infirmities. My zest and delight in my microscopical studies is unabated yet, so that every day is an unflagging holiday.'

This description of his feelings, at a time when the shadow of death had almost crossed his path, is significant, and might be taken to characterize his inward feeling, if not always his outward aspect, through the main part of the last thirty years of his life. He could even, on occasion, be merry, with a playfulness that was almost pathetic, because it seemed to be the expression of a human sympathy buried too far down in his being to reveal itself except in this dumb way. I cannot exactly describe what it was that made this powerfully built and admirably equipped man sometimes strike one as having the immatureness and touching incompleteness of the nature of a child. It was partly that he was innocent of observing any but the most obvious and least complex working of the mind in others. But it was mainly that he had nothing in common with his age. He was a Coven-anter come into the world a couple of centuries after his time, to find society grown too soft for his scruples and too ingenious for his severe simplicity. He could never learn to speak the ethical language of the nine-teenth century; he was seventeenth century in spirit and manner to the last.

No question is more often put to me regarding my father than this—How did he reconcile his religious to his scientific views? The case of Faraday* may throw some light, but not very much, upon the problem. The word 'reconcile' is scarcely the right one, because the idea of reconciliation was hardly entertained by my father. He had no notion of striking a happy mean between his impressions of nature and his convictions of religion. If the former offered any opposition to the latter, they were swept away. The rising tide is 'reconciled' in the same fashion to a child's battlements of sand along the shore. Awe, an element almost eliminated from the modern mind, was strongly developed in Philip Gosse's character. He speaks of himself, in one of his letters, as having been under 'the subjugation of spiritual awe to a decidedly morbid degree' during the whole of his life. He meant by this, I feel no doubt, that he was conscious of an ever-present bias towards the relinquishing of any idea presumably unpalatable to his inward counsellor. It was under the pressure of this sense of awe that, when his intellect was still fresh, he deliberately refused to give a proper examination to the theory of evolution which his own experiments and observations had helped to supply with arguments. It was certainly not through vagueness of mind or lack of a logical habit that he took up this strange position, as of an intellectual ostrich with his head in a bush, since his intelligence, if narrow, was as clear as crystal, and his mind eminently logical. It was because a 'spiritual awe' overshadowed his conscience, and he could not venture to take the first step in a downward course of scepticism. He was not one who could accept half-truths or see in the twilight. It must be high noon or else utter midnight with a character so positive as his.

It followed, then, that his abundant and varied scientific labours were undertaken, whenever they were fruitful, in fields where there was no possibility of contest between experimental knowledge and revelation. Where his work was technical, not popular, it was exclusively concerned with the habits, or the forms, or the structure of animals, not observed in the service of any theory or philosophical principle, but for their own sake. In the two departments where he accomplished the greatest amount of original work, in the *Actinozoa* and the *Rotifera*,* it was impossible for hypothesis of an anti-scriptural tendency to intrude, and if the observations which he made were used by others to support a theory inconsistent with the record of creation, he was not obliged to be cognizant of any such perversion of his work. He used, very modestly, to describe himself as 'a hewer of wood and a drawer of water' in the house of science, but no biologist will on that account under-rate what he has done. His extreme care in diagnosis, the clearness of his eye, the marvellous exactitude of his memory, his recognition of what was salient in the characteristics of each species, his unsurpassed skill in defining those characteristics by word and by pencil, his great activity and pertinacity, all these combined to make Philip Gosse a technical observer of unusually high rank.

[. . .]

The one art by which he was vividly affected was poetry. The magic of romantic verse, which had taken him captive in early boyhood, when he found it first in the pages of *Lara*,* never entirely lost its spell over him. Milton (though with occasional qualms, because *Paradise Lost* was 'tainted with the Arian heresy'),* Wordsworth, Gray, Cowper, and Southey,* were at his fingers' ends, and he had certain favourite passages of each of these which he was never weary of intoning. He liked Southey, because he was, as he put it, 'the best naturalist among the English poets', and had described sea-anemones like a zoologist in *Thalaba*.* He was much more interested, towards the end, in portions of Swinburne and Rossetti,* than he had ever been in Tennyson and Browning,* for neither of whom he had the slightest tolerance. Almost the latest conscious exercise of my father's brain was connected with his love for poetry. During his fatal illness, in July, 1888, when the gloom of decay was creeping over his intellect, he was carried out for a drive, the last which he would ever take, on an afternoon of unusual beauty. We passed through the bright street of Torquay, along the strand of Torbay, with its thin screen of tamarisks between the road-way and the bay, up through the lanes of Torre and Cockington. My father, with the pathetic look in his eyes, the mortal pallor on his cheeks, scarcely spoke, and seemed to observe nothing. But, as we turned to drive back down a steep lane of overhanging branches, the pale vista of the sea burst upon us, silvery blue in the yellow light of afternoon. Something in the beauty of the scene raised the sunken brain, and with a little of the old declamatory animation in head and hand, he began to recite the well-known passage in the fourth book of *Paradise Lost*—

> 'Now came still evening on, and twilight grey
> Had in her sober livery all things clad.'*

He pursued the quotation through three or four lines, and then, in the middle of a sentence, the music broke, his head fell once more upon his breast, and for him the splendid memory, the self-sustaining intellect which had guided the body so long, were to be its companions upon earth no more.

APPENDIX 4

Two letters from Sir James Frazer to Edmund Gosse

Brotherton Collection Gosse, letter 21

St Keyne's
Cambridge
20 October 1909

My dear Gosse

Thank you sincerely for the kind present of the book. I shall value it and read it for the author's sake and for its own, for dipping into it (it has just come into my hands) I find it full of interest. Indeed I had heard of it before and had intended to read it, but some-how the time has passed without my doing so. I read very little general literature, hardly ever a new book except those in my own department. I find it necessary rigorously to limit my reading, if I am to finish the literary work I have planned. But it will be both pleasurable and, I believe, profitable for my special studies to read your book; for of course I am deeply interested in the psychology of religion, of which, as I gathered from the reviews at the time of its appearance, your book is a very valuable document. When I have read it, I will write you further on the subject.

Have you read Reinach's 'Orpheus'?* and if so, what do you think of it? Do not trouble to answer just now. We can speak of that and other matters when we next meet. When will that be? We meet so seldom. I am sorry for it. I wish you would come and see me. Do come.

With kindest regards and very many thanks

    I am

  yours ever sincerely

    J. G. Frazer.

Brotherton Collection Gosse, letter 22

St Keyne's
Cambridge
10 November 1909

My dear Gosse

I have now read through 'Father and Son' with keen interest, an interest which never flagged from beginning to end. It is indeed a fascinating book. The story is a sad one, but it is delicately as well as powerfully told, and the reader cannot help sympathising with both the actors in what was hardly less than a domestic tragedy. It can scarcely be doubted that you have accomplished your object of recording a phase of education and religion which has passed, or is rapidly passing, away. As such a record, apart from its literary merit, the book is entitled to a permanent place in the archives of religious psychology. With regard to the manner, it has one of the surest marks of a good style, namely that the reader is so absorbed in the interest of the matter that he seldom attends to the style. In this respect a good style resembles a good manner in society. It is a bad manner and a bad style which attract attention.

The portrait of your father which you have drawn is deeply interesting. One would like to know more of him. Has any memoir of him been published? If not, would you give us one? He must have been a very high-minded man. His double devotion to science and religion was wonderful. And you yourself, if I may say so, become doubly interesting to your friends for the extraordinary experience you had in your youth. What a strange, sad childhood! It seems wonderful that you should have emerged from it as you have done. The long solitude and gloom would have broken or embittered for life many spirits. [. . .]

EXPLANATORY NOTES

Abbreviations: Edmund Gosse is referred to as 'EG'; Philip Henry Gosse as 'PHG'. The *Oxford English Dictionary* is shortened to *OED*. These notes are partly indebted to the work of previous editors of *Father and Son*: Cecil Ballantine (London: Heinemann Educational Books, 1970); James Hepburn (Oxford: Oxford University Press, 1974); Peter Abbs (Harmondsworth: Penguin Books, 1983); and A. O. J. Cockshut (Ryburn: Keele University Press, 1994).

1 *SCHOPENHAUER*: 'Faith is like love; it cannot be forced.' The German philosopher, Arthur Schopenhauer (1788–1860) was the author of *Die Welt als Wille und Vorstellung* (*The World as Will and Idea*) (1819), a highly influential work of pessimistic philosophy.

3 *As regards the anonymous writer . . . to conceal or to identify*: this paragraph was removed when *Father and Son* was reprinted under Gosse's own name.

5 *My maternal grandfather was born wealthy . . . a little estate in North Wales, on the slopes of Snowdon*: William Bowes, EG's grandfather, was a Bostonian by birth, a member of 'one of the most distinguished families of New England' (Edmund Gosse, *Life of Philip Henry Gosse*, 215). Bowes rapidly lost his fortune by gambling on horses.

6 *a disciple of Rousseau*: the Swiss philosopher Jean-Jacques Rousseau (1712–78) is the author of *Émile* (1762), one of the most celebrated books on education. Rousseau asserted that the 'natural' was inherently good, and the artificial irretrievably bad: we are born perfect, until society corrupts us. The neglect of subjects such as history and literature would have been inspired by an attempt to protect the child from the debilitating effects of too early a knowledge of social life. However, Emily Bowes herself felt her education to have been ' "idle, irregular" ' (Thwaite, *Edmund Gosse*, 14). None the less, it did not prevent her from having a successful career as a religious writer.

blue-stocking: a learned woman.

those days of the wide revival of Conscience: a reference to the Evangelical Christian revival of the early nineteenth century. It is intriguing that young Emily Bowes is herself shown as rebelling against her parents' way of living.

Wesleyan: a follower of John Wesley (1703–91), otherwise known as Methodists. They were known for their severe religious beliefs and practices. Again, it is worth noting here that both of EG's parents themselves rebelled and moved away from the religious communities of their childhood and youth.

7 *extreme Calvinists*: followers of Jean Calvin (or Cauvin) (1509–64). Calvinists are what we would call 'fundamentalists', believing in the literal truth and complete authority of the Bible. To Calvinists, all human beings are corrupt and sinful; in ourselves no one could be saved. God, however, has predestined the salvation of a select few people, the 'Elect', who, following repentance, reach God and Heaven by virtue of their faith. Good deeds are like filthy rags in the sight of God; human beings are justified only by faith.

'*Plymouth Brethren*': a Calvinist sect formed during the Evangelical revival, its key founding figures being J. N. Darby (1800–82), a former Anglican clergyman, A. N. Groves (1795–1853), and B. W. Newton (1807–77), in other words men of the generation of John Keats, Thomas Carlyle, and J. S. Mill. The sect split many times during the nineteenth century, usually on points of doctrine or practice.

when they married: the marriage took place on 22 November 1848, in a ceremony conducted by Robert Howard, a leading member of the Brethren, at Brook Street Chapel, Tottenham, Middlesex. The day before the wedding PHG had finished writing his book on *Popular British Ornithology*; he had begun writing it the day before he proposed to Emily, on 16 September 1848.

his mother's little house in the north-east of London: the house was at 13 Trafalgar Terrace, Mortimer Road, Hackney. Hackney is now a largely working-class area of London, with some recent gentrification. In the 1840s it was a middle-class suburb on the edge of the city.

devoted her pen to popular works of edification: Emily Gosse became a prolific author of Gospel Tracts. She published forty-one such little books, with perhaps as many as half a million copies sold around the world.

no poet later than Byron ... the Waverley Novels: George Gordon, 6th Lord Byron (1788–1824) is in some ways an unexpectedly louche choice of poet for these young Puritans. The Waverley Novels were a series of historical novels written by Sir Walter Scott (1771–1832), beginning with *Waverley* (1814). As these were published anonymously, they became known as novels by the author of *Waverley*. Byron and Scott were the two most famous authors of their day.

8 *a species of Churching*: a religious service for women after childbirth; it is presumably only a 'species' of Churching, as the sensibilities of the Brethren are so greatly anti-ritualistic.

'*dedication*': for those who do not believe in the efficacy of infant baptism, 'dedication' acts as an alternative informal ceremony in which a young child is dedicated to God; here it has a larger sense of the young EG's life being presented by others to the service of God, much as Hannah dedicates the infant Samuel: 'For this child I prayed; and the LORD hath given me my petition which I asked of him: Therefore also I have lent him to the LORD; as long as he liveth he shall be lent to the LORD. And he worshipped the LORD there' (1 Samuel 1: 27–8).

my Father's mother had lived in the house: immediately following her son's marriage Hannah Gosse bowed out of the house for the fortnight follow-ing, but her return to the family home led to perhaps inevitable discord.

9 *the small hired hall at Hackney*: this was Ellis's Rooms in Hackney.

11 *a holiday of nearly ten months in Devonshire*: the stay in Devon lasted from the end of January to mid-October 1852. The family stayed at the village of St Marychurch, then about a mile and a half to the north of Torquay. The holiday is commemorated in PHG's books, *A Naturalist's Rambles on the Devonshire Coast* (1853) and *Sea-Side Pleasures* (1853). The young Edmund appears in *Sea-Side Rambles* (at a guess) as 'a child of our party' who removes the head from a valued, but already broken china ornament (p.73). He's there too in the same year's *A Naturalist's Rambles*, dis-embarking at Torquay station for St Marychurch, as a 'little naturalist in petticoats' (p.3) with his mother, and his father, and the luggage.

'*the world forgetting by the world forgot*': these are lines from Alexander Pope's (1688–1744) poem of unhappy love, 'Eloisa to Abelard':

> How happy is the blameless vestal's lot
> The world forgetting, by the world forgot
>
> (ll. 207–8)

intellectual Thebaïd: a classical allusion to the site of desert hermit dwell-ings near Egyptian Thebes; the image is meant to convey isolation and the extreme rigours of primitive Christianity.

12 *that's the world's side . . . phrase it*: a quotation from Robert Browning's (1812–89) 'One Word More', a poem addressed to his wife, Elizabeth Barrett Browning (1806–81), with the collection, *Men and Women* (1855):

> Ah, but that's the world's side, there's the wonder,
> Thus they see you, praise you, think they know you.
> There, in turn I stand with them and praise you,
> Out of my own self, I dare to phrase it.
> But the best is when I glide from out them,
> Cross a step or two of dubious twilight,
> Come out on the other side, the novel
> Silent silver lights and darks undreamed of,
> Where I hush and bless myself with silence.

Gosse changes the passage into the past tense.

13 *My uncles were not religious men*: Emily Bowes was born in 1806; Edmund Bowes was born in 1808; Arthur Bowes was born in 1813.

in the family of an Irish nobleman: EG exaggerates. In fact Emily went to join the large family of an English clergyman, the Revd John Hawkins, at Compton in Berkshire.

Miss Edgeworth: Maria Edgeworth (1767–1849), a renowned writer of novels of Irish life, especially *Castle Rackrent* (1800), a novel narrated by Thady Quirk, the servant of the Rackrents.

13 *ultima Thule*: in classical culture the furthest island and most northerly point of the inhabited world; the end of the earth.

14 *Byronic type*: cutting the figure of a fatal man: emotionally wounded, handsome, and cynical.

an old rambling house in Clapton: Valentine House, Brook Street.

a poem which had a romantic place in my early mental history: I have been unable to identify the author of this poem.

16 *Rev. George Croly*: Croly's (1780–1860) novel *Salathiel* (1829) portrays the destruction of Jerusalem by the Romans.

chivalrous tales in verse of Sir Walter Scott: these would include *The Lay of the Last Minstrel* (1805), *Marmion* (1808), and *The Lady of the Lake* (1810), enormously popular poems throughout the nineteenth century.

17 *a little younger than Bulwer Lytton, a little older than Mrs Gaskell*: Edward George Earle Bulwer-Lytton (1803–73) was a highly successful Victorian novelist, the author of the fashionable *Pelham* (1828), the spectacular *The Last Days of Pompeii* (1834), and the occultist fantasy *Zanoni* (1842), among many others. In short, he is an unlikely point of comparison. Elizabeth Gaskell (1810–65) is more fitting perhaps, though her excellent novels, such as *Mary Barton* (1848), *Cranford* (1852), and *Wives and Daughters* (1866) also occasionally employ themes unlikely to appeal to so rigorous a Christian as Emily Gosse.

Jack the Giant-Killer, Rumpelstiltskin and Robin Hood ... Little Red Ridinghood: all fairy tale characters. Gosse's argument concerning the likelihood of an immersion in fairy stories helping to support Christian faith would seem to be ironically intended, though it is repeated in another tone by G. K. Chesterton in *Orthodoxy* (1908).

Jukes: Andrew John Jukes, a prolific author of Christian texts and biblical exegesis, publishing such works as *The Law of the Offerings in Leviticus* (1847).

18 *'The Penny Cyclopædia'*: a thirty-volume encyclopedia edited by George Long, and published by the Society for the Diffusion of Useful Knowledge between 1833 and 1858.

certain visits ... to the shores of Devon and Dorset: from April to December 1853, and described in PHG's *The Aquarium* (1854).

a house at Islington: actually quite a grand end-of-terrace house at 58 Huntingdon Street.

featherless plantigrade vertebrate, homo sapiens: designed to show EG's acquired scientific distance from a real sense of human lives; 'plantigrade' means walking with the whole sole of the foot touching the ground; A. O. J. Cockshut suggests an allusion to the famous definition of man as a featherless biped, and more specifically to Dryden's *Absalom and Achitophel*, pt. 1, p. 170: 'That unfeathered two-legged thing ...'

19 *known as his son's father!*: Philip Henry Gosse became a Fellow of the

Royal Society on 4 June 1856. The pleasantry clearly carries an Oedipal undertone of rivalry.

'the little lazy isles where the trumpet-orchids blow': from Rudyard Kipling (1865–1936), 'The Long Trail', ll. 71–2: 'And it's twenty-thousand mile to our little lazy isle | Where the trumpet-orchids blow!'

Charles Wesley . . . George Whitefield: Charles Wesley (1707–88) was the younger brother of John Wesley, the founder of Methodism. Charles was a notable composer of hymns, including 'Jesu, lover of my soul'. George Whitefield (1714–70) was one of John Wesley's circle of devout Christians in Oxford. He became a famous preacher and the founder of the Calvinistic Methodists.

20 *when the Crimean War broke out*: the war fought between Russia and Britain and her allies, France and Turkey, between 1854 and 1856.

'The Guardsman of the Alma': the Battle of Alma was fought on 20 September 1854. According to EG's *The Life of Philip Henry Gosse*, *The Young Guardsman of the Alma* was published in the autumn of 1855 by the weekly Tract society.

21 *'Jingo'*: a slang term for aggressive Imperialism or nationalist chauvinism. It derives from a music hall song written by G. W. Hunt, first performed in 1878:

> We don't want to fight, but by Jingo if we do,
> We've got the ships, we've got the men, and got the money too.

'Jings' or 'by jings' is a slang exclamation, avoiding the more profane 'by Jesus'.

geometer-moth: from a class of caterpillars, known as 'geometers' 'because they seem to measure the surface they pass over, as they walk, with a chain' (quoted in *OED* from William Kirby and William Spence, *Entomology* (1815–26)).

Vapourer, orgygia antiqua: 'a British moth of the genus *Orgyia*, esp. *O. antiqua*, the male of which flies with a rapid quivering motion' (*OED*).

22 *Princess Blanchefleur*: the Saracen heroine of an Old French romance, rescued from slavery by Floire (or Floris), a Christian prince. EG may have encountered the story in his reading of Boccaccio.

24 *one of her admirers and disciples . . . 'sowing beside all waters'*: the admirer is Anna Shipton, and the quotation appears in chapter 2 of *Tell Jesus* (1863), her book on Emily Gosse.

a Mrs Jellyby: a supposedly philanthropic lady in Charles Dickens's *Bleak House* (1852–3), who devotes herself to charitable pursuits while neglecting her own family.

'those testimonies . . . distant parts of the globe': quoted from PHG's *Memorial of the Last Day on Earth of Emily Gosse* (1857).

'her unknown day's employ': from Matthew Arnold's (1822–88) 'Lines

Written in Kensington Gardens', ll. 11–12: 'Sometimes a thrush flit overhead | Deep in her unknown day's employ.'

25 *a sensational novel*: a genre of novel that began to appear in the 1850s, but particularly flourished in the 1860s. The most famous examples of the genre would include: Wilkie Collins, *The Woman in White* (1860); Mrs Henry Wood, *East Lynne* (1861); Mary Elizabeth Braddon, *Lady Audley's Secret* (1862).

Bailey's 'English Dictionary': Nathan Bailey's *Universal English Dictionary* (1721).

26 *the Great Globe in Leicester Square*: the visit took place on 10 September 1857. EG's book is here, as elsewhere in this chapter, a little chronologically ambiguous. The trip to Leicester Square in fact took place in the months after Emily Gosse's death; on the same day at home his father's books were being packed and the parlour carpets removed, ready for their move to Devon.

the ideas of savages at a very early stage of development: EG refers to the fashionable idea of recapitulation. See the introduction to this edition for a discussion of this moment.

27 *Like the dying Falstaff, I babbled of green fields*: the drunken, fat, loquacious, and incorrigible knight in Shakespeare's *Henry IV* plays. EG alludes to Mistress Quickly's description of Falstaff's death: 'for his nose was as sharp as a pen, and 'a babbled of green fields' (*Henry V*, II. iii).

Primrose Hill: a small park with a view over London, just north-west of Regent's Park.

Donne's poem: EG refers to 'The Primrose, being at Mountgomery Castle, upon the hill, on which it is situate'. In 1899, EG published *The Life and Letters of John Donne*, which, despite its flaws of scholarship, remains one of the very first texts to foster the renewal of interest in Donne in the late nineteenth and early twentieth centuries.

Chalk Farm direction: Chalk Farm, a corruption of the area's former name as the Chalcot estate, is on the Camden side of Primrose Hill.

Poplar resembles Paradise: Poplar is a run-down, working-class area in the east of London.

28 *round the corner in the Caledonian Road*: the London road that forms the westward boundary to the Barnsbury area of Islington, where the Gosses were then resident.

a packet of spilikins: this is a Victorian game in which players took it in turns to remove a stick (or thin straw) from a pile without disturbing the other sticks.

30 *several cuts with a cane*: a brutal measure that may have looked less out of place in the context of Victorian family life. EG's reaction to it, and his suggestion that the practice is linked to social class, suggest that such familial corporal punishment would have looked harsh to the book's first readers.

'*Spare the rod and spoil the child*': see *Proverbs* 13: 24: 'He that spareth his rod hateth his son: but he that loveth him chasteneth him betimes.'

33 *local physician . . . a specialist*: the local physician was a Dr Laserson. This first examination took place on 1 May 1856. The Gosses consulted two specialists, Sir James Paget and Dr Hyde Salter, a relative of Gosse's.

34 *one of the most cruel maladies*: cancer of the breast. It is odd that EG should avoid any specific mention of the word 'cancer'. His father's frank treatment of the disease in PHG's *Memorial* had met with criticism at the time of that book's publication.

a certain practitioner: this was the American, Dr Jesse Weldon Fell (1819–90), 'who claimed to have found a new cure for breast cancer, treating the tumours by applying the essence of a root supposedly first used by North American Indians on the shores of Lake Superior. "The cancer is slowly killed and then thrown off from the healthy flesh," Philip wrote to his brother. The Gosses saw photographs of patients in different stages of treatment and the inspiring, if grim, sight of one woman at the actual moment when her tumour (dark, hard and apparently dead) was being separated by Dr Fell with his fingers from the white living flesh surrounding it. He claimed a success rate of 80 per cent' (Thwaite, *Edmund Gosse*, 30). Fell's own first wife had died of cancer. He came to London in May 1855; he was attracting interested attention while treating Emily Gosse, and shortly before her death articles appeared on his technique in the *Lancet* (31 Jan. 1857), 128, and the *Medical Times and Gazette* (31 Jan. 1857), 118, though his work was attacked later in 1857 in the same journals.

35 *Tamar*: the river that separates Cornwall from Devon.

36 *pressure of new poverty*: EG exaggerates, again. By most reckonings, the Gosses were fairly comfortable at this time—certainly well off enough to buy a house in Devon, and keep two maids and a housekeeper.

37 *Newton's 'Thoughts on the Apocalypse'*: Benjamin Wills Newton's *Thoughts on the Apocalypse* (1844).

Toplady: Augustus Montague Toplady (1740–78), the Calvinist hymn-writer, now best remembered for his hymn, 'Rock of Ages'.

38 *'The Cameronian's Dream' . . . a certain James Hyslop*: James Hyslop (1798–1827) published his poem, 'The Cameronian Dream', serially in the *Edinburgh Magazine* in 1819, while he was working as a shepherd—he went on to become a schoolmaster and a tutor on a ship. The Cameronians were a strict Protestant sect, founded by Richard Cameron in 1680.

'their last song to the God of Salvation': from lines 31–2 of Hyslop's 'The Cameronian Dream': 'With eyes rais'd to heaven in meek resignation | They sung their last song to the God of Salvation.'

Robert Louis Stevenson: Robert Louis Stevenson (1850–94) was the writer of *Treasure Island* (1883), *The Strange Case of Dr Jekyll and Mr Hyde* (1886), *Kidnapped* (1886), and the unfinished *Weir of Hermiston* (1896).

This last work bears some resemblance to *Father and Son*, dealing as it does with an only child, whose mother dies when he is young, leaving him to the care of a strict father, whose influence and power he must reject. Stevenson was a friend of EG's.

39 *Sir James Simpson received the Monthyon prize*: James Simpson was awarded this prize by the Académie des Sciences in 1856. The whole passage about anaesthetics here serves to remind the reader again of the distance of this recent past. This sudden attempt at historical perspective is central to EG's critique of his parents' religion.

The floods of the tears . . . a place for the tears!: from 'The Fountain of Tears', a poem by Arthur William Edgar O'Shaughnessy (1844–81) included in Palgrave's *The Golden Treasury* (1891–7; second series). EG makes a few errors of transcription, or of memory.

40 *Parthian shot*: the Parthians were known for their skill in firing arrows as they retreated back at the advancing enemy. Hence, a cutting remark executed on leaving, which leaves no room for the adversary to reply. The remark itself refers to Matthew 15: 14: 'Let them alone: they be blind leaders of the blind. And if the blind lead the blind, both shall fall into the ditch.'

41 *Corinthian converts . . . English men and women of the nineteenth*: EG refers to St Paul's two epistles to the Corinthians, Greek (Achaian—the deliberately estranging word carries its own point) colonists in the north-east Peloponnese, in the south of Greece. EG's central point here is that truth is not fixed; against his parents' belief in a single, continuing revelation, he constructs a sense of truth as relative and bound to personal and historical laws of development.

Trimalchion's feast . . . City dinner: Trimalchio appears in Petronius' *Satyricon*, a Latin work contemporary with the writing of the Gospels and St Paul's epistles. Trimalchio is a scurrilous and hedonistic character; the phrase 'City dinners' refers to polite, official, and implicitly staid bourgeois meals.

42 *Wormwood that fell from Heaven . . . teeth as the teeth of lions*: EG draws upon the imagery of the Revelation of John the Divine, the last book in the Bible—see Revelation 8: 11: 'And the name of the star is called Wormwood: and the third part of the waters became wormwood; and many men died of the waters, because they were made bitter'; and 9: 8: 'And they had hair as the hair of women, and their teeth were as the teeth of lions.' Like many puritans, the 'latter days' fascinated PHG, who wrote several books on the subject, including *The Prophetic Times* (1871). EG demonstrates that his parents could neither read a text historically, nor imaginatively, though clearly they could read allegorically. By implication, he sets out an alternative way of interpreting literature, religion, and experience itself.

Napoleon III and Pope Pius IX and the King of Piedmont: the anti-European and anti-Catholic bias here is interesting and typical of nonconformist Protestantism of the period. It is noteworthy that EG's parents subsume contemporary reality into the fixity of prophetic revelation. The modern world is understood through the medium of the Bible text. Napoleon III was the nephew of Napoleon Bonaparte, and Emperor of France 1846–78; Pius IX was Pope 1846–78; Victor Emmanuel II was King of Sardinia and I of Italy 1820–78.

the Wild Beast: that is, the Antichrist.

Newton and Jukes: in later editions, EG replaced the name of Newton with that of Matthew Habershon (1789–1852), architect and writer on prophecy. PHG knew Habershon personally, which may account for the substitution. Habershon was the father of one of PHG's pupils, while the latter was a schoolmaster in the 1840s, and the two men corresponded on the subject of the apocalypse and end-time prophecy.

'Horæ Apocalypticæ' of a Mr Elliott: Bishop Edward Elliott (1793–1875) published *Horae Apocalypticæ* in 1844.

Babylon the Great: it was common practice among strict Protestants to describe the Roman Catholic Church as Babylon, or as the Whore of Babylon. See Revelation 17–19.

light of the Morning Star, the harbinger of the rising sun: cf. Revelation, 22: 16: 'I Jesus have sent mine angel to testify unto you these things in the churches. I am the root and the offspring of David, and the bright and morning star.'

44 *John Henry Newman*: in the light of the anti-Catholic sentiments detailed in this chapter, the possibility of this reference on EG's part seeming cruel would have been most fresh in the reader's mind. John Henry Newman (1801–90), writer, Christian apologist, and man of the church, scandalized Protestant society when he entered the Roman Catholic Church in 1845. He was made a cardinal in 1879.

'All the trouble which the world inflicts . . . the Divine Majesty': I have been unable to find the source of this quote, and indeed wonder if it really is by Newman.

the burden of Atlas: Zeus, the father of the gods, condemned Atlas, a rebel Titan, to the punishment of upholding the heavens upon his shoulders.

45 *the newly-invented marine aquarium*: PHG coined the word 'aquarium' (previously known as a marine or aquatic vivarium) and was one of the foremost inventors and popularizers of the thing itself: his book *The Aquarium* had appeared in 1854.

46 *little-known, paternal cousin from the west of England*: Mrs Anne Morgan; far from being little known, Anne Morgan had recently visited the Gosses in London, where she nursed the dying Emily.

Clifton: a well-to-do area of Bristol. EG stayed in the house for only four weeks. There were six adolescent children there: Mary, John, Henry, William, Alice, and Ann (who was to become the grandmother of Alec and Evelyn Waugh).

46 *a menagerie*: EG wrote a delighted letter to his father, describing this visit to the Zoological Gardens.

47 *half-blind remembrances of walks, with my tall cousins waving like trees above me*: perhaps an echo of the words spoken by the healed blind man, Mark 8: 24: 'And he looked up, and said, I see men as trees, walking.'

   the foot that used to flutter with winged impetuosity, and to float with the pulse of Hermes: Hermes, the messenger of the gods, depicted as having winged feet.

   an eight-day clock: that is, a clock that requires to be wound up every eight days.

   eldritch scream: a word of Scottish origin, meaning 'weird', 'strange', 'unearthly'.

48 *a Leyden jar*: a completely sealed jar used for the accumulation of electricity, named after the place of its invention in Leiden, Holland.

   Jersey protestant: that is, from Jersey in the Channel Islands.

   Here's your rope . . . to choke him: I have been unable to find the source of this anti-Catholic rhyme.

   The tragedy of Mr Punch: the malignant and murderous hero of the children's puppet show, Punch and Judy.

49 '*with pity and terror*': an allusion to Aristotle's theory of tragedy as cathartic of these emotions. The sense that Punch and Judy is a tragedy, may depend on which version of the tale EG witnessed. Most often, and usually, Punch would end up outwitting the Devil; the attraction of such a trick is obvious for a child growing up in a home where the reality of eternal damnation was undisputed.

50 *a world of light*: possibly an allusion to Henry Vaughan's midseventeenth-century poem about the dead, 'They are All Gone into the World of Light'.

51 *microbes*: a word not coined until 1887, but already by the 1900s in common use.

52 *Mother Shipton . . . Copenhagen Street . . . Regent's Canal*: all very close to the Gosses' house in Barnsbury: Copenhagen Street is only three streets away; the canal just two blocks further. 'Mother Shipton' is presumably the pub on the Pentonville end of the Caledonian Road, named after the seventeenth-century prophetess.

   the Wesleys, Charlotte Elliott . . . and James Montgomery: for the Wesleys, see the notes to pp. 6 and 19. Charlotte Elliott (1789–1871) was a hymn writer and religious poet; this hymn appears in the *Invalid's Hymn Book* (1834). James Montgomery (1771–1854) was a Scottish poet and hymnwriter.

   '*Puseyite*' . . . '*The Christian Year*': Puseyite refers to the Anglo-Catholic movement that grew around Edward Pusey (1800–82), John Henry Newman, and John Keble (1792–1866), the author of the popular and influential work of religious verse, *The Christian Year* (1827).

Newman, Faber and Neale: for Newman, see note to p. 44. F. W. Faber (1814–63), a Roman Catholic convert, went on to become Superior of the London Oratory. J. M. Neale (1818–66) is another Anglo-Catholic hymn-writer.

53 *Horatio Bonar*: Horatio Bonar (1808–89) was a prolific Scottish hymn-writer.

'*Epistle to the Hebrews*': one of St Paul's biblical epistles, particularly concerned with salvation by faith.

'*The heavens are the works . . . fail*': Hebrews 1: 10–12.

'*laying again . . . dead works*' . . . '*crucifying the Son of God afresh*': Hebrews 6: 1; Hebrews 6: 6.

54 *the formalities of the Law of Moses in their very blood, the apostle battles with their dangerous conservatism*: it is likely that EG makes an indirect criticism of the 'Hebraic' (in St Paul's and in Matthew Arnold's sense of the word) in relation to his father's conservatism. For a consideration of Matthew Arnold's distinction between the Hebraic and the Hellenic, see his book, *Culture and Anarchy* (1869).

casuistry: a double-edged word: it could mean either the application of general moral principles to particular moral problems (itself an ambiguous process in EG's thinking); or specious and oversubtle argument.

'*Line upon Line: Here a Little, and there a Little*': a book by Mrs Favell Lee Mortimer, published in 1837, that retells and offers commentary on Old Testament stories.

'*almost all things . . . no remission of sin*': Hebrews 9: 22: 'And almost all things are by the law purged with blood; and without shedding of blood is no remission.'

fuliginous pages: sooty or smoky.

55 *the number of the Beast*: 666, the number of the Antichrist. See Revelation 13: 16–18.

Armageddon: the site of the last battle before the Day of Judgement. See Revelation 16: 16.

County Antrim: one of the six counties of Ulster, the nineteenth-century stronghold of Protestantism in Ireland.

Lord Beaconsfield's phrase . . . own silly business': EG corrected this in later editions to Lord Chesterfield (1694–1773), most famous for his letters offering advice on the ways of the world to his son. A. O. J. Cockshut: 'J. H. Jesse, *Memoirs of Court of England* (1840–3): "He once exclaimed to Anstis, Garter King at Arms: 'You foolish man, you do not even know your own foolish business'." '

the Scarlet Woman: that is, the Roman Catholic Church.

language of the seventeenth century: the sense that the Gosses are part of a culture that places them out of time, in a forgotten past, is double here:

they are both part of the vanished 1850s, and even then were part of a vanished seventeenth century. The 'language of the seventeenth century' is both the language of the Authorized Version of the Bible, but also of the Puritan writers of that period.

55 *Sassari*: a town in northern Sardinia.

56 *Naples*: Italy, of course, is a predominantly Roman Catholic country.

Miss Marks: this woman's real name was, in fact, Sarah Andrews. She worked for the Gosses from May 1857 until the first half of 1861.

57 *Mrs Pipchin and Miss Sally Brass*: Mrs Pipchin is an intimidating Brighton housekeeper who looks after the sickly child, Paul Dombey, in *Dombey and Son* (1847–8); Miss Sally Brass appears in *The Old Curiosity Shop* (1841).

58 *House of Rimmon . . . shibboleths*: the House of Rimmon appears in 2 Kings 5: 18, where Naaman prays for forgiveness for bowing in the house of Rimmon; in other words, for worshipping in the temple of an alien religion: Miss Marks (Sarah Andrews) was not a member of the Brethren. This is the first of many mentions of Naaman and Rimmon, which may suggest that his story possesses a symbolic function in *Father and Son* as an example of religious hypocrisy or expediency, or of simply being in the wrong place. A 'shibboleth' is another biblical reference, this time to Judges 12: 6, and is a word used to denote a doctrine, a practice, or a word adhered to by a group long after its original meaning has been lost.

59 *Wordsworth . . . lighted up his spirit with gleams that were like the flashing of a shield*: William Wordsworth (1770–1850), English poet, famous for his celebration of childhood experience. EG may be referring to the 'visionary gleam' of ll. 56–7 of Wordsworth's 'Ode. [Intimations of Immortality from Recollections of Early Childhood]':

> Whither is fled the visionary gleam?
> Where is it now, the glory and the dream?

'Prelude' . . . 'infirmity of love for days disowned by memory': William Wordsworth's *The Prelude*, composed 1799–1805, and published in a much revised form in 1850, is one of the key autobiographies of the nineteenth century and a seminal text in the representation of childhood. The quote comes from *The Prelude*, i. 614–15.

'drinking in a pure organic pleasure': *The Prelude*, i. 563–4.

The village . . . but half a mile inland: St Marychurch, near Torquay.

60 *Oddicombe*: a stretch of coast between Petit Tor and Babbacombe.

like those of savages: another instance of EG's recapitulatory thinking.

61 *'flinging down their golden crowns upon the jasper sea'*: from Reginald Heber's (1783–1826) hymn, 'Holy, holy, holy, Lord God Almighty!' EG

misremembered, or decided to improve, Heber's lines, which read 'Casting down their golden crowns around the glassy sea'.

Lake of Gennesaret: the Sea of Galilee.

Cascine . . . Arno . . . Mugnone: the Cascine is a mountain peak close to Florence on the banks of the river Arno. Percy Bysshe Shelley (1792–1822) famously wrote 'Ode to the West Wind' there. The Mugnone is a canal that joins the Arno near there.

Lyell: Sir Charles Lyell (1797–1875), the geologist and author of *The Principles of Geology* (1830–3), which argued for a theory of 'Uniformitarian' geology, which supposed that geological change took place slowly and over very great periods of time.

Darwin: Charles Darwin (1809–82), whose *The Origin Of Species* was to be published two years later in 1859.

62 *Hooker and Wallace, Asa Gray and even Agassiz*: Sir Joseph Hooker (1817–1911), the botanist, and, in 1857, Assistant Director of Kew Gardens (he became Director on his father's death in 1865); Alfred Russel Wallace (1823–1913), the naturalist, who independently arrived at the theory of natural selection, and he and Darwin presented the idea together at the Linnean Society on 1 July 1858; Asa (John Edward) Gray (1810–88), an American taxonomist and naturalist; and Jean Louis Rodolphe Agassiz (1807–73), a rather more conservative Swiss-American geologist, palaeontologist, and naturalist.

'The Origin of Species': published in 1859 by Charles Darwin.

Wollaston's 'Variation of Species': Thomas Vernon Wollaston (1822–78) published his book in 1856.

orang-outang: since the eighteenth century this was popularly supposed to be the great ape most akin to human beings.

'Vestiges of Creation': published anonymously in 1844 by Robert Chambers (1802–71), this work proposed an evolutionary view of nature, suggesting that laws of development control the organic world.

Owen: Sir Richard Owen (1804–92), the Superintendent of the Natural History Department of the British Museum and an outspoken critic of the evolutionary theories propounded by Charles Darwin.

Royal Society: the body founded in the early 1660s to promote scientific knowledge in Britain, and which in the 1850s still stood for the centre of national scientific life.

Carpenter: William Benjamin Carpenter (1813–85), biologist, botanist, and, from 1856 to 1879, Registrar of London University.

63 *catastrophists*: those who accounted for geological changes as evidence of past cataclysmic catastrophes.

Sir Thomas Browne: Sir Thomas Browne (1605–82), Christian apologist, who wrote *Pseudodoxia Epidemica* (1646), a sceptical work that comes close to the empirical spirit that prompted the founding of the Royal

Society. His other key works are *Religio Medici* (1642), *Hydriotaphia*, and *The Garden of Cyrus* (published together in 1658). EG wrote a study of Browne in 1905, one of several books in which he explored the lives and works of seventeenth-century Christian writers.

63 *omphalos*: the Greek word for 'navel'.

64 *'Omphalos' . . . make the lion eat grass with the lamb*: PHG published *Omphalos* in 1857; see the introduction to this edition, and App. 2. See Isaiah 11: 6: 'The wolf also shall dwell with the lamb, and the leopard shall lie down with the kid; and the calf and the young lion and the fatling together; and a little child shall lead them.'

youthful Huxley . . . Charles Kingsley: Thomas Henry Huxley (1825–95), the renowned and pugnacious popularizer of Darwinian theories, and author of *Evidence as to Man's Place in Nature* (1863) and *Evolution and Ethics* (1893). Charles Kingsley (1819–75) was PHG's great friend, a 'muscular Christian', and author of *Alton Locke* (1850), *Glaucus: or the Wonders of the Shore* (1855), and *The Water Babies* (1863).

'inspissated': thickened.

so huge a rout | Encumbered him with ruin: from John Milton's Puritan epic of the fall of man, *Paradise Lost*, vi. 873–4.

65 *'He can zing a zong, zo well's another, though he be a minister'*: William Barnes (1801–86), the Dorset poet, renders West Country dialect in a similar way (though this, of course, is Devon).

67 *Burke and Hare*: William Burke and William Hare, the famous Edinburgh grave-robbers, or 'Resurrectionists', who dug up bodies to sell to anatomists for medical dissection. They graduated to suffocating victims simply for the purpose of obtaining their bodies. Burke was tried and hanged as a result in 1829, on the evidence of his accomplice, Hare.

'the Carpet-bag Mystery': on 9 Oct. 1857, a carpet-bag was discovered close to Waterloo Bridge, containing a mutilated body without head or limbs. The murder was later supposed to be part of a conspiracy against Napoleon III.

69 *assafœtida*: a strong tasting medicine, made from resin.

Yule-Tide: originally a heathen festival of the winter solstice, lasting twelve days; later simply Christmas. The connection of the Christian feast to the pagan one is what disturbs PHG.

'Oh! Papa, Papa, I have eaten of flesh offered to idols!': Acts 15: 29: 'That ye abstain from meats offered to idols, and from blood, and from things strangled, and from fornication: from which if ye keep yourselves, ye shall do well. Fare ye well.'

72 *fœtor*: a stench.

74 *before the French Revolution*: that is, before 1789.

James Petherbridge, the Nestor of our meeting: Nestor is an aged and wise man in Homer's *Iliad* and *Odyssey*.

75 *a Methody*: colloquial term for a Methodist.

'*in her labour of teaching the young idea how to shoot*': the allusion is to James Thomson (1700–48), *The Seasons* (1726–30), 'Spring', ll. 1151–2: 'Delightful task! to rear the tender thought, | To teach the young idea how to shoot.'

phthisis: that is, tuberculosis.

76 *hepatica*: 'A subgenus of the genus *Anemone*; esp. the common spring-flowering *Anemone* (*Hepatica*) *triloba*, a native of continental Europe, cultivated in Britain, the three-lobed leaves of which were fancied to resemble the liver' (*OED*).

a converted person: a person who has been 'born again', having repented of their sins and become a Christian.

77 *factotum*: someone who controls (or meddles with) everything.

patois: a dialect spoken in a particular region, and considered distinct from literary language.

neurotic condition: a concept that arose in the 1870s and was popularized in the 1880s and 1890s.

78 *opoponax*: a medicinal but foul-smelling gum-resin.

cotoniaster: that is, cotoneaster, a genus of small trees or trailing shrubs.

in the very words of Shelley: the quotation is from the third stanza of Percy Bysshe Shelley's (1792–1822) poem, 'The Question', first published in 1822.

79 *He was not a biologist, in the true sense of the term*: EG suggests that his father is a man interested in details, and not in the whole study of life—although, of course, *Omphalos* goes a long way to providing a general theory of life.

'*affranchissant l'esprit . . . sans Dieu*': a remark made by Gustave Flaubert (1821–80), the French novelist: 'setting free the spirit and weighing up worlds, without hatred, without fear, without pity, without love and without God'.

80 *rufous promontories*: promontories of a brownish-red colour.

oar-weed: or ore-weed, which is simply seaweed.

81 *like Keats' Grecian vase, 'a still unravished bride of quietness'*: a reference to the first line of John Keats's (1795–1821) 'Ode on a Grecian Urn', a poem which explores the preserving powers of art in relation to the effects of time.

anthea . . . the fronds of the dulse: dulse is red edible seaweed.

corallines: 'A genus of seaweeds having a calcareous jointed stem, one species of which (*Corallina officinalis*) is common on the coasts of the North Atlantic; "a plant having the power of secreting lime like the coral animals" (Dana)' (*OED*).

82 '*History of the British Sea-Anemones and Corals*': a book published by PHG in 1860.

82 *a slightly timorous Andromeda*: a reference to the Greek myth in which Andromeda was tied to a rock, where she was rescued by Perseus from a sea-monster. Like the reference to Princess Blanchefleur (see note to p. 22), this is an image in which EG feminizes himself, while stressing his lonely vulnerability.

83 '*Actinologia Britannica*': published in Jan. 1860.

Susan . . . Kate: Susan Mears was the Gosses' cook; Kate is mentioned by her first name only in letters and diaries from 1857 to 1858.

horrid, tropical niggers: A. O. J. Cockshut sees this expression as EG signalling the fact that he was absolutely in tune with the prejudices of his upbringing. I disagree. In a book about rebellion, EG peppers his story with little rebellions; this moment is clearly one of these. The strength of the expression demonstrates the strength of his childish opposition to a low fate that seems set out for him.

84 *detraquée*: someone unhinged; who's 'gone off the rails', though without the usual suggestion of a drift into dissipation. *Détraquée* should have an accent on the first 'e'. This is one textual error that fails to get consistently corrected in later editions.

In the downhill of life ... o'erlooks the wide sea: from the poem 'Tomorrow' by John Collins (1724–1808), and included in *The Golden Treasury* (1891–7). See note to p. 168.

cowry-shells: 'Any gastropod (or its shell) of the genus *Cypræa* or family *Cypræidæ*, characterized by their oval shape, undeveloped spire, and narrow aperture as long as the shell; e.g. *Cypræa Europœa*, the common cowrie of the British coast' (*OED*).

86 *reticule*: a net, or a small woven bag.

'*Jack Robinson*': that is, immediately, very quickly. According to Brewer's *Dictionary of Phrase and Fable*, the phrase may derive from an exchange made by Sheridan in the House of Commons, where, making a speech on government bribery, and being greeted by calls to name the guilty parties, he declared: 'Yes, I could name him as soon as I could say Jack Robinson.'

'*without a single kiss or a good-bye*', *as the poet says*: the poet is Coventry Patmore (1823–96), and the words form l. 9 of 'Departure', yet another poem that EG found in *The Golden Treasury* (1891–7).

87 *bound hand and foot like Mazeppa*: eponymous hero of Byron's (1788–1824) poem *Mazeppa* (1819), in which, following an intrigue, he is bound to the back of a wild horse.

CARMINE: a crimson pigment derived from cochineal, a dye-stuff made from the dried bodies of the insect *Coccus cacti*.

88 *jobation*: a lengthy and tedious rebuke.

pure Johnsonian English: in the correct, balanced, and rhetorical style of Samuel Johnson (1709–84).

89 *essence of cochineal*: see note to p. 87.

my shibboleth of self-indulgence: see note to p. 58.

Belshazzar's feast, the loftiest épergne of gold: in chapter 5, verses 1–4, of the biblical book of Daniel; it was at Belshazzar's feast that mysterious writing appeared on the wall, interpreted by Daniel as a prophecy of the fall of Babylon. An 'épergne' is an elaborate centre-piece at a banquet.

90 *âme d'élite*: an élite soul.

the Sheep from the Goats: Matthew 25: 32: 'And before him shall be gathered all nations: and he shall separate them one from another, as a shepherd divideth his sheep from the goats'.

election: the condition of being chosen from eternity as a soul that God will save.

91 *His surname I have forgotten*: this was emended in a later edition to 'His surname was Jeffries'.

Pisgah-views: the mountain from which Moses glimpsed the Promised Land.

92 *hirsuta et horrida*: a Latin phrase, meaning bristly/hirsute and rough.

escalading: climbing over by means of ladders.

Charles Kingsley: see note to p. 64. He was visiting Livermead on the other side of Torquay, where his wife was living on account of her poor health.

stentorian tones: a very loud voice, derived from Stentor, a Greek herald in Homer's *Iliad*, v. 783, whose voice was as loud as that of fifty men.

'*Hypatia*': a novel by Charles Kingsley published in *Fraser's Magazine* in 1851, and in book form in 1853. This historical novel set in Alexandria in the fifth century AD expresses some criticism of the early Christian church, concentrating as it does on the murder of Hypatia, a Greek Neoplatonic philosopher by an enraged Christian mob.

94 *minnock*: EG may be making this up. The edition of Nathan Bailey's *An Universal Etymological English Dictionary* (1721), that we know the Gosses owned, defines 'minx' as 'a proud Girl'. See notes to pp. 25 and 160.

entr'ouvert: half-open.

95 *Like Aurora Leigh*: the heroine of Elizabeth Barrett Browning's (1806–61), *Aurora Leigh* (1857). The lines are misquoted from Book I, ll. 403–6: 'I learnt a little algebra, a little | Of the mathematics,—brushed with extreme flounce | The circle of the sciences, because | She misliked women who are frivolous.'

my Grandfather: probably Thomas Gosse (1765–1844), who is supposed to have carried the Bible and an edition of the Greek pastoral poet, Theocritus, with him at all times.

Virgil: a significant choice for PHG from among all the classical writers. Virgil was embraced by the Roman Catholic Christian Middle Ages. The fourth of his *Eclogues* was seen as prophetic of Christ, and Dante made the pagan poet his guide through the Christian universe in *The Divine Comedy*.

96 *Horace, Lucretius, Terence, Catullus, Juvenal*: Latin writers all of whose work can stray into sexual or profane matters. Horace (Quintus Horatius Flaccus) (65–8 BC) is famous for writing *Satires* and *Odes*; Lucretius (Titus Lucretius Carus) (*c.*99–55 BC) wrote the philosophical poem, *De Rerum Natura* ('Of the Nature of Things'), an atheist poem illustrative of Epicurus' atomic theory of the universe; Terence (Publius Terentius Afer) (*c.*190/180–159 BC) was the author of a series of brilliant comedies; Gaius Valerius Catullus (*c.*84–*c.*54 BC) is particularly remembered as the writer of epigrams and lyric poems; Juvenal (Decimus Junius Juvenalis) (*c.* AD 60–*c.*136) was the author of sixteen angry, vivid, and indignant satires.

Delphin edition of 1798: that is, an edition of the Latin classics prepared for the Dauphin of France (the son of the king).

Tityre . . . fagi: from Virgil, *Eclogues*, i. 1: 'Tityrus, you who lie under the shade of the spreading beech.'

tu, Tityre . . . silvas: from Virgil, *Eclogues*, i. 4–5: 'You, Tityrus, reclining in the shade, make the woods echo the name of beautiful Amaryllis.'

my prosodical instinct: one of the key uses of the concept of 'instincts' in an autobiography generally infused with the questions of heredity and evolutionary inheritance. This 'instinct' is key to EG's developing a sense of himself as bound to the vocation of poet.

'a breeze mid blossoms playing', as Coleridge says: the misquoted first line of 'Youth and Age', by Samuel Taylor Coleridge (1772–1834): 'Verse, a breeze 'mid blossoms straying.' Once again, this is a poem to be found in *The Golden Treasury* (1891–7; first series). The number of quotations and allusions to most of the key English Romantic poets rivals only the Bible in EG's *Father and Son*.

Formosam . . . silvas: see note to p. 96.

99 *Linnæan Society*: a London-based society for natural historians, named after Carl Von Linnæus (1707–78), the Swedish naturalist who created a system for the ordering of flora and fauna.

104 *'another infant Samuel'*: Samuel, while still a child, served God: 'But Samuel ministered before the LORD, being a child, girded with a linen e-phod' (1 Samuel 2: 18). See note to p. 8.

106 *babe and a suckling*: cf. Matthew 21: 16, itself referring to Psalms 8: 2: 'Out of the mouth of babes and sucklings hast thou ordained strength because of thine enemies, that thou mightest still the enemy and the avenger.'

'as an adult': it is crucial that EG's religious apotheosis should metaphorically entail the erasure of his identity as a child.

108 *jujube*: a sweet.

Mr S. now rose: Leonard Strong (1797–1874), a former Anglican curate, was a leading member of the Brethren, and was one of those who were behind the building of the Warren Road Room, the largest Brethren meeting place in Torquay (where the baptism presumably took place).

hieratic figure: a priestly figure.

James Smith . . . He who, in quest of quiet, . . . hubbub he imputes': James Smith (1775–1839) was the co-author, with his brother, of *Rejected Addresses* (1812), a series of imitations and parodies of poets of the day, and *Horace in London* (1813). However, James Smith does not appear, as far as I can discover, to have ever written such a remark.

109 *Titanic arms*: huge, like the arms of the mythical Titans.

113 *'backsliding'. . . 'put away'*: backsliding means to deviate, or retreat, from a full Christian life and faith; to be put away is a cultural practice, common to more than one religious group, in which an individual is ostracized and deliberately ignored, as social pressure or punishment for a perceived misdemeanour.

Mrs Pewings: this is probably Elizabeth Fewings, who was the Gosses' 19-year-old, unmarried cook—though these facts somehow do not fit the anecdote that follows about her ('old Pewings').

the church of Laodicea: in Phrygia, or modern Turkey. The Laodiceans were criticized in Revelation 3: 14–16 for being unenthusiastic and indifferent regarding their faith: 'And unto the angel of the church of the Laodiceans write; These things saith the Amen, the faithful and true witness, the beginning of the creation of God; I know thy works, that thou art neither cold nor hot: I would thou wert cold or hot. So then because thou art lukewarm, and neither cold nor hot, I will spue thee out of my mouth.'

115 *St Teresa, wild for the Moors and martyrdom*: St Teresa of Avila (1515–82) was a Spanish mystic. A. O. J. Cockshut suggests that this may be a reference to Richard Crashaw's (1612/13–49) 'Hymn to Saint Teresa', ll. 4–8: 'Since 'tis not to be had at home, | Shee'l travel for *A Martyrdome*. | No *Home* for hers confesses she, | But where she may a Martyr be. | Shee'l to the *Moores* and trade with them, | For this unvalued *Diadem*.'

no close time for souls: a metaphor derived from hunting, referring to those periods where game can not be shot.

' *"My poor work is done . . . my spirit"* ': this paraphrases St Stephen's words before his martyrdom, from Acts 7: 59: 'And they stoned Stephen, calling upon God, and saying, Lord Jesus, receive my spirit.'

nunc dimittis: the first words of St Simeon's prayer in the Temple, after he first sees the infant Christ ('now depart'), from Luke 2: 29: 'Lord, now lettest thou thy servant depart in peace, according to thy word.'

116 *'God who is a jealous God'*: cf. Exodus 20: 5: 'Thou shalt not bow down thyself to them, nor serve them: for I the LORD thy God am a jealous

God, visiting the iniquity of the fathers upon the children unto the third and fourth generation that hate me.'

116 *Archbishop Leighton's 'Commentary on the First Epistle of Peter'*: Robert Leighton (1611–84) was Archbishop of Glasgow, being particularly known for his religious moderation.

117 *this saving faith, which could move mountains of evidence*: paraphrasing Matthew 17: 20: 'And Jesus said unto them, Because of your unbelief: for verily I say unto you, If ye have faith as a grain of mustard seed, ye shall say unto this mountain, Remove hence to yonder place; and it shall remove; and nothing shall be impossible unto you.'

Antilles: a group of islands in the West Indies.

Cape Sant' Antonio to the Serpent's Mouth: that is, an entrance to the Gulf of Paria, from the western end of Cuba to Trinidad and Venezuela.

'Tom Cringle's Log': a novel by Michael Scott (1789–1835), first published in *Blackwood's Magazine* (1829–33).

118 *all-spice*: pimento trees.

febrifugal: adapted to mitigate or subdue fever.

Spanish Town: Panama, in ch. 6 and 7 of volume II of Michael Scott's *Tom Cringle's Log*.

pagan: the sense that life and energy are pagan, while Christianity is a constriction of life is a commonplace among late nineteenth-century writers like Swinburne or Pater, among whom Gosse would have liked to have counted himself.

119 *Fatima*: the last wife of Bluebeard in Charles Perrault (1628–1703), *Histoires, ou contes du temps passé* (1697). Another feminizing image analogous to the Princess Blanchefleur similitude (see note to p. 22).

Petit-tor Lane: currently renamed as Petitor Road. It goes from the centre of St Marychurch to the sea.

120 *John Brooks, an Irish quarryman, and his wife, Ann Brooks*: in Hepburn's notes, he suggests Ann's name was changed from Mary.

121 *Mary Brooks*: this was corrected to 'Ann Brooks' in the fourth impression of *Father and Son*.

a day-school ... Mr M.: the school was at Trafalgar Villa, Westhill Road, St Marychurch, and the schoolmaster was Nicholas Meneer (born 1832/3?).

122 *Poole*: a harbour town, eastwards along the southern coast in Dorset.

James Sheridan Knowles: James Sheridan Knowles (1784–1862), actor and verse dramatist, wrote *Virginius* (1820), *The Hunchback* (1832), and *The Love Chase* (1837).

123 *Hamlet and Falstaff and Prospero*: all famous Shakespearean characters, Falstaff appearing in *1 Henry IV*, *2 Henry IV*, and *The Merry Wives of Windsor*, and Prospero in *The Tempest*.

Bassanio: the 'romantic' lead of Shakespeare's *The Merchant of Venice*, who sets out to win the hand of Portia. The play, dating from 1596–8, deals with, among other things, the conflict between Venetian Christians and the Jewish money-lender, Shylock.

In Belmont is a lady . . . than that word!: from *The Merchant of Venice*, I. i. 161–2. EG misplaces two commas (which should come after 'and' and 'word') to make the quote make independent sense.

124 *Tor Bay*: the stretch of sea off the coast of Torquay.

125 *in an old house that was simply a basket of roses*: Upton Cottage, in Torquay.

Miss Brightwen: Eliza Brightwen was a 47-year-old spinster.

126 *pedobaptist*: someone who believes, unlike the Plymouth Brethren, in the efficacy of infant baptism.

127 *a lodge in my garden of cucumbers*: a reference to Isaiah 1: 8: 'And the daughter of Zion is left as a cottage in a vineyard, as a lodge in a garden of cucumbers, as a besieged city.'

128 *avoirdupois*: weight, heaviness.

quidnuncs: gossips and busybodies—the Latin word *quidnunc* literally means 'what now?'.

régime: a pun on a change of a system of government, and a change of regimen (diet, exercise, etc. for the sake of health).

129 *magnis clamoribus*: from Virgil, *Georgics*, iv. 76, meaning 'with great noise'.

a peg-top: a child's toy, consisting of a peg of wood that is spun by a whip or a cord.

130 '*The Romance of Natural History*': a work by PHG, published in two volumes in 1860–1.

'*one lamb among so many kids*': see note to p. 90.

131 '*cette tromperie mutuelle*' *of which Pascal speaks*: 'that mutual error'. Blaise Pascal (1623–62) was a French mathematician, natural philosopher, and moralist. As a Jansenist and therefore a Roman Catholic believer in predestination, Pascal is a suitable person to quote.

Tartufe: the anti-hero and religious hypocrite in Molière's play, *Le Tartuffe* (1664). The more usual spelling is 'Tartuffe', but 'Tartufe' is also sometimes used.

Molière: the pen-name of Jean-Baptiste Poquelin (1622–73), the French comic dramatist and actor.

133 *Walter Scott*: see note to p. 7. It is significant, perhaps, that EG should find himself echoing his parents' literary tastes.

134 '*The Lady of the Lake*': a poem in six cantos by Sir Walter Scott, published in 1810, describing the chivalrous and romantic adventures of James Fitz-James, Roderick Dhu, and Malcolm Graeme, all suitors for

the hand of Ellen, daughter of the outlawed Lord James of Douglas. The following names are all references to the poem.

134 *A sharp and shrieking . . . On Beala-nam-bo*: from *The Lady of the Lake*, III. x. 31–4.

allows 'The Lord of the Isles' and excludes 'Rob Roy': the former is a poem by Walter Scott, published in 1815, the latter is one of his novels, published in 1817.

'*Pickwick*': *Pickwick Papers* was Dickens's first novel, published 1836–7, and a great portrait of unworldly innocence.

135 *Old Crome painting . . . Cotman*: John Crome (1768–1821) was an English landscape painter, and founder of the Norwich School of painting. John Sell Cotman (1782–1842) was the drawing master of Norwich School, and a fine painter in his own right. This paragraph's denigration of PHG's artistic interests and abilities is unfair: PHG had trained at the Royal Academy and was a fine artist in his own right, as the illustrations to his books demonstrate. Perhaps EG wishes to establish an antagonism between the artistic temperament and the scientific (and puritan) character; in such a schema the fact that PHG was a talented artist is undoubtedly an inconvenience.

Liber Studiorum: J. W. M. Turner's (1775–1851) 'book of studies', a series of engravings published in fourteen parts (with five engravings in each part) sporadically between 1807–19, depicting landscapes as seen in different artistic genres (i.e. pastoral, epic or elevated pastoral, maritime, architectural, mountainous, and historical).

Creswick: Thomas Creswick (1811–69), a landscape painter and illustrator.

136 *Royal Academy*: the Royal Academy of Arts, founded in 1768; at the time about which EG is writing it was housed in the National Gallery, prior to its move in 1869 to Burlington House on Piccadilly.

Mr Holman Hunt's Finding of Christ in the Temple: William Holman Hunt (1827–1910) was one of the English Pre-Raphaelite Brotherhood, and the member who longest stayed true to the Brotherhood's principles. PHG's interest in the painting sits uneasily with EG's declaration that it was his stepmother who fostered his love of art. The painting was exhibited nationally in 1860. Its symbolic appeal is obvious in a book which describes a child apparently marked out for a glorious religious future. This symbolic appeal may have outweighed EG's sense of accuracy, as it was another Holman Hunt picture, *The Light of the World*, that was exhibited at Croydon's Royal Library in Torquay in 1861, whereas the *Finding of Christ* was not shown there until 1865.

my Father pointed out to me various details, such as the phylacteries and the mitres: this may sound a terribly literal approach to a painting, in keeping with PHG's scientific illustrations being the wrong thing. In fact, as EG goes on to suggest, the same impulse to the elucidation of detail underlies both Hunt's picture (it was praised for precisely the kind of thing that PHG attends to) and PHG's illustrations. A phylactery is a small leather case containing strips of parchment inscribed with religious texts; a mitre is, in Christian terminology, the liturgical headdress of a bishop.

'*Preraphaelite*': the Pre-Raphaelite Brotherhood, founded in the winter of 1848, in a house on Gower Street in London, were a group of young artists committed to painting in imitation of the clarity, colour, and detail found in Italian paintings before the flourishing of Raphael (Raffaello Sanzio) (1483–1520)).

chiaroscuro: an Italian word literally translatable as 'light–dark', and referring to painterly effects intended to represent light through the arrangement of light and dark areas in a painting.

139   *Campbell . . . Byron*: a fairly typical selection of Romantic period poets for the period: Thomas Campbell (1777–1844), Robert Burns (1759–96), John Keats (1795–1821), and George Gordon, Lord Byron (1788–1824).

'*The Last Day*' *of Dr Young . . . Samuel Boyse*: Edward Young (1683–1765), rector of Welwyn and the author of *The Complaint, or Night Thoughts on Life, Death and Immortality* (1742–5), published *The Last Day* in 1713. Robert Blair (1699–1746), minister of Athelstaneford, published *The Grave* in 1743. Bishop Beilby Porteus (Porteous) (1731–1808) was Bishop of London. Samuel Boyse was born in 1708 and died in 1749. It is probable that the book bringing together these melancholy, religious poems was a volume edited by C. Whittingham in 1823.

the reign of George II: that is, from 1728 to 1760.

140   *autochthonous*: native to the soil; something peculiar to the place from which it derives.

Jukes' 'On the Apocalypse' . . . 'The Javelin of Phineas': for Jukes, see note to p. 17. The other book is Revd William Lincoln's *The Javelin of Phineas* (1863). Its title derives from Numbers 25: 6–8, in which Phineas kills Zimri, a Jewish man, and Cozbi, the Midianitish woman, he has deigned to marry against the wishes of God.

'*The Last Day*': see note to p. 139.

Father of mercies! . . . a clod with misery?: Young, *The Last Day*, iii. 164–9.

sanctimonious rector of Welwyn: that is, Edward Young. It is interesting that EG should declare that he derived a pleasure from the poem that is other than that intended by its religious author, and therefore that texts permit more than one interpretation.

Now charnels rattle . . . the feet: Young, *The Last Day*, ii. 23–6. The punctuation is slightly different in the original.

142   '*Casabianca*' *. . . 'We are Seven*': typical anthology pieces of the period and both concerning the exploits of children, 'Casabianca' is a poem of Felicia Dorothea Hemans (1793–1835) and 'We are Seven' is one of William Wordsworth's (1770–1850) *Lyrical Ballads*.

Calverley: Charles Stuart Calverley (1831–84) was a barrister, a parodist, translator, and a writer of light verse. His legal career was blighted by the effects of a skating accident.

142 *If death were nothing . . . then might the debauchee*: this is from Robert Blair, *The Grave*, ll. 382–5.

143 *the Mabille*: the Jardin de Mabille in Paris was famous in the nineteenth century for dancing (especially the polka) and 'loose women'.

144 *Philemon and Baucis*: in Greek mythology, a virtuous couple who unknowingly entertained the gods.

to parody the poet Gray: the line parodied is 'How jocund did they drive their team afield', l. 27 of Thomas Gray (1716–71), *Elegy in a Country Churchyard*.

Sandford and Merton: Thomas Day (1748–89), *The History of Sandford and Merton* (3 vols., 1783–9), a didactic book for children in which the rich and nasty boy, Merton, contrasts with the poor but goodly farmer's son, Sandford.

145 *Yes Tor*: or 'West Tor', a high, bare hill on nearby Dartmoor.

146 *Apollo . . . Venus . . . Diana . . . Jupiter*: all Greek and Roman gods: Apollo is the god associated with perfect male beauty; Venus is the beautiful goddess of love; Diana, the huntress, is the symbol of chastity; Jupiter is the king of the gods.

Cities of the Plain: Sodom and Gomorrah, destroyed by God for their wickedness in Genesis 19: 28–9. The contrast between a Hebraic Christianity and Hellenic paganism is central to the tensions in the book, and to the culture of Britain in the period.

some Hellenic hippodrome: a course of chariot races, though I would guess that EG is suggesting something even more violent or lewd than horse-racing.

without any external suggestion: another instance of EG possessing instincts that do not appear to derive from immediate heredity or the culture into which he was born.

147 *Crystal Palace*: a large building of glass and iron erected in Hyde Park, London, for the Great Exhibition and subsequently moved to Sydenham.

'in the very temple of Belial': Belial is a Hebrew word meaning worthless, reckless, lawless. Although taken to stand for a particular demon, really it should be regarded as a way of suggesting worthlessness. However, in many literary texts (and the word recalls various mentions of Belial in Milton's *Paradise Lost* (1674)), Belial had become a symbolic figure for the demonic and the worldly.

unbridled hysteria: EG again uses the modern language of pathology to describe individual actions.

iconoclastic Susan, I at least would be ardent on the other side: EG draws up battle lines, arranging himself on the side of the physical manifestation of beauty versus the Puritan inner light; of the Hellenic versus the Hebraic; of the urbane and lovely versus the brooding and ungenerous. It is crucial, of course, that both opposing views should be held 'ardently'.

'*Hellas*': a lyrical drama by Percy Bysshe Shelley (1792–1822) published in 1822. The original lines (232–8) read:

> Apollo, Pan, and Love
> And even Olympian Jove
> Grew weak, for killing Truth had glared at them;
> Our hills and seas and streams,
> Dispeopled of their dreams,
> Their waters turned to blood, their dew to tears,
> Wailed for the golden years.

148   *Hermes and to Aphrodite*: the messenger of the gods, and the goddess of love.

     S. T. Coleridge: Samuel Taylor Coleridge (1772–1834), Romantic poet. See note to p. 96.

     the Sin against the Holy Ghost: this is the one sin that can never be forgiven, cf. Mark 3: 29: 'But he that shall blaspheme against the Holy Ghost hath never forgiveness, but is in danger of eternal damnation.'

149   *Behold him . . . singed his cheek!*: misquoted (for 'hair' read 'beard') from ll. 473–4 of Dante Gabriel Rossetti's (1828–82) poem, 'Dante at Verona' (1870), referring to the superstitious belief that Dante Alighieri (1265–1321), the medieval poet, really had descended into hell, as described in *Inferno*. The allusion to a literal interpretation of a fiction is another telling example of EG's critique of his father's Protestantism.

150   *gimlet*: penetrating or piercing, deriving from a gimlet which is a tool used for boring small holes in wood.

     Colossians: one of St Paul's Epistles.

152   *a neighbouring sea-port town*: Thorn Park Classical and Mathematical School in Combe Vale in Teignmouth, along the coast to the north from Oddicombe and St Marychurch. The 'elderly couple' were the Edgelows. EG became a full boarder in 1863 and apparently remained there until the close of 1866.

153   *Promised Land*: the place to which the Jews fled after escaping from their long captivity in Egypt.

     as Elkanah and Hannah . . . lent unto the Lord': a very full comparison derived from the relationship of the infant Samuel as described in 1 Samuel 1 and 2. Like PHG, Elkanah is also a man who has (or had had) two wives. Samuel is described as 'girded with a linen ephod', a Jewish priestly garment in 1 Samuel 2: 18. The last quotation is from 1 Samuel 1: 28: 'Therefore also I have lent him to the LORD; as long he liveth he shall be lent to the LORD. And he worshipped the Lord there.' The sense is of a life of a child dedicated by his parents to the service of God; the child's life belongs neither to itself, nor to the parents, but to the Father in heaven. See notes to pp. 8 and 104.

153 *Faith could move mountains*: see note to p. 117.

154 *in custodiendo sermones Dei*: observing the word of God.

Gehazi: a covetous servant of Elisha, punished with leprosy ('he went out from his presence a leper as white as snow', from 2 Kings 5: 27) for fraudulently obtaining a present from Naaman. See 2 Kings 5: 20–7. The following allusions are all to this story. See note to p. 58.

156 *I 'wandered lonely as a cloud'*: the first line of a poem by William Wordsworth (1770–1850); another poem from *The Golden Treasury* (1891–7).

'*the child is father of the man*': another line from a Wordsworth poem, this one being l. 7 of 'My Heart Leaps Up'. This is also included in *The Golden Treasury* (1891–7).

as Montaigne explained them, 'parceque c'était lui, parceque c'était moi': Michel Eyquem de Montaigne (1533–92) the author of *Essais* (1580–95). The quotation refers to Montaigne's explanation in Book I, Essay 38, of why he loved his friend, Étienne de la Boëtie: 'because he was he, and I was I.'

157 *But this is not an autobiography*: EG reminds the reader that this is in fact 'a study of two temperaments', and not a simple account of the author's childhood and adolescence.

phthisic lad: suffering from tuberculosis.

'*chum*': a slang word for friend, in the mid nineteenth century mostly used in the south of England, and prevalent among the working classes in particular.

158 *I was the liberator, the tyrannicide*: it is tempting and obvious to point out that there is an element of an Oedipal fantasy in this.

159 *like that chimerical flower, the Rose of Jericho*: *Anastica hierochuntina*, a desert flower which uncurls if exposed to moisture.

When I read Shakespeare: EG refers to *The Tempest*, I. ii. 355 ff. (the last word in the quoted speech should be 'known'). Caliban's famous reply to Prospero's speech (does EG intend the reader to remember it?) is: 'You taught me language; and my profit on't | Is, I know how to curse' (I. ii. 365–6). The change of wording endows the adolescent Gosse's purposes with greater agency.

160 *Bailey's 'Etymological Dictionary', a book published early in the eighteenth century*: Nathan Bailey, *An Universal Etymological Dictionary* (1721). This interest in etymology and in words as 'instruments of expression' clearly fits with EG's eventual career as a man of letters, and is also relevant to the abstruse language sometimes ostentatiously employed in this book.

Warbury Hill: Warberry Hill, to the south-west of St Marychurch.

chine: a ravine, cut like a fissure into the cliffs.

161 *Shakespearean necromancy*: necromancy is magic that either uses the dead to effect its operation, or conjures up spirits of the dead.

the Strand: a street in central London, parallel to the north (Middlesex) bank of the River Thames, running between Aldwych and Charing Cross.

an immense hall, somewhere in the north of London: the conference took place on 9, 10, and 12 May 1864, in Freemason's Hall, Great Queen Street, in Covent Garden (really in the centre of London).

162 *a blasphemous celebration of the birth of Shakespeare*: the third centenary of his birth was on 23 April 1864 (the traditional but conjectural birth-date of Shakespeare). The man who denounced Shakespeare was Henry Soltau (1805–75), who made the speech on 10 May 1864.

Stratford: Stratford-upon-Avon is, of course, the birthplace of Shakespeare.

163 *mumbo-jumbo*: nonsense, but originally a word given by Europeans to describe a grotesque idol worshipped by certain African tribes. The link between savage and Christian religion may well be intended by EG.

'testified': borne witness to one's Christian faith.

165 *nirvana*: the Buddhist state of extinction of the individual existence through its absorption into the divine state. Still a self-consciously foreign word for EG, intended perhaps to introduce an awareness of other religions into his study of Protestant Christianity.

166 *Ben Jonson and Christopher Marlowe*: Ben Jonson (1572–1637) and Christopher Marlowe (1564–93) both poets, dramatists, and contemporaries of Shakespeare.

'Hero and Leander': an unfinished poem, an epyllion or little epic, by Christopher Marlowe, published in 1598 in a version completed by George Chapman (?1559–1634). It tells the story of how Leander drowns while trying to swim across the Hellespont to reach his beloved, Hero, the priestess of Aphrodite.

Buskins . . . behold: from *Hero and Leander*, i. 37–40.

Amorous Leander . . . Musaeus sung: *Hero and Leander*, i. 57–8. Musaeus was a mythical singer closely related to Orpheus.

modern romanticists: as EG has already demonstrated that he does know the Romantic poets (see note to p. 139), although in a way which may suggest that he had not as yet actually read them, this could refer to poets of the generations of Coleridge, Keats, and Shelley, or perhaps to EG's contemporaries, Dante Gabriel Rossetti (1828–82) and Algernon Charles Swinburne (1837–1909).

the description of Leander's person: cf. Christopher Marlowe, *Hero and Leander*, i. 61–96. The passage, like much of the poem, is imbued with a homoerotic sensuality.

167 *innocently pagan mind*: EG, despite his upbringing, characterizes his mind as pagan and innocent, a deliberate affront to his father's hopes and beliefs.

plethoric elders: an excessive number of elders. The term 'elders' suggests a contrast between his youth and their age.

168 *Keats*: John Keats (1795–1821) remains a decisive if vague influence on EG's own poetry.

Shelley, whose 'Queen Mab': Percy Bysshe Shelley (1792–1822), whose *Queen Mab* was published in 1813. It is a visionary and political poem, whose fierce polemical attacks on the monarchy and commerce might have left the apparently unpolitical EG cold, though the assault on religion in cantos VI and VII might have been expected to appeal to him.

Wordsworth: perhaps EG implies that the poetry of William Wordsworth (1770–1850), with its reflections on the loss of youthful vision, was less appealing to him than the youthful visions of Keats and Shelley.

Southey's stony verse: Robert Southey (1774–1843) was once considered one of the major Romantic poets, though in the twentieth century he was very little read. His key works are the long narrative poems, *Thalaba* (1801) and *Madoc* (1805), and *Wat Tyler*, a drama written while studying at Oxford but published in 1817. He is perhaps a better prose writer than a poet, producing histories and an enjoyable *Life of Nelson* (1813).

'The Golden Treasury': Francis Palgrave's (1824–97) anthology of poems, published in 1861. EG's step-aunt, Maria Brightwen, was married to a brother of Francis Palgrave, which may be why his stepmother possessed a copy to lend. The influence of this book—and its subsequent editions—on EG is witnessed by how many of the poetic references used in *Father and Son* are to be found there.

169 *Unitarian (or 'Socinian' as he preferred to say)*: a Unitarian denies the doctrine of the trinity, believing that God is one being; a Socinian similarly denies the doctrine of the trinity, and disbelieves in the divinity of Christ, and in original sin, holding that those who follow the moral teaching of Christ will find salvation.

170 *Puginesque cathedral*: built in the Gothic revival style of Augustus Welby Northmore Pugin (1812–52).

in the house of Rimmon: cf. 2 Kings 5: 18: 'In this thing the LORD pardon thy servant, that when my master goeth into the house of Rimmon to worship there, and he leaneth on my hand, and I bow myself in the house of Rimmon: when I bow down myself in the house of Rimmon, the LORD pardon thy servant in this thing.' The phrase refers to Naaman's asking permission of Elisha to worship a Babylonian god while with his Babylonian master, and therefore means to act insincerely, to do one thing and feel another. Here the phrase clearly has a more literal application. See also notes to pp. 58 and 154.

171 *a huddled mixture of 'Endymion' and the Book of Revelation, John Wesley's*

hymns and Midsummer Night's Dream: a mixture of English poetry and the Protestant inheritance. John Keats's *Endymion* (1818) and Shakespeare's *A Midsummer Night's Dream* (1595–6?) share a style that is consciously 'poetic', sensuous, faery, and beautiful.

Jesus and Pan held sway together: EG's sense that his taste in English poetry tends towards the 'pagan' (in the sense of easy, joyful, nature-worshipping, unconstrained by petty moralism), and that the inheritance of the particular kind of English literature he chose as his own (Shakespeare, Marlowe, Keats, Shelley) is Hellenic, is central to EG's self-portrayal and to the nature of his rebellion.

as in the great chorus which so marvellously portrays our double nature, 'the folding-star of Bethlehem': this is the same chorus ('Worlds on worlds are rolling ever', ll. 197–238) from Shelley's *Hellas* (1822), already quoted by EG—see note to p. 147. EG imagines himself, indeed imagines *us* (as the word 'our' suggests) as doubly possessed of the Hellenic and the Hebraic, the pagan and the Christian. The chorus suggests that religious belief, like everything else, is mutable and changes as mankind progresses. Intriguingly, EG had used 'the folding-star' image long before in an early essay (1873) on Ibsen's *Emperor and Galilean*, and collected in *Northern Studies* (1890: 74). There it is used to suggest that Julian the Apostate cannot be truly interesting as his pagan beliefs are culturally dead and backward-looking: 'To resuscitate their ghosts was the dream of a morbid scholar, ignorant of the hearts of men, and blind to the deeper significance of all the signs of the times.' This sense that beliefs operate in an evolutionary manner, and can become outmoded through cultural progress, is prevalent in the period (it is central to the thought of D. H. Lawrence), and is at the heart of EG's critique of his father and his Christianity.

I wrote a tragedy in pale imitation of Shakespeare: this was *Jonathan: a lyric drama in three acts*, written in 1865, presumably on the subject of the passionate friendship between David and Jonathan. (See 2 Samuel 1: 26: 'I am distressed for thee, my brother Jonathan; very pleasant hast thou been unto me. Thy love to me was wonderful, passing the love of women.')

'Prometheus Unbound': a poetic drama in four acts written by Percy Bysshe Shelley in 1818–19, and published in 1820. Its subject is an apt one: a suffering Prometheus (a Christ-like figure) tormented by Jupiter, the father of the gods.

Apollo and Bacchus: Apollo is the god of poetry and music; Bacchus is the Latinization of Dionysus, the god of wine and revelry. It would be interesting to know for certain if EG was aware of Friedrich Nietzsche's *Die Geburt der Tragödie* (*The Birth of Tragedy*) (1872) with its consciously anti-Christian division of experience, and of the artistic impulse, into the Apollonian and the Dionysian. An English translation of *The Birth of Tragedy* by William A. Haussmann appeared in 1909, in Oscar Levy's edition of the complete works of Friedrich Nietzsche, but knowledge of Nietzsche was fairly widespread among intellectual and literary circles in the period. In the years before the publication of *Father and Son*, Nietzsche's ideas were disseminated in various translations, notably a projected edition of his works, edited by Alexander Tille, as well as by Thomas Common (translator and compiler of the anthology, *Nietzsche as Critic, Philosopher, Poet and Prophet* (1901), which specifically alludes to the idea of the Dionysian), A. R. Orage (author of *Friedrich Nietzsche, the Dionysian Spirit of the Age* (1906)), W. B. Yeats, and George Bernard Shaw, among others.

171 *boys who were 'going up for examination'*: that is, for entry to Oxford or Cambridge, something which EG was not to do.

172 *'the thick o' the world between us'*: from William Ernest Henley (1849–1903), 'I.M.R.L.S. (1850–1894)': 'For Time and Change estrange, estrange — | And, now they have looked and seen us, | O, we that were dear, we are all-too-near | With the thick of the world between us' (ll. 5–8).

173 *the new life in London*: in Dec. 1866 or early Jan. 1867, EG went to live at 6 The Terrace, White Hart Lane, in Tottenham, then a countrified suburb in the north of London. His landladies were Miss Anne Buckham and Miss Mary Ann Baker, both Plymouth Brethren who had been friends of Emily Gosse. EG had been appointed to the British Museum as a cataloguer, through the influence of Charles Kingsley (see note to p. 64).

neophyte: a new convert to a religion.

174 *The letter . . . to breakfast*: in reading the ensuing pages it is interesting to note that in her recent biography of Philip Henry Gosse, *Glimpses of the Wonderful*, Ann Thwaite records that in actuality EG was the more constant correspondent, and that his letters reveal an ongoing affection and need for his father's attention (273–7).

175 *Quixotism*: used to refer to anyone committed to a pointless, visionary, and imaginary quest; from Miguel de Cervantes (1547–1616), *Don Quixote* (1605/1615).

176 *the last of their disciples*: as before, PHG stands for the seventeenth century in opposition to EG who represents the modern.

Bossuet . . . fondre le cœur': Jacques Bossuet (1627–1704), the Bishop of Meaux and theologian, writing of 'the cry of misery around us which should melt the heart'.

'Rule and Exercises of Holy Living' . . . Jeremy Taylor . . . Salvation lassie: Jeremy Taylor (1613–67), seventeenth-century chaplain to Charles I and later Bishop of Down and Connor. He published *The Rule and Exercises of Holy Living* in 1650. The 'Salvation lassie' is a woman member of the Salvation Army, founded in 1865 by William Booth.

177 *Dean Alford's edition of the Greek New Testament*: Henry Alford (1810–71), Dean of Canterbury and first editor of the *Contemporary Review*, published his edition 1849–61.

ennui: boredom, lassitude, weariness (originally from a want of occupation, but here from the pressure of one).

Carlyle or Ruskin: Thomas Carlyle (1795–1881) and John Ruskin (1819–1900) are two of the major 'Victorian prophets', secular writers who wrote of political, artistic, and religious issues for the public as professional men of letters.

'*lay bedridden in the dormitory of the soul*': from the first of the 'Introductory Aphorisms' by Samuel Taylor Coleridge (1772–1834), *Aids to Reflection* (1825): 'Truths, of all others the most awful and interesting, are too often considered as *so* true, that they lose all the power of truth, and lie bed-ridden in the dormitory of the soul, side by side with the most despised and exploded errors.'

a Minor Prophet: a phrase used of a group of twelve prophetic works in the Old Testament from Hosea to Malachi.

178 *Leviticus or Deuteronomy*: two works of Hebrew law from the Old Testament.

'*The Continuity of Scripture' by William Page Wood, afterwards Lord Chancellor Hatherley*: William Page Wood (1801–81) was Chancellor 1868–72. *The Continuity of Scripture* was a series of excerpts from the Bible designed to show evidence of continuity (as the title suggests) between the Old and New Testaments. It was first published in 1867.

the glorious rhetoric of the Orient: again an estranging tactic meant to demonstrate the strangeness of the Bible.

'*pitfalls*': originally an animal or bird trap, but from the sixteenth century used metaphorically to mean any device or snare that might entrap the unwary.

an old edition of Bunyan: John Bunyan's (1628–88) *The Pilgrim's Progress* (1678).

Holy Job: PHG sees himself through the analogue of the biblical story of Job, the suffering patriarch.

179 *Elihu the Buzite, of the kindred of Ram*: from Job 32–7. The allusion is complex, but I think refers to the following verses: 'And Elihu the son of Barachel the Buzite answered and said, I am young and ye are very old; wherefore I was afraid, and durst not shew you mine opinion. I said, Days should speak, and multitude of years should teach wisdom. But there is a spirit in man: and the inspiration of the Almighty giveth them understanding. Great men are not always wise: neither do the aged understand judgement. Therefore I said, Hearken to me, I will also shew mine opinion' (32: 6–10). Apart from the sense of youth and age at odds, perhaps the significant thing in this allusion is that EG can quote the Bible just as well and as knowledgeably as his father.

that intellectual Abdera: Abdera is a city in Thrace, whose inhabitants were renowned for their stupidity.

180 *papier-mâché fastnesses*: made from the moulding of damp paper-pulp; in other words, a weak structure.

plains of Jericho: cf. Joshua 6: 5–21.

Zedekiah the son of Chenaanah prepared for the encouragement of Ahab: cf. 1 Kings 22: 11: 'And Zedekiah the son of Chenaanah made him horns of iron: and he said, Thus saith the LORD, With these shalt thou push the Syrians, until thou have consumed them.'

181 *the Prussian war with Austria*: the war of 1866.

Virgil . . . Claudite . . . biberunt: from Virgil's *Eclogues*, iii. 111: 'Boys, now close the streams: the meadows have drunk enough.' See note to p. 95.

house of Rimmon: see note to pp. 58, 154, and 170.

Ibsen: Henrik Ibsen (1828–1906) was early championed by EG, who effectively introduced him to an English audience. EG published a book on Ibsen in 1907, the same year as *Father and Son*.

182 *'The Wild Duck'*: Ibsen's play *The Wild Duck* was written in 1884. In that play, Gregers Werle is seized with a passionate desire to unmask hidden hypocrisy and sin, including the sins of his own father.

in the house where there are many mansions: cf. John 14: 2: 'In my Father's house are many mansions: if it were not so, I would have told you. I go to prepare a place for you.'

the faithful steward of a Master who might return at any moment: cf. Luke 12: 36–40.

183 *which reminded my Father of the tropics in his youth*: the sudden reminder of PHG's own youth is striking.

185 *Plato, Socrates, Cicero*: Greek philosophers, Plato (429–347 BC) was the pupil of Socrates (469–399 BC); Cicero (106–43 BC) was a Roman orator and philosopher. All three are chosen as symbols of the highest limits of pagan wisdom.

186 *the necessity of religious independence*: a rejection of Protestantism infused with the language of Protestantism.

Appendix 1

188 *Mr Paget*: James Paget (1814–99) was one of the leading London surgeons from the early 1860s onwards.

instant excision was recommended: Mary Stacey took Emily to Edward Laseron, himself a member of the Plymouth Brethren and formerly a missionary. He was director of the Deaconesses' Institute in Tottenham. The 'relative' they consulted the next day was Dr Henry Hyde Salter, a grandson of an aunt of PHG. It was Salter who recommended Dr Fell's treatment.

an American: Dr Jesse Weldon Fell, a doctor from America, who treated cancer using an ointment composed of zinc chloride or lead oxide mixed with a plant root. Perhaps Fell hastened the death of Emily Gosse, by deceiving her and her husband into pursuing a mode of treatment that he knew was futile. See note to p. 34.

Dr S——: that is, Henry Hyde Salter.

190 *mucilage*: the viscous pulp of Dr Fell's ointment.

annular: formed like a ring.

194 *best wine . . . (Song vii. 9)*: paraphrased from the original verse.

Appendix 2

196 *JAMES iii. 6*: the course of nature.

MacLeay, Swainson, and others: William Sharpe MacLeay (1792–1865) first suggested the 'quinary' or circular system, arguing that the relationships within a zoological group can be expressed by a series of interlocking circles. William Swainson (1789–1855) was a zoologist and disciple of MacLeay's 'quinary system', though his adherence to this mistaken theory was ruinous for his career.

cotyledons: the primary leaf in the embryo of higher plants.

plumule: the rudimentary shoot, bud, or bunch of leaves of the embryo plant.

pistil: the female organ of the flower, situated in its centre and comprising ovary, style, and stigma.

197 *protococcus*: a genus of microscopic, unicellular algæ.

monad: monad came to be taken as a hypothetical simple organism, assumed in evolutionary speculations as the first term in the genealogy of living things. PHG may be using it in this way, though without the evolutionary framework, or he may simply be referring to a protozoon of the genus *Monas* or *Monadidea*.

199 *cicatrice*: the scar of a healed wound.

Sir Thomas Browne: Sir Thomas Browne (1605–82) was a doctor; he wrote works on religion and natural philosophy, including *Religio Medici* (1642) and *Hydrioptaphia* (1658). See note to p. 63.

Vrbin, Angelo, and others: that is, in the art (presumably engravings) of Raphael (of Urbino) (1483–1520) and Michelangelo Buonarotti (1475–1564).

Pseudodoxia Epidemica: Thomas Browne published *Pseudodoxia Epidemica: or, Enquiries into Very Many Received Tenets and Commonly Presumed Truths*, also known as *Vulgar Errors*, in 1646. It is a key work in the new spirit of empiricism in natural philosophy, investigating popular myths and superstitions, including the notion that badgers have legs longer on one side than on the other.

gemmation: almost a metaphor here, a term borrowed from botany and zoology—in botany, referring to the way in which the young leaf is enfolded in the bud; and in zoology, the process of reproduction by buds, the formation of a new individual by the protusion and separation of a part of the parent.

200 *ex nihilo nihil fit*: 'nothing is made from nothing.'

Appendix 3

203 *Faraday*: Michael Faraday (1791–1867) one of the greatest British scientists of the nineteenth century, was also a devout Christian, who had been brought up within the benign fundamentalism of the Sandemanian Church.

Actinozoa and the Rotifera: Actinozoa are a class of radiated animals, containing the sea-anemones and coral polypes. Rotifera are a class of minute animalcules, which swim with the aid of rotatory organs.

204 *Lara*: a poem by George Gordon, Lord Byron (1788–1824) published in 1814.

Milton . . . Paradise Lost . . . Arian heresy: John Milton (1608–74) published *Paradise Lost* in ten books in 1667, and then in its final twelve-book form in 1674. Following the fourth-century Alexandrian, Arius, Arians denied the Trinity, arguing that Christ was not of the same substance or essence as God.

Wordsworth, Gray, Cowper, and Southey: all English poets—William Wordsworth (1770–1850), co-author of *Lyrical Ballads* (1798) and author of *The Prelude* (1850); Thomas Gray (1716–71), author of 'Elegy Written in a Country Churchyard' (1751); William Cowper (1731–1800), co-author of *Olney Hymns* (1782) and author of *The Task* (1785); Robert Southey (1774–1843), author of *Madoc* (1805).

Thalaba: *Thalaba the Destroyer*, a poem by Southey, was published in 1801.

Swinburne and Rossetti: two contemporary poets, known for their wayward lives—Algernon Charles Swinburne (1837–1909), a friend of EG, was virulently anti-Christian. EG may be referring to the similarly scandalous Dante Gabriel Rossetti (1828–82), or (less likely) to his sister, the pious poet, Christina Rossetti (1830–94).

Tennyson and Browning: the chief poets of the preceding literary generation (in a way, PHG's own), Alfred, Lord Tennyson (1809–92), and, presumably, Robert Browning (1812–89), though EG might possibly (it is unlikely) be referring to Elizabeth Barrett Browning (1806–61).

'*Now came still evening on . . . all things clad*': the lines comes from Book IV, ll. 598–9, of John Milton's *Paradise Lost*. The poem reads:

> Now came still Evening on, and Twilight gray
> Had in her sober Liverie all things clad;
> Silence accompanied, for Beast and Bird,
> They to thir grassie Couch, these to thir Nests

> Were slunk, all but the wakeful Nightingale;
> She all night long her amorous descant sung;
>
> (iv. 599–603)

Appendix 4

205 *Reinach's 'Orpheus'*: a reference to the recently published history of religion by Salomon Reinach, *Orpheus, Histoire Générale des Religions* (Paris: Alcide Picard, 1909), translated by Florence Simmonds as *Orpheus, A General History of Religions* (London: William Heinemann, 1909).

A SELECTION OF   **OXFORD WORLD'S CLASSICS**

JOHN BUCHAN
Greenmantle
Huntingtower
The Island of Sheep
The Thirty-Nine Steps

JOSEPH CONRAD
Chance
Heart of Darkness and Other Tales
Lord Jim
Nostromo
An Outcast of the Islands
The Secret Agent
Typhoon and Other Tales
Under Western Eyes

ARTHUR CONAN DOYLE
The Adventures of Sherlock Holmes
The Case-Book of Sherlock Holmes
The Hound of the Baskervilles
The Lost World
The Memoirs of Sherlock Holmes
A Study in Scarlet

FORD MADOX FORD
The Good Soldier

JOHN GALSWORTHY
The Forsyte Saga

JAMES JOYCE
A Portrait of the Artist as a Young Man
Dubliners
Occasional, Critical, and Political Writing
Ulysses

RUDYARD KIPLING
Captains Courageous
The Complete Stalky & Co
The Jungle Books
Just So Stories
Kim
The Man Who Would Be King
Plain Tales from the Hills
War Stories and Poems

A SELECTION OF   **OXFORD WORLD'S CLASSICS**

D. H. LAWRENCE   The Rainbow
                        Sons and Lovers
                        The White Peacock
                        Women in Love
                        The Widowing of Mrs Holroyd and Other
                            Plays

KATHERINE MANSFIELD   Selected Stories

VIRGINIA WOOLF   Between the Acts
                        Flush
                        Jacob's Room
                        Mrs Dalloway
                        Night and Day
                        Orlando: A Biography
                        A Room of One's Own and Three Guineas
                        To the Lighthouse
                        The Voyage Out
                        The Waves
                        The Years

W. B. YEATS   The Major Works

A SELECTION OF   **OXFORD WORLD'S CLASSICS**

JANE AUSTEN	Emma
	Mansfield Park
	Persuasion
	Pride and Prejudice
	Sense and Sensibility
MRS BEETON	Book of Household Management
LADY ELIZABETH BRADDON	Lady Audley's Secret
ANNE BRONTË	The Tenant of Wildfell Hall
CHARLOTTE BRONTË	Jane Eyre
	Shirley
	Villette
EMILY BRONTË	Wuthering Heights
SAMUEL TAYLOR COLERIDGE	The Major Works
WILKIE COLLINS	The Moonstone
	No Name
	The Woman in White
CHARLES DARWIN	The Origin of Species
CHARLES DICKENS	The Adventures of Oliver Twist
	Bleak House
	David Copperfield
	Great Expectations
	Nicholas Nickleby
	The Old Curiosity Shop
	Our Mutual Friend
	The Pickwick Papers
	A Tale of Two Cities
GEORGE DU MAURIER	Trilby
MARIA EDGEWORTH	Castle Rackrent

A SELECTION OF **OXFORD WORLD'S CLASSICS**

ROBERT LOUIS
STEVENSON

Kidnapped and **Catriona**
The Strange Case of Dr Jekyll and
    Mr Hyde and **Weir of Hermiston**
Treasure Island

BRAM STOKER

Dracula

WILLIAM MAKEPEACE
THACKERAY

Vanity Fair

OSCAR WILDE

Complete Shorter Fiction
The Major Works
The Picture of Dorian Gray

DOROTHY WORDSWORTH

The Grasmere and Alfoxden Journals

WILLIAM WORDSWORTH

The Major Works

A SELECTION OF   OXFORD WORLD'S CLASSICS

ANTON CHEKHOV
: Early Stories
Five Plays
The Princess and Other Stories
The Russian Master and Other Stories
The Steppe and Other Stories
Twelve Plays
Ward Number Six and Other Stories

FYODOR DOSTOEVSKY
: Crime and Punishment
Devils
A Gentle Creature and Other Stories
The Idiot
The Karamazov Brothers
Memoirs from the House of the Dead
Notes from the Underground and
   The Gambler

NIKOLAI GOGOL
: Dead Souls
Plays and Petersburg Tales

ALEXANDER PUSHKIN
: Eugene Onegin
The Queen of Spades and Other Stories

LEO TOLSTOY
: Anna Karenina
The Kreutzer Sonata and Other Stories
The Raid and Other Stories
Resurrection
War and Peace

IVAN TURGENEV
: Fathers and Sons
First Love and Other Stories
A Month in the Country

A SELECTION OF   **OXFORD WORLD'S CLASSICS**

HANS CHRISTIAN ANDERSEN — **Fairy Tales**

J. M. BARRIE — **Peter Pan in Kensington Gardens** and **Peter and Wendy**

L. FRANK BAUM — **The Wonderful Wizard of Oz**

FRANCES HODGSON BURNETT — **The Secret Garden**

LEWIS CARROLL — **Alice's Adventures in Wonderland** and **Through the Looking-Glass**

CARLO COLLODI — **The Adventures of Pinocchio**

KENNETH GRAHAME — **The Wind in the Willows**

ANTHONY HOPE — **The Prisoner of Zenda**

THOMAS HUGHES — **Tom Brown's Schooldays**

ANTHONY TROLLOPE

An Autobiography

The American Senator

Barchester Towers

Can You Forgive Her?

The Claverings

Cousin Henry

Doctor Thorne

The Duke's Children

The Eustace Diamonds

Framley Parsonage

He Knew He Was Right

Lady Anna

The Last Chronicle of Barset

Orley Farm

Phineas Finn

Phineas Redux

The Prime Minister

Rachel Ray

The Small House at Allington

The Warden

The Way We Live Now

	Women's Writing 1778–1838
WILLIAM BECKFORD	Vathek
JAMES BOSWELL	Life of Johnson
FRANCES BURNEY	Camilla
	Cecilia
	Evelina
	The Wanderer
LORD CHESTERFIELD	Lord Chesterfield's Letters
JOHN CLELAND	Memoirs of a Woman of Pleasure
DANIEL DEFOE	A Journal of the Plague Year
	Moll Flanders
	Robinson Crusoe
	Roxana
HENRY FIELDING	Joseph Andrews and Shamela
	A Journey from This World to the Next and
	The Journal of a Voyage to Lisbon
	Tom Jones
WILLIAM GODWIN	Caleb Williams
OLIVER GOLDSMITH	The Vicar of Wakefield
MARY HAYS	Memoirs of Emma Courtney
ELIZABETH HAYWOOD	The History of Miss Betsy Thoughtless
ELIZABETH INCHBALD	A Simple Story
SAMUEL JOHNSON	The History of Rasselas
	The Major Works
CHARLOTTE LENNOX	The Female Quixote
MATTHEW LEWIS	Journal of a West India Proprietor
	The Monk
HENRY MACKENZIE	The Man of Feeling
ALEXANDER POPE	Selected Poetry

A SELECTION OF   **OXFORD WORLD'S CLASSICS**

ANN RADCLIFFE	**The Italian**
	The Mysteries of Udolpho
	The Romance of the Forest
	A Sicilian Romance
SAMUEL RICHARDSON	**Pamela**
FRANCES SHERIDAN	**Memoirs of Miss Sidney Bidulph**
RICHARD BRINSLEY SHERIDAN	**The School for Scandal and Other Plays**
TOBIAS SMOLLETT	**The Adventures of Roderick Random**
	The Expedition of Humphry Clinker
	Travels through France and Italy
LAURENCE STERNE	**The Life and Opinions of Tristram Shandy, Gentleman**
	A Sentimental Journey
JONATHAN SWIFT	**Gulliver's Travels**
	A Tale of a Tub and Other Works
HORACE WALPOLE	**The Castle of Otranto**
MARY WOLLSTONECRAFT	**Mary** and **The Wrongs of Woman**
	A Vindication of the Rights of Woman

A SELECTION OF   OXFORD WORLD'S CLASSICS

HENRY ADAMS — The Education of Henry Adams

LOUISA MAY ALCOTT — Little Women

SHERWOOD ANDERSON — Winesburg, Ohio

CHARLES BROCKDEN BROWN — Wieland; or The Transformation and Memoirs of Carwin, The Biloquist

WILLA CATHER — O Pioneers!

KATE CHOPIN — The Awakening and Other Stories

JAMES FENIMORE COOPER — The Deerslayer
The Last of the Mohicans
The Pathfinder
The Pioneers
The Prairie

STEPHEN CRANE — The Red Badge of Courage

J. HECTOR ST. JEAN DE CRÈVECŒUR — Letters from an American Farmer

FREDERICK DOUGLASS — Narrative of the Life of Frederick Douglass, an American Slave

THEODORE DREISER — Sister Carrie

F. SCOTT FITZGERALD — The Great Gatsby
The Beautiful and Damned

BENJAMIN FRANKLIN — Autobiography and Other Writings

CHARLOTTE PERKINS GILMAN — The Yellow Wall-Paper and Other Stories

ZANE GREY — Riders of the Purple Sage

NATHANIEL HAWTHORNE — The Blithedale Romance
The House of the Seven Gables
The Marble Faun
The Scarlet Letter
Young Goodman Brown and Other Tales

A SELECTION OF **OXFORD WORLD'S CLASSICS**

WASHINGTON IRVING   The Sketch-Book of Geoffrey Crayon,
                       Gent.

HENRY JAMES   The Ambassadors
                       The American
                       The Aspern Papers and Other Stories
                       The Awkward Age
                       The Bostonians
                       Daisy Miller and Other Stories
                       The Europeans
                       The Golden Bowl
                       The Portrait of a Lady
                       The Spoils of Poynton
                       The Turn of the Screw and Other Stories
                       Washington Square
                       What Maisie Knew
                       The Wings of the Dove

JACK LONDON   The Call of the Wild
                       White Fang and Other Stories
                       John Barleycorn
                       The Sea-Wolf
                       The Son of the Wolf

HERMAN MELVILLE   Billy Budd, Sailor and Selected Tales
                       The Confidence-Man
                       Moby-Dick
                       White-Jacket

FRANK NORRIS   McTeague

FRANCIS PARKMAN   The Oregon Trail

EDGAR ALLAN POE   The Narrative of Arthur Gordon Pym of
                       Nantucket and Related Tales
                       Selected Tales

HARRIET BEECHER STOWE Uncle Tom's Cabin

HENRY DAVID THOREAU   Walden

A SELECTION OF   **OXFORD WORLD'S CLASSICS**

Mark Twain   Adventures of Huckleberry Finn
                             The Adventures of Tom Sawyer
                             A Connecticut Yankee in King Arthur's
                                 Court
                             Life on the Mississippi
                             The Prince and the Pauper
                             Pudd'nhead Wilson

Lew Wallace   Ben-Hur

Booker T. Washington   Up from Slavery

Edith Wharton   The Custom of the Country
                             Ethan Frome
                             The House of Mirth
                             The Reef

Walt Whitman   Leaves of Grass

Owen Wister   The Virginian

The Oxford World's Classics Website

www.worldsclassics.co.uk

- Information about new titles
- Explore the full range of Oxford World's Classics
- Links to other literary sites and the main OUP webpage
- Imaginative competitions, with bookish prizes
- Peruse the Oxford World's Classics Magazine
- Articles by editors
- Extracts from Introductions
- A forum for discussion and feedback on the series
- Special information for teachers and lecturers

www.worldsclassics.co.uk

American Literature

British and Irish Literature

Children's Literature

Classics and Ancient Literature

Colonial Literature

Eastern Literature

European Literature

History

Medieval Literature

Oxford English Drama

Poetry

Philosophy

Politics

Religion

The Oxford Shakespeare

A complete list of Oxford Paperbacks, including Oxford World's Classics, Oxford Shakespeare, Oxford Drama, and Oxford Paperback Reference, is available in the UK from the Academic Division Publicity Department, Oxford University Press, Great Clarendon Street, Oxford OX2 6DP.

In the USA, complete lists are available from the Paperbacks Marketing Manager, Oxford University Press, 198 Madison Avenue, New York, NY 10016.

Oxford Paperbacks are available from all good bookshops. In case of difficulty, customers in the UK can order direct from Oxford University Press Bookshop, Freepost, 116 High Street, Oxford OX1 4BR, enclosing full payment. Please add 10 per cent of published price for postage and packing.